DAVID S. PAYNE

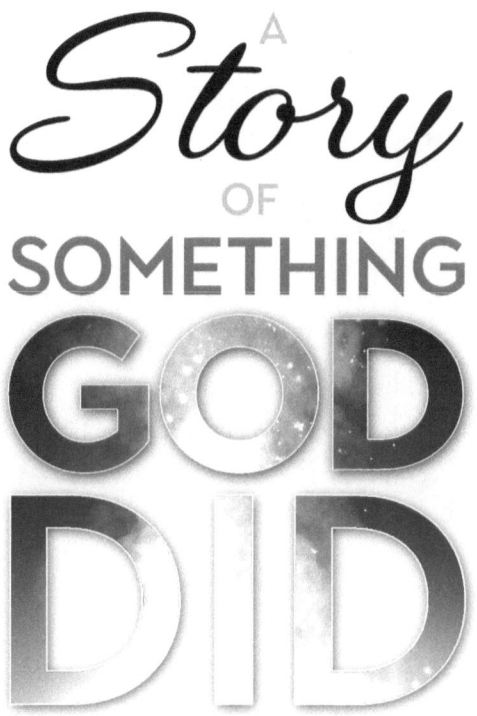

A Story of Something GOD DID

A FAITH JOURNEY

A STORY OF SOMETHING GOD DID
Copyright © 2025 by David S. Payne

All rights reserved. Neither this publication nor any part of this publication may be reproduced or transmitted in any form or by any means, electronic or mechanical, including photocopying, recording or any information storage and retrieval system, without permission in writing from the author.

Unless otherwise indicated, scripture quotations are taken from the Holy Bible, New Living Translation, copyright ©1996, 2004, 2015 by Tyndale House Foundation. Used by permission of Tyndale House Publishers, Carol Stream, Illinois 60188. All rights reserved. Scripture quotations marked MSG are taken from The Message, copyright © 1993, 2002, 2018 by Eugene H. Peterson. Used by permission of NavPress. All rights reserved. Represented by Tyndale House Publishers.

ISBN: 978-1-4866-2689-2
eBook: 978-1-4866-2690-8

Word Alive Press
119 De Baets Street Winnipeg, MB R2J 3R9
www.wordalivepress.ca

Cataloguing in Publication information can be obtained from Library and Archives Canada.

To my wife, Diane, for her steady partnership and support.
To my three children, Jeremy, Rebecca, and Sarah, who journeyed with us.
To their spouses, Bonnie, Chris, and Ian, who joined the journey.
To the next generation, in the interest of leaving a godly legacy.

Author's Note

WHY AM I writing this book? My reason is to tell a story—a story that is not dramatic or sensational but shows how God works in both ordinary and extraordinary ways in the life of an average person. I began my writings primarily as a memoir to pass on to my children and grandchildren. But the more I wrote and developed this book, it seemed to become something more.

Recently, something happened to remind me why I needed to keep writing. I heard the *ping* on my phone, telling me that I had received a text from my eleven-year-old granddaughter, Sierra. She had heard that I was writing another book and wanted to talk about it.

"Hi Grandpa," she wrote. "Have you finished your book yet? If so, can you make me a copy so I can read it? If not, that's okay!"

I replied, "Hi Sierra. That's so sweet that you want to read my book. That makes writing it all the more worthwhile. No, I haven't finished the book yet. It will take at least another year to finish it."

"Oh wow! Another year! Okay, perfect. Well, remember, I would love to read it."

"Yes, it takes a long time to write a book," I said. "But I'll remember to give you a copy."

"Are you making a front cover and everything?" she asked.

"Yes, if I finish the book, I will need to give it a front cover. I will send it to a publishing company and they will then make it into a book with a front cover."

"Oh, that's so cool!"

I felt enthused by her passion for what I was doing.

"I can see that it takes good effort and hard work to get a book done," she added. "I would love to read it because you are spending so long writing it. The fact that it takes so long to write a book means that it must be worth something. Also, I love reading your books."

"Yes, it sure does take a lot of effort and hard work," I said. "Probably the main reason I write books is so that when you and all my other grandkids grow older, you will read them and they will help you to live your lives for Jesus."

"Yes, I totally agree, Grandpa!" Then she said something profound: "Once I'm done reading your book, I can pass it on to my kids. And then once they are done reading it, they can pass it on to their kids. We can all learn from you. I think that's what I'm going to do."

I was gobsmacked. She understood the concept of legacy.

"That's wonderful," I responded. "And that's why I write books. That's why it is worth all of the effort doing it."

"Yes, of course! You don't just spend all that time writing a book and then just leave it or throw it away. You actually have to use it and make something good out of it… if you know what I mean."

"I know exactly what you mean, Sierra. You are so right. You understand the idea perfectly behind why I would write a book. Love you, sweetheart."

"Love you, Grandpa."

As for why I write, I really can't add anything to that.

Preface

THIS IS THE story of a church. It is my story. It is the story of my wife, Diane, and our family. It is the story of so many others who journeyed with us.

I was the pastor of three churches over a period of forty-five years. I pastored the Campus Church in Aurora, Ontario, for thirty-three of those years. They weren't easy years. In fact, there were some very dark days. But God's plan and call kept our hand to the plough.

This is also a story of sowing in tears and reaping in joy. A story of God's unfailing love and unmitigated grace. A story of God's faithfulness. It is a story of something God did. A story worth putting pen to paper.

It is a faith story. Do you remember the well-known account of Peter leaving the security of the fishing boat and walking on the water to Jesus? You have to give it to him. All the others stayed in the boat. Peter was the only one who stepped out—and he walked physically on water.

But when Peter began to think about the inconceivability of walking on water, he was quickly overwhelmed by fear. He began to sink.

Jesus watched all this unfold, then reached down into the waters that engulfed his follower and pulled him up. When they had time to reflect on this experience, Jesus said to Peter, "You have so little faith."

Jesus saw this whole event as a faith lesson. In fact, the whole of life—the good, the bad, and the ugly—is the spiritual classroom in which we learn our most valuable and consequential faith lessons.

We like to stay in our boats where we feel safe and secure. But God allows circumstances into our lives that call us to step outside of the boat. Jesus wasn't in the boat on this occasion. He was out on the waves.

And he often calls us to follow him there.

Faith hears God calling. Faith obeys the call and steps out into the unfamiliar. Faith means that we keep our eyes fixed on Jesus in the midst of uncertainty and the unknown. Faith means trusting beyond our own strength, ability, and visibility and going where God is. Faith means doing things, going places, and seeing things that are only possible with God.

Jesus said that if we have faith, nothing is impossible (Matthew 17:20). In faith, we understand that if we do everything we can do and trust God beyond that, we will see him do what only he can do. Faith sees the invisible, believes the incredible, and receives the impossible.

In this story, every step forward came with seemingly insurmountable challenges and setbacks. My family and I became cognizant of our fragility, limitations, and insufficiencies. At times, our faith was as small as a mustard seed.

But that was enough to move mountains. Little faith was enough because it rested in a loving, powerful, sovereign God who reigns over everything.

As you journey with us, it is my prayer that this story will inspire your faith.

Introduction

AS I BEGAN writing, something peculiar happened that reinforced a fundamental message I wanted to underscore. While grocery shopping and placing the items in the back of my vehicle, I absentmindedly did something stupid.

I placed my wallet in the shopping cart.

When I got home, I unloaded the groceries and reached to take my wallet out of my pocket. It wasn't there. I immediately got that sick, panicky feeling. Where was it?

I searched all of my pockets. I rummaged in the grocery bags. I hunted through the vehicle. I searched everything all over again.

It was nowhere to be found.

Feeling nauseous, I wondered whether I had left it in the grocery cart back at the store. Forty minutes had passed since then, but I sped off in search of the wallet. My wife, Diane, phoned the store to see whether anyone had handed it to someone in the office.

They hadn't.

Arriving at the store, I ran to the location where I had left the grocery cart and searched every cart several times. Nothing. I then went inside the store and inquired at the office. They still didn't have anything. I left my name and phone number in case my wallet showed up.

Before leaving, I scoured the counter where I had paid for my groceries. Nothing.

I hurried outside to check the carts again, but it seemed clear what had happened: someone had found the wallet and taken it. Maybe they would call me. Maybe not.

I had just been to the bank and withdrawn $400. The money was sitting in my wallet along with all my credit cards. I decided to return home and quickly cancel those cards.

As I began to walk away from the carts, a car pulled up. Inside was a guy with long hair and unshaven face. His eyes followed me as I walked—and as I got closer to him, he beckoned me over.

I bent down and looked at him through his passenger side window, my face flushed with anxiety and frustration.

"Looking for something?" he asked.

"Yes," I replied and told him the story.

He asked a few more questions about the wallet, including its size, material, and colour. He asked whether there was money in it and how much. I answered.

He then smiled. "I think that I may have it."

I stared at him with a look of disbelief. I was speechless!

He leaned over, reached into his glove compartment, and pulled out a wallet. Sure enough, it was mine.

The whole event seemed surreal. A whole hour had passed since I'd left it in the cart, driven home, unloaded the groceries, and returned to the store. In the meantime, this stranger had discovered my wallet and driven away, vanishing for a period of about forty minutes. He then returned and drove by at the exact same moment I was walking away.

And we met.

This couldn't have been coordinated more precisely. All the money was still in the wallet, and the cards were undisturbed.

Coincidence? Coincidence is the word we give to something we can't explain. The encounter is too improbable. The timing is too perfect. The paths of two people intersect in the most incredible way in the most unlikely place. Is it just chance? Or is there something more complex at play?

There seems to be too much design, order, and precision in the world to brush things off as chance or coincidence. Consider the intricate and interconnected workings of the human body or the brain. Think of the delicate balance of nature, the finely tuned universe, or the perfect orbits of the planets and moons in space.

While witnessing a recent total lunar eclipse, I was forced again to recognize the wonder of it all. Such an eclipse is the rare alignment of three separate celestial bodies. For it to happen, you need to be on a certain planet at a certain distance from its sun, with a moon at a certain distance from the planet and relative size to the sun.

Whatever belief system or worldview one has, it's impossible to experience something like this without feeling awe. For me, the only logical and reasonable explanation is the existence of a creator God who is intelligent, all-knowing, and all-powerful, and who sovereignly governs all things with absolute perfection.

The Bible teaches that not only does this amazing God exist, but his loving governance applies to the everyday details of our lives. He is a God who oversees every component of my life, coordinating everything all the time. It's not a despotic kind of control but a loving control. That is why I'm writing about something God has done.

Now that doesn't mean that everything in life is going to work out the way we would hope all the time. It doesn't mean that God is going to solve every problem we encounter or answer every prayer the way we want. What if my wallet hadn't been found or it was found with all its contents missing? Would that mean God no longer loves me or cares? Would that mean that God isn't in control? Not at all. Bad things happen. Injustices occur all the time. We live in a fallen world. There exists the tension between good and evil. That is also reality.

It is reassuring, however, to know *"that God causes everything to work together for the good of those who love God and are called according to his purpose for them"* (Romans 8:28). Note the phrase *"God causes everything."* When things don't work out as we hope, God is still working in everything and working out everything—not just isolated incidents—for the ultimate good of those who love him and to accomplish his purpose for them.

The next verse says that God's primary purpose is that we die to self and become like Jesus (Romans 8:29). Adversity is the means of growing in character and Christlikeness. We need the tough times to shape us.

These are truths I have learned, sometimes slowly, through my life and pastoral ministry. They lie at the heart of everything I write in this story. Through the good and the bad, the victories and defeats, the successes and failures, when facing perplexity and disappointment, a sovereign and loving God is in control. He has this. He is writing the script. So persevere in faith.

One

WE ARE ALL born into a particular set of conditions that greatly impacts our lives. The most impactful is the family and home we are raised in. What one learns and experiences, especially in those early formative years, is critical to making us who we are as adults.

And there are other contributors. The era in which one is born. Geographical setting. Cultural context. Economic situation. Social milieu and status. Political conditions. Our environment hugely influences us as human beings.

But we are not victims of our environment. Our existence isn't determined by our surrounding conditions. Life isn't a chain of random events and experiences, good and bad, happy and unhappy, passively carrying us along like the current of a great river. A divine plan interconnects us. A divine will interacts with our human will and decision-making, always operative despite the conditions and circumstances of our lives.

The Bible teaches that God's plan and purpose for us began before our births. What an amazing truth! God said to Jeremiah,

> Before I shaped you in the womb, I knew all about you. Before you saw the light of day, I had holy plans for you: a prophet to the nations—that's what I had in mind for you. (Jeremiah 1:5, MSG)

The apostle Paul wrote the same thing regarding himself: *"But even before I was born, God chose me and called me…"* (Galatians 1:15) The psalmist wrote, *"You saw me before I was born. Every day of my life was recorded in your book. Every moment was laid out before a single day had passed"* (Psalm 139:16).

There is a foundational truth here that will hold us when the harsh realities of life bear down. My life was known, planned out, and settled by the Creator before I was born. I am part of a divine plan. I'm not a meaningless mistake or insignificant creature drowning in existential nihilism. I didn't get flushed onto this planet to wander aimlessly. I don't just exist. I began in the mind of my Creator and am on a journey with him. That means that I have purpose, direction, and worth.

From conception to birth, from childhood to adulthood, this loving God has his eye on us and his hand upon us, preparing and equipping us as his plan unfolds. I have believed that from as far back as I can remember.

I was a child of the 50s. If I had been writing this book back then, I would have written it on an old black vintage typewriter. You can almost hear the clacking of the keys striking the paper with every letter typed. I would've spent as much time erasing letters as typing them!

We didn't have electronic devices of any sort in those days. No one had computers or cell phones. If you wanted to make a phone call, you had to dial the number and speak into the receiver at the end of a three-foot cord.

At my house growing up, we had a party line which made life both frustrating and fun. Frustrating, because it meant that there were multiple homes on one line. If the line was in use, you could wait for a long time. Sometimes the constant clicking from other people lifting the phone to check would make a person hang up. But it was also fun, because a favourite pastime was sitting and quietly listening to someone else's conversation and getting in on all the neighbourhood gossip. There was a way of quietly lifting the phone receiver from its cradle so as to remain undetected.

And yes, if you wanted to make a long-distance phone call, you needed to do it after 6:00 p.m. when the rates were cheaper. You'd go through an operator—and even she often listened in on your conversation.

We didn't have a television set until I was about ten years old. I remember the day my parents brought one home. It was the size of a Volkswagen. I also still remember the first time I saw the blurred images of my hockey heroes skating up and down the ice with no helmets to take slapshots on goalies with no facemasks. I was exhilarated!

I had always been a Toronto Maple Leafs fan and couldn't believe that I was watching Dave Keon, Frank Mahovlich, Eddie Shack, George Armstrong, Tim Horton, and of course goalie Johnny Bauer actually skate and stick-handle the puck in living black and white. I already had their photos plastered all over my bedroom walls, but this was different.

The reception on TV was never great. We often peered at it through billows of snow with the sound fading in and out. We would run around the room with the rabbit ear antenna trying to find the spot where reception was best. On the night when one's favourite program was on, sure enough, one of the tubes would blow and my father would need to phone the TV repairman to come as quickly as possible and replace the tube.

All of this meant that we spent a lot of time outdoors. Summers were spent biking, swimming, go-carting, building forts in the forest, climbing trees, picking raspberries, weeding the garden, cutting grass with the old hand pushmower, and hunting squirrels with a slingshot and pocket full of acorns.

I loved trading hockey cards and comic books. I owned stacks of both and often spent time rummaging through these valued possessions to decide which ones to trade and which to protect and keep. I loved the musty smell of comic books while the hockey cards always emitted the scent of bubblegum.

A frequent pastime was sitting on the riverbank at my favourite fishing hole with a pole. I could easily fill a six-quart basket with small perch, sunfish, smallmouth bass, and sometimes a few nice speckled trout. I would take them home, clean them, and give them to my mother for the frying pan for supper that same evening.

I didn't have money to buy snacks, so many days I pulled my wagon and searched the ditches along the road for empty pop bottles to return for small refunds. This practice also introduced me to experimentation with cigarettes. Everyone seemed to smoke back then. There were ample cigarette butts along the roads and I lit a few to get the feel—that is, until my father found out!

Anyway, I took the empty pop bottles to the old general store across the bridge and placed them up on the high wooden counter to be grudgingly tallied by Mr. Cottrill, the grumpy store owner. The pennies and nickels I received in exchange were used to purchase a soda, popsicle, or some candy. I particularly loved the butterscotch toffee that was packaged in a red tartan box. Any remaining coins were put into my metal bear piggybank.

I received ten cents a week for an allowance. One cent went faithfully to God—tithing was taught to me from the earliest age—a few pennies were dropped into the piggybank, and the rest went toward buying blackballs at a corner store in the nearby town. These were little marble-looking black candies, and every time you took one out of your mouth it was a different colour. One blackball lasted about an hour and left your tongue varied colours and your lips black.

I could purchase ten blackballs for one cent, which to me seemed like the best deal in town.

We rode our bikes on gravel roads with no protective gear. More than once, my front tire got caught in the loose gravel and I flew headlong over the handlebars. You had to learn how to fall because there was no easy landing. I would return home scratched and bleeding for my mother to tenderly bandage me up and tell me to be more careful next time.

My mother always made sure we were scrubbed up, and of course we received a good scrubbing with our weekly bath every Saturday night in order for us to be clean and ready for church on Sunday morning.

Our winters were spent shovelling snow, tobogganing, playing road hockey, building snow forts, trading hockey cards, and piling wood into the basement of our home. We had a wood-burning furnace which ate up a lot of wood. As kids, the benefit we enjoyed was that we could crowd onto the metal rad above the furnace every morning to get dressed and stay warm.

I grew up on peanut butter. When we opened our lunchboxes at school—and mine was always a Roy Rogers lunchbox—the smell of peanut butter and bologna sandwiches would permeate the halls. The sandwiches were wrapped in wax paper, which had to be neatly folded to be used again and last the whole week. When my sister, brothers, and I returned home from school, we often entered our house with the aroma of freshly baked homemade bread wafting in the air. There was nothing like fresh-baked bread and a lump of butter to satisfy a boy's salivation.

Each night we enjoyed a home-cooked meal made from scratch out of a wood-stove oven. Every meal my mother cooked was delicious, except perhaps for liver and cauliflower. Liver was an undesirable staple and cauliflower made me gag.

I always looked forward to Sunday dinner after church. We'd sit around the table, usually with guests, and enjoy a roast beef dinner with mashed potatoes and Yorkshire pudding covered in rich gravy.

Interestingly, I married a girl who was an equally good cook, and also made it a Sunday tradition to spread a delicious dinner of roast beef and roasted potatoes covered in rich gravy on the table before her family and any guests we had invited into our home. And she also filled our home with the smell of fresh-baked bread, much to her family's delight.

As a boy, suppertime was a sacred time. It was a time to talk as a family about our days. And after dinner we listened to my father read from the Bible and pray with us before running outdoors for another hour of playtime before bed.

Everything was second-hand—clothing, bikes, baseball gloves, and hockey sticks. Goalie sticks were unaffordable, so we constructed them from the handles of broken sticks and nailed slabs of board to the bottom, securely wrapping it all with duct tape. Goalie pads were cut from old carpet. We were rarely handed anything new, except perhaps on one's birthday or at Christmas. But it all worked and we were happy.

We learned at a young age to be frugal. One day, my dad brought home a large bucket of twisted, bent, rusted nails which had been salvaged from an old shed that had been torn down. Nothing went to waste. My siblings and I were given the job of straightening each nail, one by one, so it could be used again. It took us over a year to complete the painstaking task.

We played with simple toys like tin trucks, toy guns, marbles, and hula hoops, not to mention toys that would today be considered sharp choking hazards covered in toxic paint. Somehow we survived. Every boy carried a pocketknife and no one ever seemed to get hurt other than the odd time when someone got a knife stuck in their toe while playing stretch on the school playground.

In the game of stretch, two contestants stood about four feet apart, facing each other, with their feet together. They had jackknives in hand. The first person to go would throw the jackknife near the foot of their opponent, but not more than the distance of a stretched hand. If successful, and if the knife stuck in the ground, the second person had to move their foot out to where the knife had landed. They would take turns, the object of the game being to make the other fellow finally stretch their legs far enough that they lost their balance and fell over.

Our family attended the little Baptist church down the road from our house. It was an active church and much of our lives revolved around it. Sunday school began at 9:30 every Sunday morning. We sang lots of lively action choruses, but the primary emphasis was on Bible stories and scripture memorization.

Everything was a contest. I remember looking up at a big chart covered with rocket ships. When every person in one's group could quote a Bible verse from memory, their rocket ship would go up a notch. The first three rocket ships to reach the moon would win a prize. These competitions were intense.

I particularly enjoyed the sword drills. With our Bibles shouldered, we were given a scripture reference. Upon the command "Fire!" we attacked our Bibles ferociously in search of the verse. The first person to find the verse stood and read it. We took these competitions very seriously.

When Sunday school was finished, the morning service began. Our family always sat at the front left corner by the organ—because my mother was the organist.

Every time the doors squeaked open, curiosity would compel me to turn my head to see who was entering. One old gentleman regularly reprimanded me for turning around and told me, "If you want to look at the back, sit at the back!" But I couldn't. I had to sit at the front left corner.

We sat in old wooden theatre seats that were so hard that I would pray earnestly for the service to end. At least I was praying! The seats were connected to each other and rattled and creaked when everyone sat down. If a row of kids sat too close to the front edge of the seats all at once, the whole tier would tilt forward and collapse to the floor. People would jump up and rush to the rescue to lift the seats off the bodies trapped underneath. There'd be little sympathy from the pastor, who just reminded us to sit back down. At least it made for an amusing and entertaining, though highly disruptive, interlude in an otherwise rather uneventful service!

Whispering was common, but it was risky, as the pastor would stop his sermon in the middle of a sentence and scold you. Everyone's eyes would glare at you with disapproval. There was no nursery, so the hour could become noisy as the preacher tried to speak above the cries of one or more babies.

I could always tell when the pastor hadn't had time to prepare his Sunday sermon that week. He would begin by saying, "Turn for this morning's sermon to Psalm 23." We heard a lot of sermons on Psalm 23!

Salvation was the dominant theme of most church gatherings. The question of whether we were saved was uppermost in our minds and often posed. I remember my father once asking a particular man if he was saved. The man replied, without missing a beat, "As saved as anyone in this church." I thought this was witty, but the question was sincere and important.

Every Sunday evening, we had an evangelistic service where the gospel was preached vigorously. It began with a rousing hymn sing. We'd open the small red hymnbooks and enthusiastically sing our favourite songs. The building was always packed.

The community drunk, Reuben, whom I knew well, usually arrived late and stumbled through the back doors to sit somewhere in the back row. You knew when he had shown up because he would greet the pastor with a loud, "Evenin', pastor!"

The pastor would preach a gospel sermon and always give an altar call at the end, asking anyone who wanted to receive Jesus into their heart to raise their hand.

"Every head bowed, every eye shut, and no one looking around," he told the rest of us.

But of course that was an invitation for any young boy to covertly cup his hand over his eyes, peek one eye open, and subtly look around. Whether out of nosiness, or just honest curiosity to see who wanted to receive Jesus, I could never help but look around. I couldn't understand why the pastor should be the only one to know.

"I see that hand," the pastor would acknowledge when someone raised their hand. He'd then ask them to walk the aisle to the front for prayer. Reuben walked the aisle to receive Jesus numerous times.

It's interesting to reflect upon the things one learns by osmosis as a child. These are the things that help to form one's character. I learned to be happy with the basic necessities of life and creatively compensate for the things I didn't have. Frugality was a virtue. A simple life was a good life. I didn't need a lot of things to be happy. And I greatly benefitted from being given a strong spiritual foundation. Such realities were fundamental in my later life and ministry.

We had to be out the door early each weekday morning to catch the school bus. Just before we left the house, my mother would line me and my siblings up for a big spoonful of cod liver oil. It was the cure-all of the day, and it was horrible. It tasted like, well... oil. I'd gag and convulse. My mother tried mixing it with jam, but nothing worked.

In my younger years, cod liver oil and school ranked at the same low scale of things I didn't like.

School mornings were an anxious time for me. Depending on what was happening in class, I often feigned feeling sick. I became adept at making myself bring up my breakfast just so I could stay home and evade some challenge or worry at school.

One of life's tough realities is that there will be people who come into our lives who demonstrate unkindness and insensitivity. I've met a few.

My Grade Four teacher was one of them. Her influence was worse for me because she attended our church. After church, she would often pat me on the head and tell my parents in a soft and gentle voice that I was a wonderful child and it was such a pleasure to teach me.

But she was like Dr. Jekyll and Mrs. Hyde. In class, she could be nasty. She was a stout lady and strutted the aisles in her heavy black-laced shoes. You could only pray she would pass you by. If the clomp of the shoes stopped behind you, you'd feel the glowering stare of her eyes peering over your shoulder to scrutinize your work. If she was unhappy with you for some reason, and her reasons often weren't apparent, she would grasp your ear with her sharp nails and pinch and twist. On many occasions, I remember being lifted from my desk as her nails cut into the skin of my contorted ear. She did this to other students as well, although never to her favourites.

I will never forget the day she sorely humiliated me. At the time I had a urinary problem and had been granted special permission to be excused to go to the washroom whenever I needed. One afternoon during class, I put up my hand and asked to go to the washroom. She was in a particularly miserable mood and refused me permission to go. I held on as long as I could and tried to ask a second time. She saw my raised hand but ignored it.

When I could hold it no longer, I remember the hot humiliation of wetting my nine-year-old self.

And it got worse. I asked to go home and used the reason that I felt ill. She called me to the front of the classroom to explain my manner of illness. That was the ultimate shame! Even she was embarrassed when she saw, along with everyone else, the evidence of what I had done.

But it was too late. I may as well have been tied to a public post to suffer the ignominy of disgrace. This was a lesson learned: there are malicious people in the world along with the good. They will enter and exit our lives and we must learn how to deal with them.

Fortunately, there were many more good people in my life. My Grade Five teacher, Mrs. Oak, was one of the most caring people I can remember. She was also a wonderful storyteller. I would sit at my desk listening to her tell stories of the early explorers. When she wove the story, I imagined that I was in the canoe exploring new rivers with Radisson, crawling on my hands and knees with David Livingstone to get a view of the great falls on the Zambezi River, or standing beside Corporal James Walsh while he shook hands with the great Chief Sitting Bull.

I learned from her the importance of cultivating the art of storytelling. While I didn't understand it at the time, in the years to come I used this skill as a teacher.

She also gave me a deep appreciation for history. Over time, I especially fell in love with early Canadian and American history, church history, and biblical history. I grew to understand that history is foundational for understanding ourselves, where we come from, and where we're going.

And then there was Mrs. Smith, my Grades Seven and Eight teacher. She always wore her hair up in a bun and had a severe, old-fashioned look. She would stroll up and down the rows between the desks and lecture us on the importance of diligence and excellence, virtues which I never forgot. She demanded discipline and good behaviour and reinforced this with a leather strap that came out of her desk drawer weekly in case there was any doubt as to the import and consequence of her words.

At the time, I sat under her reign of terror, scared to death of her. It seems like the dark ages now, but I lived to tell the story. As I look back, while I may not agree with her methodology, I am incredibly indebted to her. She instilled discipline, excellence, and a high regard for vigilance and hard work. She drilled the rules of spelling and grammar into my head. These things served me well in the years to come when I wrote essays and articles and crafted sermons and books. Even back in Grade Eight, I had a childlike appreciation for what she taught me. In fact, I painted my first oil painting to give to Mrs. Smith as a thank-you gift when I graduated.

It's not only our environment, the things that happen to us, or the people who come into our lives that shape us. There is also the way God made us. He gave me a sensitive nature and tender heart.

I have always hated to see people hurting. I empathize with the underdog and am always willing to help. When I was young, before I went to sleep, I would call out to my siblings and ask whether there was anything I had done to hurt them that day—and to please forgive me. I'm sure they thought it strange and repetitive, even humorous, but it was genuine. I had a strong God-consciousness, always cognizant of his presence and love and the need to serve and obey him.

I never closed my eyes at night without thanking God for his help and asking for his forgiveness for any sin I had committed. This sensitive nature was who I was. It's who I am still. Some things just can't be changed. This served me in later years as both a strength and liability.

Two

OUR PARENTS ARGUABLY impact who we are more than anyone else. My mother was born in Wimbledon, England, just outside the city of London. Her name was Eileen. She loved music and was a wonderful singer who was told by her music teacher that she sang with perfect pitch. As a girl, she sang the scales up and down with such gusto that her family's neighbour on the other side of the thin dividing wall would complain by banging on the wall.

That didn't stop her. She just took her rehearsal to the bathroom where she shut the door, put her head in a pillow, and continued to sing.

When she got a little older, she accepted an opportunity to sing second soprano with a large London choir that performed in such esteemed venues as the Royal Albert Hall. She enjoyed participating in many oratorios, such as *Elijah*, *The Passion of Christ*, *Hiawatha*, *The Pied Piper of Hamelin*, and of course *The Messiah*.

A most remarkable story my mother once related to me was about her close connection to the familiar Christian hymn "How Great Thou Art" and its entrance into the English-speaking world. The song was a traditional Swedish melody written by Carl Boberg in 1885. The song as we know it today was influenced by Stuart Hine, an English missionary to Russia who translated the song from Russian into English.

When World War II broke out in 1939, Stuart and his wife Mercy returned home to England. For a while, they attended Haydon Hall, the same Brethren chapel that my mother and her parents attended. Stuart became my mother's youth leader. She described him as a likeable, active, and happy man who seemed to be everyone's friend. She called him Uncle Stu. He was a great musician who played a wide variety of instruments. My mother told me that the young people loved to sit around and listen to him play, especially the large piano accordion which he played fantastically.

One day after a service, he beckoned to my mother and told her that he had written and added some original verses to the hymn "How Great Thou Art." He had actually written two sets of new lyrics and explained that the Lord seemed to be saying to him, "Do something with this, Stuart."

He could only afford to publish one set of lyrics, however, and couldn't decide which one. He recognized my mother's musical talent and experience and wondered whether she would take the lyrics home and pray fervently regarding which set she preferred.

My mother happily agreed and returned the following week with her decision. She had chosen the lyrics we know today as verses three and four:

> And when I think that God, his Son not sparing,
> sent him to die, I scarce can take it in,
> that on the cross my burden gladly bearing
> he bled and died to take away my sin.
>
> When Christ shall come with shout of acclamation
> and take me home, what joy shall fill my heart!
> Then I shall bow in humble adoration
> and there proclaim: "My God, how great thou art!"[1]

Stuart expressed his deep gratitude for her decision.

That same week, as it so happened, he was called to another church to serve as pastor. She never saw him again and also never heard anything more about their new hymn—that is, until after the war and she attended a Billy Graham crusade. After the opening song, George Beverly Shea, the gospel singer who served alongside Billy Graham, introduced a new song. Shea walked to the podium and began to sing in his deep baritone, "O Lord my God, when I in awesome wonder, consider all the worlds Thy hands have made…"

My mother recognized the song immediately. It was the song she had assisted Stuart Hine with several years before.

Unable to contain herself, she grabbed the knee of the man sitting beside her, whom she did not know, leapt to her feet, and cried out, "That's Stuart's song! That's our song!"

"Sit down and be quiet!" someone called out. There was a whole lot of shushing from the crowd.

---

[1] Stuart J. Hine (translator), "How Great Thou Art," 1949.

But my mother's excitement could not be quieted.

When Shea began to sing the last stanza, "When Christ shall come with shout of acclamation and take me home, what joy shall fill my heart," the crowd began to clap. The lyrics had resonated in the hearts of all those many thousands. The song exploded in popularity and became the signature song for the Billy Graham crusades for many years, and one of the most well-known songs ever written. Elvis Presley earned two Grammys for his rendering of the song. Most of us are familiar with Carrie Underwood's 2011 chart-topping rendition.

My mother passed along to me her love of singing. When I was very young, she would turn on the radio every Saturday morning for me to listen to country music. She gave me a cookie rack to strum like a guitar and I sang away. As I got older, she recruited me to sing alto alongside her in church. She always encouraged me to use my gift of singing for the Lord. I carried that passion through my many years of ministry.

Life changed dramatically and forever for my mother one Sunday morning as she sat in church. Just fifteen minutes into the service, the air raid sirens began to wail and the congregation heard airplanes overhead. The chapel immediately emptied as people panicked and began to run home. The streets filled with people frantically running this way and that. War had arrived.

That same week, every household was instructed to keep their blinds and curtains closed tightly after dark. The ARP (air raid precaution) wardens walked the streets and kept a sharp lookout for any chinks of light coming from windows. Every individual was given an identity card and personal number and was asked to wear an identity bracelet for rescue purposes.

Several weeks later, everyone was issued a gas mask, which was to be kept on one's person 24/7. The ARP wardens carried little black books and recorded the name of anyone who was caught without their mask.

My grandmother made two shelter coats, one for herself and one for my mother. They were hooded, floor-length, and made from a heavy material. Once zipped up, they were very warm. They also contained large pockets for carrying a flashlight and identity papers. They were red in colour so as to be easy to spot in the case of needed rescue.

Food became scarce. Each person was given a food ration card, like a book of stamps. These stamps were exchanged for food. Long lineups were the norm at grocery stores, especially for bread. My mother was allowed a weekly ration of one egg, two ounces of butter, four ounces of sugar, a half-cup of jam, enough cheese for one sandwich, a few ounces of lamb meat, one piece of bacon, powdered eggs (sometimes), and a daily portion of a third-pint of milk. Fruit simply wasn't available. Recipe leaflets were distributed, suggesting such meals as seagull pie with fatless pastry and banana pudding made from pureed parsnips and banana essence. No coupons were required for rabbits, horse meat, or whale meat.

During the first few years of the war, my mother trained to be a nurse, a profession which dictated her speedy call into active duty. Every day during the Battle of Britain and London Blitz (1940–1941), a relentless bombing offensive carried out by the German Luftwaffe, she risked her life to travel into central London and care for the injured and dying. At night she made her way home by rail, or some other means if the tracks had been bombed or the underground Tube network had been disrupted. She often had to take cover inside random stores or pubs when she heard the sirens wail, the roar of a bomber overhead, or the hissing of a falling bomb. My grandfather always met her partway to help her arrive home safely and together they'd run for the safety of the six-by-five-foot steel bomb shelter in their back yard. It was buried in a hole four feet deep, the excavated dirt spaded over the curved roof to a depth of two feet. It mostly served as a protection from shrapnel, fragments of metal and debris that were blown around by the force of bombs. Five people slept side by side on a double mattress, like sardines in a can.

As soon as darkness settled, they would hear the sound of German bombers approaching and need to run to the shelter. No one slept much; it was too noisy to sleep. Guns went off all the time. The frightening roar of the bombers came in wave after wave and one could hear the whine of British Spitfires swooping and diving in chase. When a searchlight caught a plane in its beam, all the other searchlights would swing onto it while antiaircraft guns fired volleys of ammunition. When a bomber was hit, it would release its bombs—and some of those bombs dropped uncomfortably close to my mother's home. The neighbour's house was hit one night. On two occasions, all the windows of my mother's house were blown out. My grandfather often poked his head out of the small door of the shelter to give a running commentary on what was happening all around.

The Germans began sending V-1 and V-2 rockets over the city. These were like bombs with engines. When they reached their destination, the engine would cut out and the bomb would descend at a forty-five-degree angle. When the bomb went silent, everyone waited, wondering where the bomb would explode.

This was how my mother and her parents lived for months on end, night after night, without fail—except Christmas Day. Everyone's home sustained damage, and every morning neighbours helped one another sweep up the glass and shrapnel from the night before.

My mother's family sang a little chorus whenever they felt frightened:

> Jesus is with me all through the raid.
> He is my comfort. Be not afraid.
> When bombs are dropping and danger is near,
> Jesus is with me till the "All clear!"

They received many answers to prayer. One night a plane was hit and released its bombs. As my mother's family lay in the shelter, they counted the bombs explode upon hitting the earth, each one getting successively louder as they came closer to their small refuge.

One... two... three... four...

"This next one's ours!" my grandfather shouted. "Keep us safe, Lord!"

But it never came. It was a dud. The Lord had kept them safe.

My mother witnessed amazing answers to prayer on a large scale. Twice, King George VI and the government called for a day of national prayer. In 1940, the British Expeditionary Force was trapped on the beaches of France between the sea and the enemy bearing down upon them. All churches were opened and everyone was expected to attend at some point during the day to pray for the deliverance of the troops.

The following day, while walking along the banks of the River Thames, my mother saw scores of boats, large and small, even small rowboats, making their way downriver. She had never seen anything like it and had no idea where they were going.

It turned out that all registered boats had been ordered to the English Channel on a rescue mission to save the lives of the hundreds of trapped soldiers on the French shores.

Prayer was answered that day in that the Channel, renowned for its rough water, was as smooth as glass. Sailors said they had never seen the waters so calm. Soldiers waded out into the water to meet the incoming boats, be picked up, and taken home.

God had clearly answered the prayers of the nation with a remarkable miracle.

Another day of national prayer was called prior to the landing of the Allied troops on the shores of Europe, known as D-Day. It was a momentous occasion and the beginning of the end of German occupation and aggression. Despite heavy losses, the attempt was successful. General Montgomery, the man who commanded all Allied ground forces and was affectionately known as "Monty," was quoted as saying, "It is the Lord's doing, and it is marvellous in our eyes."

Three

MY MOTHER AND father met around an organ in the home of an older Christian couple, Mr. and Mrs. Godwin, who had invited a few nurses, my mother being one of them, and some Canadian soldiers together for an evening of singing.

My father was in the Canadian army training in England and preparing to advance into Europe. He was one of the soldiers invited to the Godwins' that night, and the rest is history.

His name was Donald and he trained as a wireless operator, relaying coded messages in a Sherman tank with the Canadian Grenadier guards. He was sent into Belgium and from there into the Netherlands where he witnessed the worst bloodshed and warfare in the hard-fought liberation of Holland. He lost many friends and comrades, young men who cried out for their mothers as they bled to death. During battle, his tank rang with the ear-splitting sound of hundreds of bullets hitting the metal sides. The enemy was pushed back to the German border and my father soon found himself engaged in active warfare in Germany until the end of the war.

These years remained etched in his mind for the rest of his life.

The joy of liberation was also etched in his memory, though, and he spoke about it many times in later years. As the Canadian tanks rolled into Dutch towns and villages, people streamed out into the streets shouting, crying, and celebrating. Women threw flowers up onto the tanks, covering them with colour. My father looked out at the faces of the children emaciated from years of hunger. He took a pair of long underwear, knotted the bottoms, and filled the legs with cans of food, then lowered them down into the outstretched hands.

During the war, Dad realized that he would either live for Jesus or not. There was no middle ground or room to compromise his witness and faith. He decided, along with a few fellow soldiers, to make a stand to live for Jesus. He was often mocked for his stand and nicknamed the Reverend. However, in the thick of battle a radio message would often come through from the other tanks asking him to pray.

While serving in Holland and Germany, there were times when my father thought he wouldn't survive. During one of those times, in the midst of a flaming barn where he had been sleeping under a hay wagon, he promised to serve God in any way he was called should God get him out of the situation alive.

Well, God got him out alive and that promise always held a space in his mind.

At the end of the war, my father returned to Canada, but he never forgot the beautiful girl he had met around the organ in England. They wrote letters back and forth and my father promised that he would return to marry her.

And he did! Two years later, he was on a ship headed for England.

My mother recently went home to be with Jesus, and in her old age she recounted this part of the story, how she stood with hundreds of people on the wharf in Southampton, waving as the ship came into port. She wore a cranberry-coloured linen skirt and jacket so she would be easily distinguished. All she could see were hundreds of heads looking over the rail on the port side of the ship. Her eyes scanned the crowd, back and forth, looking for my dad.

Then, amidst the throngs, their eyes locked. She waved frantically, tears running down her face. My father waved back from the deck of the ship and then disappeared from sight.

She waited.

A few minutes later, she felt two arms envelop her tightly from behind. Decades later, she could still remember the prickly tweed jacket he wore. She turned and the two lovers held each other in their arms for a good half-hour, kissing and weeping with joy.

"We will not be parted again," Dad said to her.

She described that as one of the happiest days of her life.

Just before she died, she told me that this was the picture she had in her mind of what it would be like to meet Jesus. The ship of life would come into port and Jesus would be waiting to receive her into his arms forever, never to be parted. It was to be the happiest day of her life.

That became her reality on Christmas Day 2020.

Upon his arrival, my father got a good job with the London Toll Exchange, monitoring telephone lines. He sat directly behind a young Japanese gentleman named Kay Kitamura. My father had long legs and stretched them out under Kay's chair in front of him. Every time Kay looked down, he saw a pair of large shoes and diamond-knitted socks.

When Kay looked around to see who owned them, he met my father. The two became best of friends.

My dad witnessed often to Kay about his faith, and Kay had lots of questions. One day Dad had the joy of praying with his friend and leading him to Jesus.

When I was born, I was given Kay's middle name, Stanley, as my middle name.

My father always had a passion for sharing Jesus with others. He did so boldly. He joined a group of young men called Village Workers, and every weekend they rode their bicycles into the countryside to the towns and villages. They would set up in the village green and go door to door inviting people to a gospel service. These gospel services were always well-attended.

When the day arrived for my mom and dad to be married, my grandmother purchased a surplus Japanese parachute in a London market and, excellent seamstress that she was, made from it a beautiful silk wedding dress for my mother.

Two weeks after the wedding, my parents were on a boat, the *RMS Queen Elizabeth*, heading for Canada. It was a rough voyage, but they did it together.

It's difficult to imagine what was going through the mind of my mother as she peered westward from the bow of the ship toward a new life. It was an enormous change. She had left behind everything familiar to live in a land she knew so little about. In her imagination, Canada was a land of snow and ice, bears and wolves. My dad had to keep reassuring her that it was a land of opportunity for the Lord. This resonated with her.

Interestingly, she had experienced a strong feeling of divine call on her life in the years just before the war, intending to travel to Labrador in northern Canada to serve as a missionary nurse with the Grenfell Mission. Obviously, the prolonged war had interrupted those aspirations.

My parents both felt the same thing: a sense of divine call. And that was instilled in me from my earliest days.

When I was born just one year after their return to Canada, the trauma of the war was still recent—and all those experiences they'd had now impacted me as well. As a result, they instilled values in me that remain to this day. Values like persevering through tough times, determination, resilience, duty, learning to be content with just a little, appreciating simplicity, showing compassion for the hurt and marginalized, understanding the priority and power of prayer, embracing the reality of God's presence and providence in every situation, never giving up hope, living one's faith, and letting one's light shine for Christ in the world.

Four

I WAS BORN in Toronto, Ontario. About the same time, the Holy Spirit was stirring the hearts of my parents to make another life-altering change. Two words kept coming to their minds: *go north*. He gave no specific leading as to any particular location. Just *go north*.

They prayed much about it and the two words persisted. So my father purchased an old 1926 Pontiac for $200. They packed a tent and everything they owned into the back seat, including me, and like Abraham of old set off for a country that God would show them. They had no idea where they would end up, only that they should set off for the north country.

My father was raised in the city, but he was a country boy at heart. My mother was also raised in a city, but she was not so much a country girl. She envisioned *north* to mean the wilds of Canada, resurrecting the old foreboding thoughts of ice and snow, bears and wolves. They both felt apprehension, but stronger was their faith that God was leading them. They prayed fervently for the Lord to show them his will about where they should settle.

On the way north, they stopped at a friend's home for a short visit, and this friend gave them a box of ten chickens. They loaded the chickens in the back seat, along with the luggage and me, and set off again.

The old car heated up quickly and they had to stop regularly to let the engine cool down. They also discovered that the roof leaked water. When it rained, they had to open an umbrella to stay dry.

At night they stopped and set up the tent. My mother had never camped before and she wasn't dressed for it. She was dressed in silk stockings, a Harris Tweed suit, and a cashmere sweater. But she did it!

After a couple of days, they neared the small town of Huntsville in the beautiful lake district of Muskoka in central Ontario. About seven miles before Huntsville, they rounded a large bend in the road. As the road straightened, they saw a little Anglican church in the middle of a field and a small single-story house just past the church in a grove of trees. It had a for-sale sign in the front yard.

They looked at each other and cried out, "There it is!"

They used the little money they had saved to put a small downpayment on the house. It was just a shell, very simple, but adequate. They worked on the house all summer, insulating, painting, making curtains, and doing whatever was necessary to make it into a comfortable little home. Dad built a chicken shed at the back of the property to house the chickens.

The property included a lovely brook bubbling down over the rocks. Dad was thinking, *A new house and brook trout!* Mom was thinking, *A new house and a comfortable bed!*

They called the property Sunnybrook, attesting to the beauty of the sparkling brook when the sun shone upon it. Rich, green grass surrounded the house. The community was called Grassmere.

My father found a job with the T. Eaton Company in Huntsville. Just as he walked into the store, the boss had fired a man for stealing. That's when he turned around to see my dad.

"Yes, sir," the man said. "Can I help you?"

"Sir, I was wondering if you had a job opening," Dad replied.

"Yes. Go up to my office and apply. You can begin right away."

My father started his new job by serving coffee to the employees. Over the next few years, he moved from one department to another until he worked his way up to becoming the assistant manager of the store.

God's providence is amazing. Providence means that God sees before us or ahead of us and provides. Well, God provided over and over again. He did it for my parents as they raised their small family, and he would do it for me and my wife and our family in equally amazing ways.

Five

A FEW YEARS later, we moved into a home closer to Huntsville and began attending the little Baptist church down the road. My parents became very active serving in that church. However, they were always looking for innovative ways to share the gospel in places where there was no gospel witness.

One day someone gave my father a pair of loudspeaker horns for the top of the car. These came as a direct answer to prayer, as Dad had been praying for a means of sharing the gospel in the open air.

This gift opened up doors all over the Huntsville area. It certainly seems inconceivable today, but he acquired permission to hold open-air gospel services in provincial parks. We would drive into the park and walk from campsite to campsite inviting campers to the service in the outdoor theatre. Campers strolled into the theatre, curiously attracted by the sound of music. They would sit down and listen to a short program and a gospel message delivered by my father. We were thrown out of a few provincial parks but were well-received in others.

One Sunday in Algonquin Park, thirty-five people responded to the gospel invitation and remained after the service to receive Jesus into their lives.

Both my parents had a passion to reach out to people in the outlying rural communities around Huntsville. Many of them were poor and relatively isolated. My parents started mission works in numerous locations.

Those years had a lasting impact on my life. My mother played the accordion—we called it a "squeeze box"—and as she played, my siblings and I burst our lungs singing the action choruses. She was a wonderful storyteller and told Bible stories to the kids using flannelgraph. I would sit riveted to the flannel board, listening to every word.

Over the years, I learned most of the stories of the Bible just by listening to her tell the stories. And I witnessed the effectiveness of good storytelling. Meanwhile, my father would give a twenty-minute message to the adults, always concluding with an invitation to respond.

I remember a particular mission my parents started in a small rural community called Yearly. It began one day when my parents were driving through the backwoods. They pulled into the driveway of a rundown farmhouse where a large number of children were playing. They knocked on the door, introduced themselves, and asked the parents if they would like them to return the following Sunday morning to tell the kids Bible stories. The kids were eager and the parents happily obliged.

We returned the following Sunday and told stories to all the kids lined up on wooden benches.

The following Sunday, the parents stayed for the stories.

The Sunday after that, the grandparents showed up.

Every Sunday the numbers increased until someone suggested we should move into the one-room schoolhouse up the road. So we did. From that day forward, we were bursting at the seams. I still remember the picture of Queen Elizabeth hanging at the front just above the blackboards. A woodstove in the middle of the room served as the only source of warmth in the winter.

The summers at Yearly were particularly eventful. My father drove his blue '56 Chevy along the dusty backroads to pick up anyone waiting at the end of their driveway. Poverty and alcohol abuse had left their mark on many families.

At one particular place, we would pick up seven or eight children. These kids lived a meagre and pitiful life, but they loved to attend the meetings. My dad would honk the horn at the end of the driveway, then usually walk up to the house and step over the body of their alcoholic father lying drunk in the doorway. The mother had died several years earlier giving birth in the barn outback. Yes, the barn.

When my father gave the call, kids emerged from all corners, jumped over their drunken father, and bounded toward the Chevy. These were the days before seatbelts, so we could load fifteen or more people into the car. I often sat in the trunk with three others, with the lid up of course. By the time we got to the schoolhouse we'd be blanketed in a thick layer of white dust. Those were the days! As our car rolled over gravel roads, we sang heartily, belting out our favourite songs. We were like a singalong on wheels.

Many people gave their lives to Jesus during those years. My dad always closed the service with a certain chorus:

>Into my heart, into my heart,
>Come into my heart, Lord Jesus.

> Come in today, come in to stay,
> Come into my heart, Lord Jesus.[2]

As mentioned, he always closed with an altar call, asking anyone who wanted to receive Jesus to get out of their chair and walk to the front of the room where he would pray with them. I felt convicted most times to go forward.

One young man who gave his life to Jesus in those days was a lad from that same home that was so broken by alcoholism. After returning home from the schoolhouse one day, he sat looking out of the window in his bedroom and sang the chorus: "Into my heart, into my heart, come into my heart, Lord Jesus." He sang it with more meaning than he had ever sung it before and knew that something had truly happened deep inside his heart.

This young man was poorly educated, barely able to read and write, but he understood that God was calling him to serve full-time in some kind of Christian ministry. He made the decision to go to seminary and become a pastor. My parents assisted and supported him over the next few years, and upon graduation he returned to the same community where he had grown up and continued the ministry my parents had begun.

Another young man from that congregation became a missionary to Haiti.

While I didn't fully recognize it at the time, I was witnessing the supernatural power of the simple gospel to transform a human life and give it a whole new direction.

We used to pick up two old gentlemen for church by the side of the road. Both in their nineties, Sam and Tom would walk several miles to the main road every Sunday from their homestead and wait for us to pick them up.

One morning, they weren't at the roadside and my father felt concerned, and of course they had no phone for us to call and check on them.

He decided the next day to drive out to their home and invited me to come along with him. I was more than ready to do so.

We parked the car at the end of their road, as it was impassable for a vehicle. When we arrived at their place, my dad rapped on the door and called out for them. There was no answer. Clearly something was wrong.

I remember entering the house. We saw some scanty food on the table, mouldy cheese and stale bread. Tom was lying on a cot over in the corner, weak and sick. Sam had fallen down the stairs and was lying near the bottom of the stairs with a nasty gash on his head. Fortunately we discovered them before the situation got worse.

---

[2] Harry D. Clarke, "Into My Heart," 1924.

We cleaned them up, got them to drink some water, and told them that we would return after going for help. We then walked to a small farm several miles away and informed the farmer, who was more than ready to help. He hitched a small wagon to a team of horses and we returned. Back at the homestead, we lifted them out into the wagon and made them as comfortable as possible in a bed of straw. We returned down the bumpy lane to the main road, loaded them into our vehicle, and made the journey home.

My mother prepared a good healthy dinner for them that evening. We sat down, gave thanks for the safe arrival of our two guests, and began to eat. Sam and Tom just nibbled away at what was on their plates.

That's when it happened—both men belched what little they had in their stomachs onto the table. All four kids jumped up and beat an immediate retreat, leaving my parents to attend to the cleanup. They cleaned the table, the chairs, the floor, and up the wall. It amazed me how much had spewed up from their almost empty stomachs. Both men were then escorted to the bathtub where they were cleaned and scrubbed.

They continued to live with us in our home until my parents found them a place of their own, a small cabin just down the road. They lived a few more years and my parents cared for them daily. As kids, we visited them often and listened to the stories they told about the early pioneer days.

All this time, God was preparing the heart of a young boy. I was learning what it meant to reach out to the poor and underprivileged. I was witnessing what it meant to serve and practice what Jesus had meant when he washed the disciples' feet and told us to do the same. I was digesting a life lesson on what it means to do whatever it takes to help those in need.

Every Saturday morning, I would pull up a chair beside the fridge, reach up for the radio, and listen to a broadcast called *Back to the Bible*. The broadcast always included a fifteen-minute mystery story from the life of a fictional character named Danny Orlis. I loved the mystery, but I also learned things such as commitment to Jesus, putting him first in your life, faith, courage, love, and serving God and others.

And whenever I listened, I felt an inner tug. I didn't fully understand it then, but now I know that it was the Holy Spirit.

At the Baptist Camp just down the road from our home, I was challenged to walk to the front of the room at a camp meeting and commit my life to serving Jesus. My parents had already led me to faith in Jesus as my Saviour, but now I made a public commitment to serve him. I was saying to Jesus, "Anything, anywhere, anytime." I meant it. I signed a small commitment card which I have to this day.

Six

ONE DAY EVERYTHING changed for our family. My mother sat all four kids down for a conversation. She seemed sombre and we knew something was wrong.

She told us that our dad was not well. He had been to many doctors, but they couldn't diagnose the problem. He was losing strength and the specialists were beginning to question whether he would recover. It was serious.

Late one night, my father shook my mother to awaken her. She was startled, but Dad was even more startled. He told her that the Lord had just spoken to him—and there was no doubt in his mind what God had said.

"Are you going to keep the promise you made to me twenty years ago in that burning barn on the battlefield in Germany?" the Holy Spirit questioned. It was just a whisper, but it struck like a bolt of lightning. "You promised me that if I got you through this war alive, you would serve me for the rest of your life and do whatever I asked. You know what I've been asking. I've been calling you into full-time pastoral ministry. If you don't act, I'm going to take you home. What is your answer?"

My father had been working at the Eaton's store in Huntsville. Over a period of about twelve years, he had successfully worked through various departments to finally become assistant manager. He had a promising future with the company. In fact, he had recently been offered the manager's position at the T. Eaton store up in Sault Ste. Marie.

But the next morning, after my father was roused from sleep, he walked into his manager's office and handed in his resignation… along with the reason: he would be going into full-time pastoral ministry.

The manager looked up at him. "You're mad!"

"No," replied Dad. "I've never been more certain. I mean it."

And he did.

That same day, my father phoned a seminary in Toronto and began the application process for pastoral studies. He was just in time to begin a new semester.

Interestingly, at his next doctor's visit he learned the reason for his medical condition, and with the right medication and treatment he was predicted to make a full recovery. God had spoken.

That was a challenging and stretching year for our family. My father attended classes in Toronto during the week and hitchhiked home every Friday. Most Friday nights, he was picked up by truckers who were going directly to Huntsville or nearby. God looked after the details.

My mother got a job as a private nurse at Huntsville Hospital in addition to looking after the home. All four of us kids took on responsibilities to help compensate for our dad's absence.

I grew up a lot that year.

God was active in the life of our family. He was certainly working in the life of a boy to make him a young man. As I navigated that year, it became clearer that my life was in God's hands. He was looking after both the big picture and the small details. And I was increasingly aware that God had a call on my life. I wanted to be attentive when He spoke—and obey.

Seven

AFTER MY FATHER completed his seminary training, he received a call to a church in northern Ontario in a village called Desbarats, pronounced Debra, just east of Sault Ste. Marie. So our family found ourselves moving north.

We lived in a little house out in the middle of a field. We called it the little house on the prairie. It was more than a hundred years old, had walls insulated with straw, and was very small for a family of six. There was a kitchen, a small living room, one bathroom, a small room that Dad used as a study, and three small bedrooms at the top of a long, narrow staircase. I slept in a room with my two brothers. My dad had me tie a rope to the leg of my bed for a fire escape out the window in case the place ever caught fire in the night.

We heated the house with a small oil stove. The stove pipe went up through my parents' bedroom and served as the source of heat upstairs. Needless to say, getting up on a cold winter morning was invigorating and we had to get dressed briskly. Frozen water pipes were common. We always left a pot of water on the stovetop overnight so we would have some hot water for washing each morning.

My mother made it into a cozy home. Though it lacked in space, it never lacked in laughter. The experience of living in that little house was more fun than I can express. We were poor but didn't know it.

I loved the north. The summers were hot and dry. We lived in a large farming community and I learned to work hard, bailing hay from dawn to dusk, ploughing fields, milking cows, cleaning calf pens, slaughtering pigs, and taking care of whatever farmwork needed doing. I found farmers to be people of principle. The farmers who went to our church wouldn't work on Sunday, choosing instead to take a sabbath rest, and they never broke with that principle even if rain was in Monday's forecast.

While working on a farm, I experienced one of my strangest but most memorable encounters. My friend and I, returning home with the last wagonload of hay for the season, stacked the bales particularly high to save us from needing to return to the field for a second load. The wagon was in motion when I scrambled up onto the top of the hay load and stretched out at the front to catch the breeze. At one point, the road wound down a short, steep hill with a sharp bend at the bottom. As we crested the hill and began our decline, the gravitational force of the heavy load began to push the tractor uncontrollably.

The driver panicked. He pushed his foot down on the brakes, causing the tractor to slide sideways as the large wheels dug into the dirt. The hay began to shift frontward. I felt this and reached out my hand to grasp the limb of a tree that hung out over the road.

Suddenly everything gave way. My feet swept out from beneath me and I felt myself falling. I remember clearly hitting my back on the iron tongue of the wagon. In that split second, I anticipated being dragged underneath the wagon and killed under several tons of hay.

God had other plans. Unexpectedly and swiftly, I felt a hand—this is the most adequate way to describe it—lift me from the iron tongue. I sprang to the side of the road as though catapulted by a heavy elastic band, landing safely away from the carnage.

What had happened made no sense! One doesn't fall flat on one's back on an inflexible iron tongue, attached to a moving tractor pulling a full heavy load of hay that's avalanching upon you... and walk away unscathed. It was as if I had been flung by an unseen hand out of harm's way. All in a split second.

The driver came running back up the hill, shaking and shocked to see me sitting on a bale of hay alive. Debris lay scattered all over the hill.

I sat for several moments trying to process what had just happened.

"I think that I was just rescued by... an angel," I said to my friend, whose own look of panic had turned to relief.

I wonder how many times such things happen in our lives, with less drama and without our awareness. The Bible does say, *"For he [God] will order his angels to protect you wherever you go"* (Psalm 91:11). These angels guard, protect, care, and support us in our weakness.

Such episodes in our lives serve to remind me that God knows and holds control over every detail of my life.

Well, if the summers were hot and dry, the winters were long and cold. But there was no shortage of ponds on which we could shovel off the snow and enjoy a good game of ice hockey. What we lacked in skill we made up for in passion. We would play so vigorously that I'd need to strip down to the waist even when the temperature was well below zero—Fahrenheit—and of course every Saturday night we gathered in unbroken tradition around the television and watched *Hockey Night in Canada*.

In the early fall, I enjoyed hunting along the rocky ridges, keeping my eyes peeled for grouse.

In winter, I loved to slip into moccasins, strap on the snowshoes, and trek as far back into the forest as possible. I still recall the sound of the snow crunching under my hide-covered feet. I absorbed the silence and serenity of the deep woods. And nothing tasted better than a hot dog roasted over an open fire on a cold winter's morning.

Our whole family was very busy with the church's ministry. We were also busily engaged in a second ministry, a Sunday school in another farming community. There, we gathered in a bare-bones community hall and sat on hard wooden benches with no backrests. We looked for every opportunity to stand and stretch!

We soon outgrew the community centre and decided to move into the village of Echo Bay, a tough little steel town just outside the Garden River First Nation. We knocked on every door in the village to inform people about who we were and inviting them to church. I often took my life in my hands, as most homes had a hungry guard dog on the lookout for something to eat.

We arrived at the larger Echo Bay community centre early every Sunday morning, opening the doors wide to exchange the stale smell of food and booze with fresh air. We cleaned up beer bottles and garbage from the night before and got the coffee on. We transformed the centre into a place of worship in a half-hour. The sense of community was great! Everyone who had bought into the vision of the church was ready to lend a hand and do whatever needed to be done.

The church community grew and we eventually recognized the need for our own church facility, so we purchased land and worked hard that year to construct a building. Everyone—men, women, and whole families— willingly and eagerly gave their time and skills. I worked every Saturday at the site, all the while learning about more than just construction; I was learning firsthand how to plant the seed of a church and cultivate and water it for growth. The experience was rewarding. God's hand was on me, personally cultivating my spiritual growth and training me for the calling he had on my life.

We completed the building debt-free and opened on Thanksgiving Sunday. It was an exciting day. We named the church Faith Baptist Church because the story of the church had been one of faith from the beginning. That small church became a glowing light in this tough little northern town where many people came to faith in Jesus and found salvation, healing, and community.

In those days, I learned a lot about ministry from experience. Faith is essential, but faith without works is dead. A lot of hard work goes into ministry. There's no way around it.

Sundays were particularly busy. In the morning, we held worship services at Faith Baptist Church. Then we raced home and grabbed a quick lunch in time for the worship service at Calvary Church in Desbarats. After dinner, we drove over to St. Joseph Island for a community service there. We had to take a ferry over to the island; during the summer it wasn't unusual to wait in line for several hours before being able to catch the ferry home. It made for a long and tiring day.

Through the week, there were prayer meetings and vibrant youth ministries for both churches. As the churches prospered, more and more opportunities opened for ministry in addition to the ongoing care of the congregation.

Yes, hard work! There's no way around it if you want to flourish as a church.

In the years of our ministry in the north, another critical lesson was impressed upon me by the Holy Spirit in his classroom of spiritual growth: when we move forward by faith, God provides for our needs.

My father's income was inadequate, especially for a family of six. But God always provided. People often brought the produce of their gardens, not to mention the produce God provided out of our own garden. Sometimes a farmer would share a butchered cow and our freezer would be filled with meat.

The dairy farmer next to us told us that we could take as much milk as we required from his milk vat. When my mother asked him if he realized how much milk four teenagers could drink, he replied that he did since he had teenagers of his own. In the morning, after the milk had sat in the fridge all night, two inches of fresh cream would have risen to the top of the jug. A scoop skimmed off the top was to die for.

Once in a while, a large box of clothing would arrive at our doorstep, sent from someone we knew from southern Ontario. I must admit that it wasn't always the best clothing. As teenagers, we would have fun parading around in outfits that were well past their expiry date. But while lots of secondhand clothing wasn't suitable for wear, we did get some that was, and for that we were grateful.

We never suffered. We never went without. And while we didn't have a lot, we had enough. God always provided.

My wife and I would experience that same lesson years later with the same results.

Eight

EVERYONE TOLD ME that I would be a pastor like my father. I would nod agreeably just to escape the conversation since I couldn't really see myself as a pastor. While I was very aware of the rewards of ministry, I had been in a pastor's home long enough to question whether I really wanted the stress and struggle of it. That kind of life wasn't easy. I knew that. I had witnessed up close the anguish my parents had endured because of criticisms and attacks. I had seen the burdens they carried. I had experienced the hard work and felt the pain of ministry.

Anyway, I was too shy, very much an introvert. I could get up and sing in front of an audience behind my guitar, but to preach? I thought I could never do that.

I tried preaching once. I spent hours preparing my sermon and thought I was good to last for at least twenty-five minutes. When I got up to speak, I got through everything I knew in ten minutes and sat down. Going into pastoral ministry would require me to hear a definite call from God.

So as I neared the end of high school and ruminated about what direction I should go, I decided to enter teachers' college.

That was an extremely difficult year of study. The course load was heavy, the instructors strict, and the practical classroom teaching intimidating. I often thought about packing it in. But I stuck with it.

Looking back, I can again see how the Holy Spirit was leading me. I loved teaching and it seemed natural to me. It seemed like God had made me to teach. But formal training equipped me to understand the art of lesson preparation. It cultivated my communication skills and gave me confidence to stand in front of people, which would serve me well in the years to come.

While in one sense I was running away from pastoral ministry, in another sense God was preparing me for it.

I taught elementary school for two years in northern Ontario. I enjoyed those years immensely. The children I taught came from communities ravaged by social problems. Some of them had experienced trauma.

After my first year of teaching I was asked to meet with the superintendent of the board of education. I entered the meeting with no idea what he wanted to say. Had I done that badly in my first year of teaching?

But I could hardly believe what I heard him say. He asked whether I would be willing to move to another school. The reason? This new school had many children who came from extremely dysfunctional homes without a healthy male influence. He wanted to place a male teacher in the school who practiced strong Judeo-Christian values and would display a positive male image. He was looking for someone to instill healthy family and community values. And that person was me.

I was shocked. I hadn't any idea that he knew anything about me, let alone what my values were or that I was a person of faith. But there was no way to say no, so I made the move.

During those years, the Holy Spirit reinforced in me the importance and high priority that children hold in the mind and heart of God. Jesus placed children on a pedestal one day when parents brought their children to him to be blessed. His disciples went into immediate action, acting like Jesus's security detail, and pushed everyone away.

Jesus's response was swift. He called the children to him and gathered them around. He then made a poignant statement: the kingdom of God belongs to those who are like children.

Another time, Jesus listened to a conversation amongst his disciples about who was the most important among them. Jesus responded by stating that whoever wanted to be first among them should take last place and be the servant of everyone else. He drove the lesson home by taking a child in his arms and informing them that anyone who welcomed a child welcomed him. He added that the greatest in his kingdom was the one who became as humble as a child.

The mind of a child absorbs everything, the good and the bad. What a child's mind and heart absorb in childhood has the potential to inspire and ignite hopes and dreams, but also to destroy those hopes and dreams.

Young minds are easily opened to become receptive to the wonders of their heavenly Father and the purposes he has for their lives. These are the years when truth can take deep root and influence a life exponentially.

Children have always held a unique and special place in my mind. Throughout my years as a pastor, I personally worked hard to communicate truth to them on a level they could understand. I sought intentionally to establish vibrant ministries to children that the Holy Spirit could use to awaken a powerful God-consciousness within and stimulate them to a deeper relationship with him, godly action, and a sense of divine purpose.

During those two years of teaching elementary school, the Holy Spirit clearly impressed upon my heart the need to go into full-time pastoral ministry. I knew what he wanted me to do.

So just like my father had done years before, I quit my job and applied to seminary.

Nine

IT WAS A shock to my system moving from northern Ontario to the sprawling city of Toronto. I looked forward to my theological studies, but getting accustomed to the urban culture was difficult. The pace of life was so much faster and impersonal.

I became laser-focused on my studies, with a clear sense of where God was leading me. I took as many courses as I could in the books of the Bible, dissecting and understanding their history, content, and message. I poured my energies into Greek and Hebrew, Old Testament and New Testament surveys, biblical and church history, systematic theology, and pastoral theology.

I became a student of the Reformation and was particularly inspired by the devotion of the sixteenth-century Anabaptists who led a countercultural movement and remained faithful in living for Jesus in the face of appalling persecution and death. Their example of faithfulness kindled within me the desire to have the same spirit. I studied intensely and enjoyed it immensely. I was like a sponge soaking in as much content as I could.

I also had my eyes on a girl. She was tall with long dark hair and brown eyes. People had rebuked me and told me that one doesn't go to seminary to find a wife, but I believed that finding the right girl to marry would greatly impact both me personally and the ministry to which God was calling me, probably more so than all the studies I pursued. And what better place to find a good and godly wife than at seminary? I had prayed that if it was God's will, he would show me the right girl before I completed my studies.

It was only the second day when I saw her. While sitting in the lunchroom with a new friend, I saw her walk past the doorway. The glimpse was quick but irresistible. She glanced my way and our eyes locked.

And then she was gone.

I'm sure that I read much more into it than she did. I remarked to my friend that this was the girl I was going to marry one day.

He looked at me with a smirk. "You don't even know her."

I found out two things about her several days later from my friend. Firstly, she had a name: Diane. And secondly, she was engaged to be married.

Engaged! I couldn't believe that the one girl I wanted to marry was engaged to someone else. Two days into seminary and my hopes were already torpedoed.

So for the next few years I focused on my studies.

On weekends, I worked as the youth pastor at the church where my father pastored an hour outside Toronto. I pastored about forty to fifty students, which kept me extremely busy. For two summers, I also pastored another large group of teens and college students at a different church. I wanted to gain as much experience as possible in pastoral ministry. I loved working with youth, helping them set their sights on God's purposes for their lives while they were young and making critical decisions.

One summer I served alongside my brother-in-law with the Shantymen's Christian Association. SCA sent missionaries into many isolated regions within Canada to share the gospel with such people as loggers, miners, fishermen, and Indigenous people.

Our mission was to travel to Junior Ranger camps throughout northern Ontario. These were young men who at the time worked for the government's Department of Lands and Forests in bush camps. It was wonderful to get the northern air into my lungs again.

We travelled in a little blue half-ton truck over almost impassable roads into very remote areas. We would drive into a camp and ask whether we could show a Christian movie, do some singing with our guitars, and answer questions on life and the Bible. Some camps had no interest in anything religious and showed us the gate and the way out. Most camps, however, were hungry for something to do in the evenings and we were well-received.

It was an unforgettable experience. Our discussions about faith sometimes continued long into the evening. We even witnessed a few young men receive Jesus as Saviour. From others, we met resistance.

With one year left in my studies at seminary, I specifically asked the Holy Spirit to show me who he wanted me to marry—and if he didn't want me to marry, I would accept that.

Later that same week, I attended a missions conference at a church I was attending. While sitting next to the aisle of a packed room, I saw Diane walk past me with her parents and sit four rows directly in front of me.

I have no recollection of what the preacher had to say that evening, but I do recall staring at the back of Diane's head throughout the entire meeting. I decided that I would wait to make my move until the end of the service, when she had to walk past me on her way out and wouldn't be able to avoid me.

And that's what happened. As she walked my way, she glanced at me shyly, since we knew each other a little by now from attending the same seminary. I stood up, said hello as though surprised by her unexpected appearance, and stumbled around for words to engage her in conversation. Her mother smiled at me and kept walking, but Diane stayed back.

As it turned out, this meeting was more of a divine appointment than a chance encounter. She was at a very low juncture in her life, having recently experienced the abrupt breakup of her engagement only six weeks before the wedding day. She had found out via a letter in the mail. Plans had been made. Gifts received. Venue paid for. And then it was over! It felt like the bottom had fallen out of her life.

She had a very good job as a medical secretary for a well-known urologist in the city, but when she came home after work she often just went to her room to cry. Her heart was truly broken. That night, her mother had encouraged her to get out of the house and go to the service, since maybe God had something to say to her.

As it turned out, God did have something for her. And for me!

Time got away on us and before we knew it we were the last two people in the building. The custodian told us politely that he wanted to lock up. We looked around for her mother, but she had left the building and gone home.

"That's okay," I interjected. "I'll take you home."

That was the beginning of it all.

It would be several more years before I finished my studies in seminary and university, but Diane waited for me. I didn't have money for an engagement ring but assured her that I would save up and get one as early as possible. She came up with a very generous plan to take her previous engagement ring to a pawn shop and use the cash to purchase a new ring.

Then, on June 25, 1977, we were married. She was clearly the girl God had chosen for me as a life partner, and I was the guy he had chosen for her. Neither one of us ever doubted that, even through some extraordinarily difficult times that would test our love.

Our honeymoon was spent at a rundown cabin on an island in northern Ontario. We arrived at it by canoe. It so happened that the cabin was overrun with mice, and I hadn't taken into consideration that there was only an outdoor facility attached to a woodshed. This outhouse was also home to a family of flying squirrels.

As I sat there on the first occasion, peering at the rough wooden door only a few inches from my nose, I got a strong sense that I was being watched. I looked up and found myself face to face with a critter with large bulging eyes and bushy tail. I'm sure I had woken it from its daytime sleep.

It rained all week. Not one sunny day.

Our first meal was fish sticks, which we only needed to heat in the oven. I thought that would be easy enough. But we left them in the oven too long at too high a heat, so our first meal together was very burnt fish sticks.

And the rain continued to fall.

Diane was an invaluable partner in the ministry to which God called us. She understood the truth about God's call on one's life. The call to pastoral ministry was critical to both of us and something we shared. She was educated with a bachelor's degree from seminary, possessed a keen administrative mind, and had already exercised the richness and benefit of that gift leading the preschool department in a large church in Toronto.

Just a few years down the road, I would discover the benefits of her administrative skills in running our busy family and ministry.

She was also musical, deeply spiritual, and had a passion for knowing God and serving him. Something I loved was her quiet and gentle spirit, which was precious to God and treasured by me. She was never outspoken and didn't like the limelight. But she was a diligent, persevering, committed worker behind the scenes. She always finished what she began. She was deeply loyal, too. She had strong opinions but was never opinionated, strong but never overbearing, assertive but never officious. She could absorb a lot, and in the years to come would prove herself able to carry immense pain while maintaining a healthy outlook and gentle smile. Whenever I needed wise counsel, she was able to see through the surface of an issue and speak into my life with wisdom and discernment.

Ten

OUR FIRST CHURCH was a small Baptist congregation in Peterborough, Ontario. It was a little church with a long history of struggles. There were about thirty people, most of whom were over the age of fifty, with few children and no teenagers.

On my first Sunday morning, I stood behind a pulpit facing my thirty congregants all crowded into the back three rows and separated by six empty rows between us. I figured it would probably be easier to fill the front six rows with new attenders than it would be to convince the present back-row attenders to move forward.

That morning I decided that I would fill the front rows with as many youth as possible.

I rented the gymnasium of a local high school, planning to host a youth ministry there. It was a faith step since at that point we had no youth. In the coming week, I then visited the entire community around the church and invited as many teens as possible to come to the school on Friday evening to play floor hockey.

That Friday, to my amazement, about forty teens showed up. I told them the program for the evening was simple: they play floor hockey for one hour, then sit in a large circle and listen to me speak for ten minutes. They complied.

And they kept coming back. We went through an entire winter with a good-sized group attending every Friday evening for floor hockey and a short challenge from the Bible. I was amazed at how quietly they sat and listened to me share the gospel or some lesson from the Bible.

That first year, Diane and I also began a kids club every Friday evening. We called it Happy Hour—although we needed to change the name in years to come as the name took on other connotations. We copied the words of gospel choruses onto a wallpaper book. Thirty to forty kids turned out each time to sing, memorize Bible verses, play games, earn prizes from our "treasure chest," and listen to Bible stories.

I was still looking for a way to get as many of the neighbourhood youth as possible into the front pews on a Sunday morning, but they weren't that interested. So I began a hockey team. We joined a Christian hockey league and invited the teens to sign up. The only catch was that they had to attend church every Sunday.

They agreed.

I remember the first Sunday they showed up. They didn't know enough about church culture to squeeze as far to the back of the room as possible, so they crowded into the first two rows. The older crowd sat and stared at the newcomers in quizzical silence. Who were these teens? They hadn't ever seen a teenager in church.

The church hockey team played every Saturday night and attended church every Sunday morning. They didn't understand the words of the hymns, but they stood with open hymnbooks and listened politely to the sermon. Some began to slowly grasp what we were really all about and show genuine interest in Christianity and the Bible. In time, they invited Jesus into their lives.

I taught them the basics of the Christian faith and they were soon asking to be baptized. They seemed to breathe new life into our church.

I hadn't baptized anyone up to that point and I was nervous about it. The night before our first baptism service, I practiced on Diane. I baptized her about two dozen times just to make sure I went into the baptismal tank the next morning with experience.

The church was packed. Our new believers had invited friends and family, people who had never been in church before. They all arrived to witness this strange practice of immersing people in water.

Most of those I baptized that morning were hockey players. The first person into the tank was a big guy, about six feet tall with broad shoulders and three hundred pounds of solid mass. I was afraid of getting him down into the water and not being able to get him back up, so I plunged him down in an effort to lift him up in one smooth manoeuvre. What I hadn't expected was that his body size would send a tidal wave over the tank wall, splashing onto the platform on the other side. The incident emptied half the water out of the tank. Some gasped. Most laughed.

I remember one particular couple whom God brought into my life. Someone mentioned David and Jeannie and their significant needs to me one day and I felt led to drop by and see them. That was the beginning of a friendship.

As I listened to their story, I learned that they had held executive positions in a large Toronto firm. They lost everything as victims of fraud and their lives spiralled downward. Soon they were suffering the debilitating effects of alcohol abuse. They had three young children and the heavy drinking and hangovers greatly impaired their ability to maintain parental responsibilities. There were times when I actually put the kids in my car and took them out of the home.

But David and Jeannie deeply loved each other and their children and truly wanted help. My love and concern for them kept me coming back weekly. I did everything I could to help.

One day Jeannie brought me a cup of tea. As I drank it, she began to laugh. I wasn't sure what was so funny. Seeing my quizzical look, she confessed apologetically that earlier that morning her young son had peed in that same cup and she had forgotten to wash it. I smiled as though amused, but inwardly I cringed.

From that day on, I always excused myself from a cup of tea, or a cup of anything Jeannie offered.

They were a family in crisis, though, and I was there to show them Jesus's love. I was never sure who God would bring into my life, nor what surprises awaited on any given day.

The people who had been in the church for many years were excited about what was happening. The influx of young people, in addition to some newly arrived younger families, produced an exhilaration for the new thing God was doing. The walls of our small church building were beginning to burst at the seams.

But trouble was brewing. New people brought new ideas and ways of doing things.

I had introduced a new type of music to the church. It was called Scripture in Song, and the songs were exactly what the name suggests—scripture put to music. Some saw this as a threat to the priority of hymns. While the new songs were scripture, which was difficult to argue against, they were also less familiar.

One Saturday night late, I got a phone call from our longstanding church organist. She informed me that if we sang even one more of those new songs, she would quit playing the organ. She knew we had planned to sing one or more the next morning and I appealed to her to work with me for the sake of unity and the younger people who resonated with the new songs.

But she was adamant, and the next morning she didn't show.

Her obvious absence caused a huge stir amongst the old guard of the congregation. She had played the organ since the inception of the church.

Diane stepped in to play the organ in the weeks to come, but her presence seemed only to antagonize the friends and supporters of the previous organist. They said that things had gone too far, and for the first time I began to feel the attack from the back rows.

The rumblings and grumblings continued for a good number of weeks, sometimes erupting into open debate in the parking lot after the service. It wasn't long before the grumbling boiled over into open antagonism.

One morning after the service, a gentleman came up to me, pointed his finger in my face, and threatened to get rid of me. I wasn't sure what that meant, but it shocked me.

To add insult to injury, a new group of people arrived at the church championing something that could be potentially divisive—the practice of speaking in ecstatic tongues to evidence one's salvation and the Spirit's presence and fullness in one's life. The charismatic movement was big at the time and had now set foot in our church.

I didn't challenge anyone's right to personally practice their beliefs, but I did take issue with this group's overt and aggressive proselytizing of it. Their zeal for charismatic theology caused confusion and disruption. I urged them to stop for the sake of the unity of the Spirit, but they resisted my appeals and continued to stir things up. Rather than inviting the Spirit's presence and power, I'm sure it deeply grieved the Spirit as people took sides.

By this time, Diane was pregnant with our first child. It was a difficult pregnancy with the church problems always tormenting our minds.

When our son Jeremy was born, he brought pure delight into our lives. We faithfully enjoyed one day off each week as a sabbath. Sometimes we hiked along an old historic railroad line near our home. Other times, we followed a trail along the edge of a bubbling stream. In the winter, we bundled Jeremy in blankets, placed him in a box, and pulled him on a toboggan. He loved it, and so did we. This helped distract from what we were facing in the church. Family was our sanctuary.

Over the next few years, God gave us two beautiful daughters, Rebecca and Sarah. Diane was an amazing mother and homemaker. She placed strong value on family and home. Family meant everything. She was unashamedly invested in the futures markets—that is, the futures of our children. And whenever I or any of our children needed a refuge, the home she created was a place of safety, shelter, and security.

I must admit that witnessing the birth of each of our children was like watching a miracle unfold. Our lives fundamentally changed. Every time, I was struck with a profound sense of responsibility. It was my task to train and guide each precious life in the ways of Christ. As a father, my heart was acutely stirred to give my son and daughters a secure foundation for life by incarnating the love of their heavenly Father through my unconditional love and care for them. And speaking of love, there was ignited within me a depth of love that was different from any kind of love I had experienced before.

I also contended with a new sense of vulnerability. I had no idea what lay ahead for any of my children. I could love them. I could guide them. I could pray for them. But their life and future were in God's hands, and I needed to willingly place them in his hands and trust him.

This was driven home to us one day when Rebecca was a newborn. While changing her diaper one evening, her eyes rolled back right before my eyes and her body went completely limp. I wasn't sure how to respond but knew I needed to do something immediately.

I yelled for Diane to come and then did the first thing that came into my mind: I picked my daughter up, tipped her upside down, placed her onto her tummy, and tapped her back.

She revived.

Greatly relieved, but still unsettled, I put her on her back again and cautiously continued changing her diaper.

Then it happened a second time.

Alarmed, I repeated what I had done the first time. To our relief, she revived again.

Well, as you can imagine, we rushed her to the hospital for examination. She was kept in the ICU for a whole week while the doctors observed her and investigated.

At the end of a week, she was sent home without any diagnosis.

For the next week, we kept her right beside our bed where we could listen to her breathing and keep a watchful eye on her. Every whimper was like an alarm bell, causing us to jump up and check her. And when there was no sound, we also jumped up and checked her.

The resulting sleep deprivation brought us to the point where we realized we couldn't go on this way much longer. So one night we knelt beside Rebecca's crib, placed our hands on her head, and prayed. We thanked God for our daughter. We prayed for her health. We prayed that God would grant her a long and happy life. But if not, if he willed to take her, then she was his daughter too. His love was perfect. His will was flawless.

We then carried her back to her own bedroom and placed her in the hands of her heavenly Father. We returned to our bed and went to sleep.

This is something we need to do for all our children and grandchildren. We do everything we can for them but must entrust them into the hands of their heavenly Father who loves them more than we do, without measure.

By the way, Rebecca has grown up to be a healthy and very capable mother and has given us four wonderful grandchildren.

Back at the church, Diane and I worked hard, usually well into the evenings. We visited homes, counselled individuals, and led Bible studies and new believer classes. Diane led a group of women in a weekly Bible study and poured herself into others one on one to disciple them in their faith. She had intended to use her education and training to lead and supervise the children's ministry, but unfortunately the church leadership was hesitant to grant her this role because of her relationship to me as the pastor. They called it a conflict of interest.

Disappointingly, every church we served in took the same viewpoint and she was never allowed to do what she had been trained to do. But it didn't stop her. She found other ministries.

I persevered every week on top of everything else to prepare a Bible study for the Wednesday night prayer meeting and two Sunday sermons.

There were still dissenting voices, but the Holy Spirit was cultivating healthy spiritual growth in many people. And the church continued to increase numerically. At times our hearts felt sadness, and at other times we were filled with joy and gratitude, sometimes all in the same day.

Eleven

WHEN WE LEFT our church in Peterborough, it was flourishing. We were called by God to pastor a church in Port Perry, Ontario—the same church my father had pastored many years earlier. It was also the church where I had served with him as the youth pastor during my years at seminary. So we knew the church well.

The church had experienced numerical growth several years before, but that growth had since stalled. The congregation was meeting in a building too small for its size and had purchased land for a new facility. It needed a pastor to help restore the soul and spirit of the church and lead it to a place where it could build and support a new and larger building. The leadership asked whether I would consider coming to be their pastor.

After prayer and fasting, Diane and I believed it to be an opportunity and challenge from the Lord, and we agreed to come.

Over the period of the next two years, the church was rejuvenated and plans got underway to begin construction. We experienced an abundance of blessings from God's hand. People came to faith in Jesus and deepened their spiritual growth. The size of the congregation increased to the point that the walls were bursting. Financial giving was healthy, unity was strong, and enthusiasm was keen. The church thrived.

Construction of the new facility went extremely well. We watched it grow brick by brick, and by year's end we were inside the building and enjoying its much-needed space.

We continued to grow numerically. That same year, we paid for most of the cost of our new facility and began initial plans for a major expansion. I had never envisioned a church thriving to the point of such blessing.

But I hadn't been paying close attention to my inner state. While lots of things were happening as a result of the Lord working through me, my soul was slowly drying up. I wasn't giving the Holy Spirit the space to work in me.

My focus was increasingly becoming the church, not Jesus. There was a severe imbalance in my life—a lot of doing but little being. Lots of action, but no resting. Lots of care for others, but little self-care.

My soul was losing its bearings and drifting. I don't know how else to describe it. I felt like a drowning man. I only share this part of my life as a warning to others who may be falling into the same vulnerable state.

I experienced collapse. I felt the deepest, most intense and profound sense of brokenness, and it was crushing. I tried not to think, because when I did it elicited bitter tears. As the nights grew longer and colder, each time the furnace came on in the house I would awaken and my mind would fill with anxiety and grief. Even now, hearing a furnace switch on is a trigger.

I was contending with what the psalmist experienced when he wrote, *"Day and night I have only tears for food"* (Psalm 42:3). At these low points, especially during the long hours of the night, the devil whispers softly but persistently into the soul, chastising and castigating, trying to erode the foundation of one's being. Loser! Worthless! Useless!

I resigned from the church. I thought that would bring some relief, but the weight of grief and sense of loss came crashing in upon me in wave after wave of increasing intensity.

A fellow pastor in the church took it upon himself to discredit my sincerity, prejudicing people against me—and one day I approached him on the matter. He just turned away, jumped into his car, and sped off in a rage.

The church was no longer a safe place for me. Sometimes my thoughts wandered and I wondered whether even God had abandoned me, without ever believing that he had.

However, our marriage was strong. Diane held on to me when my emotions were dropping. One day I found a note she had left for me: "Being married to you is the best thing that ever happened to me. Please let me be your wife forever." She knew just how to lift me and give me hope.

A few friends stood by us, encouraging and supporting us, and one day one of them handed me a note with a rendition of Ephesians 3:20 written out:

> He is able to do…
>   able to do exceeding…
>   able to do exceeding abundantly…
>   able to do exceeding abundantly beyond all… that we ask or think.

The Holy Spirit focused my mind and heart on the psalms, especially the first fifty. The sentiments of the psalmist were mine and I prayed them fervently. In these scriptures I found huge comfort, assurance, and release. They gave me a voice with which to cry out to God. They gave me permission to express my true feelings. They undergirded me with the truth I needed to counteract the lies I was being told, the lies I was believing. They reminded me to whom I belonged. I was God's child, loved, accepted, and secure in him.

God directed my attention to two books that really helped reorient my thinking and give me hope.

The title of the first, *Failure: The Back Door to Success*, got my attention because it seemed to fly in the face of the general sentiment in Christian culture.[3] The author, Erwin Lutzer, wrote that his book was intended for those who believed they were failures and for those who falsely believed they weren't. I ate up every word. The things he wrote answered a yearning within and gave me light and hope.

The second book, *Another Chance: How God Overrides Our Big Mistakes* by Dean Merrill, reinforced the truth that God is truly the God of second chances... and third... and fourth.[4] For one whose sanity was being hammered by confusion and self-doubt, I remembered that I could run into the welcoming arms of my heavenly Father, who loved me unconditionally.

---

[3] Erwin W. Lutzer, *Failure: The Back Door to Success* (Chicago, IL: Moody Publishers, 2015).

[4] Dean Merrill, *Another Chance: How God Overrides Our Big Mistakes* (Grand Rapids, MI: Zondervan, 1981).

Twelve

AT THE TIME, we were living in the church manse. Its walls protected me from the outside world but also made me vulnerable to whoever might show up at the door. We received visits from people, some comforting, but others not.

One day there was a rap on the door. A man stood on the steps, and as I opened the door he pushed his way inside. I had no idea why he had come, but he seemed angry and erupted into an irrational tirade. I had never experienced anything quite like this before.

My two young daughters who weren't yet school-age began to cry while Diane scurried them away. I tried to gain control of the situation but quickly discerned that the words this man spoke were from the devil, whose purpose is to accuse and destroy.

I asked him to leave the house. He refused. I prayed audibly, opened the door, and ordered him out a second time. At this point he moved toward the door and stormed out.

I was visibly shaken. We all were.

Not five minutes later, after only a brief moment to process what had just happened, the doorbell rang again. My heart jumped as we went to the side window and peered out to see whether the same hostile individual had returned.

He hadn't.

But what we saw baffled us. There were two big, broad-shouldered men dressed head to foot in white. White suits. White boots. And large, white wide-brimmed Stetsons. We didn't know what to think. These men were either Texas Rangers or angelic visitors.

I guardedly opened the door, more out of curiosity than anything else.

They greeted me with wide smiles, tipped their Stetsons, and asked in loud, cordial voices, "Are you Pastor David?"

I nodded with some apprehension.

"We've been sent to pray for you."

There was no explanation of who they were, where they were from, or who had sent them. They invited themselves in, which seemed to have become commonplace, then literally picked me up by the arms and carried me to the living room as though they knew where they were going.

They planted me on my knees, placed their big burly hands on my shoulders and head, and began praying. And praying. And praying. They prayed that I would know God's presence in the most real way. They prayed that God would fill me with his Spirit, his comfort, hope, joy, vision, love, strength, and courage. They interceded for me so I would know God's restorative hand in my life. They spoke into my soul as they prayed, assuring me that God had a purpose for me, a dream no man could thwart. They prayed for divine spiritual protection around me and my family. They prayed on and on. I felt myself being drawn up into the very presence of God. It was surreal.

When they finished, they got up, helped me up from my knees, and enveloped me in a huge bear hug. I could feel the strength and love of God flow through them. It was like being hugged by Jesus himself. The timing was incredible in light of what had occurred just moments earlier.

Then they left as quickly as they had come. Coincidence? I don't think so. This was something God had done.

I experienced days when I felt stronger, but there were many other days when darkness engulfed me. I felt disillusioned and disappointed with people, church, but most of all myself. I had no desire to return to pastoral ministry.

We had moved out of the manse by this time, which was a good thing. God had provided a home for us out of the ashes of a near tragedy. The house belonged to Diane's parents, who had suffered a near-fatal car accident and spent a long year of recovery in hospital. They'd kindly given us their house to live in at no cost. It was a quaint home located in the country, and it afforded us a sense of safety. It gave our family a refuge and opportunity to enjoy fun times together. We tobogganed on the hills. We skated on a small pond we cleared of snow. I got my exercise and relished pulling all three kids on a toboggan through the snow to the small pond to skate. They loved it, and so did I.

We actually moved a total of six times that year. Six homes. We moved our belongings into one particular house for only ten days.

While it was tempting to focus on what we didn't have, it was becoming clearer that God was active in our lives and providing at each step. We hadn't spent one night on the curb. We always had a roof over our heads and a bed to sleep in.

We lived by faith. Living by faith can be exciting; it can also be accompanied by trepidation. But whenever there was a need, there was provision. We seemed to be living the life of the widow in the story of Elijah. She gave him refuge and fed him when there was nothing in the pantry. We discovered, as she did, that there was always just enough flour and olive oil at the bottom of the barrel.

One day, we received a bill for a car expense of $178. We had no idea how we would pay this bill. The next day, someone handed me an envelope that contained a cheque for $175. Clearly, there was a divine hand active in our lives and God's voice was saying, "I am here." God was teaching us to focus on Jesus alone—his presence, provision, protection, and peace.

I sent out dozens of resumes for work other than pastoral ministry, all to no avail. We spent many days in fasting and prayer, but heaven seemed silent. All along, Diane told me that God might want me back in the pastoral ministry. But I couldn't be convinced.

Thirteen

MORE THAN FIVE hundred years ago, St. John of the Cross penned a masterly poem and commentary entitled *Dark Night of the Soul*. When you reduce what John of the Cross wrote, I would say that he described the journey through brokenness as an overwhelming sense of God's absence. It's not that God is absent; it's that one feels such oppressive darkness, defeat, and emptiness that God seems hidden behind a wall of silence. One cannot make sense of what is happening, and hope evaporates.

St. John of the Cross's description resonated with me. But as I navigated through this time in my life, I learned that at no time is one closer to God than when one's heart is breaking. God's seeming silence only means that he is silently working. He is quietly breaking and softening the soil of the heart to become more sensitive, receptive, and responsive to the Holy Spirit's presence.

God's seeming absence strangely draws us into an overwhelming sense of his nearness. The Holy Spirit whispers in our ear through a passage of scripture that penetrates the softened heart, just as the gentle rain of heaven penetrates and soaks the softened ground. Suffering prepares and tenderizes the soil of the heart to recognize the Spirit's presence and activity through an event, such as the visit I described from the two men in white suits and Stetsons.

I discovered another life-transforming truth in those days. God sometimes allows his child to follow a dark path to the point of absolute helplessness to reach the end of one's own resources. But while he allows us to get there, he doesn't want us to stay there. It's not his purpose for us to get stuck in this space and become paralyzed by fear, anxiety, or failure. God doesn't want us to give in to the temptation to loathe ourselves.

Neither is it his will that we wallow in self-pity or fall into the abyss of resentment, cynicism, or bitterness. It is not his will that we stagnate on a shelf somewhere, accepting God's second best for our lives, or resigning ourselves to the thought that we are disposable and no longer usable to God.

And yes, we may need to reject and ignore what others think about us. God allows us to get to this vulnerable place to discover that our end is his beginning and that when we are emptied, he fills us. To discover his presence and power in a new life-transforming way. To learn that when all else fails, he doesn't. To recognize that when he's all we've got, he is enough.

It may be a painful place, but it is a good place. It is the place where surrender begins.

One day Jesus forewarned his disciples about his impending death. His approaching crucifixion shed a new discomfiting perspective on what it meant to follow him. He continued, *"If any of you wants to be my follower, you must give up your own way, take up your cross daily, and follow me"* (Luke 9:23).

Jesus used a shocking and sickening word picture that the first-century Galileans would have been all too familiar with: Roman soldiers parading poor victims along the roads to be executed by crucifixion. Each prisoner was forced to carry the crossbar of their own cross to the place of torture and death.

Jesus drew from this image to speak of the need for our self-lives to carry a cross to the point of death. Crucifixion of the self-life is painful. It's bitter because only the most desperate of circumstances gets one to that point. For example, the trauma of life's assaults and losses, Satan's attack, the betrayal of friends, or personal failure. God allows and uses these things to get us where he wants us to be: the end of ourselves.

The self-life is consumed with personal rights and expectations. It is characterized by selfish desires, self-absorption, self-importance, self-will, self-sufficiency, and pride. These are powerful and impactful characteristics of human nature that get in the way of becoming what God made us to be in relation to him.

It accomplishes nothing to mask the self-life. It cannot be fixed. It cannot be rehabilitated. It cannot be repaired. It must die. But when it dies, its absence makes space for Jesus to fill with his resurrection life.

The essential human component is surrender. The apostle Paul wrote, *"I plead with you to give your bodies to God because of all he has done for you. Let them be a living and holy sacrifice..."* (Romans 12:1) To give your body to God means putting your self-life to death and surrendering to Christ.

When an Old Testament priest sacrificed an animal, he killed it, cut it up into pieces, and placed it on the altar. There was no doubt that the animal was dead.

Death is an absolute surrender. One cannot be half-dead. One is either dead or alive. We are called to be *living* sacrifices.

This act of surrender must be a daily decision. Note that Jesus told us to take up our crosses *daily*. Surrender must encompass this kind of regularity because a living sacrifice habitually keeps crawling off the altar.

Every day we must intentionally die to self by deliberately surrendering our lives to Christ so we live daily in the power of his resurrection life. His life surges through us just as the life of the vine flows into a branch, giving it life and fruitfulness (John 15:5). Without him, I can do nothing. By contrast, *"I can do everything through Christ, who gives me strength"* (Philippians 4:13). All I need is who he is.

Fourteen

> I waited patiently for the Lord to help me, and he turned to me and heard my cry. He lifted me out of the pit of despair, out of the mud and the mire. He set my feet on solid ground and steadied me as I walked along. He has given me a new song to sing, a hymn of praise to our God. Many will see what he has done and be amazed. (Psalm 40:1–3)

THESE VERSES GIVE expression to what happened in our lives over the next months and years. God orchestrated things that I couldn't do for myself and made it so evident that his hand was upon us. He lifted me out of the quagmire through which I found myself slogging and made his presence tangible and provision unmistakable, causing us to walk again and sing again.

God had a dream for my life that no one and nothing could thwart. We saw God do things only he could do, things that always amazed us. Not only did we see and praise him, but many others saw the things he did and gave glory to him.

God provided me with a job in a welding shop for a brief time to help provide for our needs, but I knew this wasn't what God wanted me to do long-term. It helped to keep food on the table. We clothed ourselves with second-hand clothing. We relied on hand-me-downs for winter coats and boots for the children, and God always provided.

As I said earlier, I sent resumes in as many directions as I could think. I was looking for a job in teaching or social work, but God was closing all the doors. Diane continued to be the lone voice encouraging me to consider that God might be calling me back into pastoral ministry.

There are times when something happens, something seemingly insignificant at the time, that changes the direction of one's life. One day, we received a phone call from a friend who asked whether we would be willing to entertain a visit from two men from a small church in Aurora, Ontario. She happened to have spoken to one of them about our situation and he had asked if she would contact us regarding them coming to speak with us.

Diane was excited. I was hesitant.

But in the end, we decided that it could do no harm.

Ron and Jay knocked at the door one evening after supper. We invited them in and sat down with a cup of coffee to listen to what they had to say. They represented a group of Christians who were meeting in a school and called themselves Community Bible Church. The church went back many years, but over the years it had lived and died many deaths. The congregation were few in number and their greatest need was someone who would be willing to be their pastor and build the church from the ground up.

I knew nothing about the town of Aurora. Our visitors went to great lengths to stress to us the spiritual need that existed there. Aurora had the reputation for being a dark town, home to various satanic groups, which was later confirmed to me by trustworthy sources. Evangelical churches had come to Aurora before but subsequently either disbanded or moved on. There was presently very little spiritual light in the town.

It wouldn't be an easy task, but they reiterated the unique and extraordinary opportunity that existed for an evangelical church to establish a strong gospel witness in this particular place.

We listened intently.

I told them that I had left pastoral ministry and the reasons for my departure. I honestly admitted that I couldn't see myself being a pastor again, but that we would pray much about it.

They then said something that became wedged in my mind and got my attention in a way I couldn't have imagined. They replied that it was because of what I had been through that they believed I would be a good fit for their church.

I searched for a response to that statement but found none.

Diane and I spent many days in prayer and fasting, trying to determine from God how we should respond. My primary feeling, I think, was fear. Fear of getting back into full-time ministry. And emptiness. I didn't know if I had the inner strength or courage to step back into a church context, especially as the pastor.

My initial thought was that maybe our family could attend on Sunday mornings. After all, the town of Aurora was only about forty-five minutes from where we lived. I could help them with the teaching ministry without the responsibility of pastoring. We were in need financially, and maybe this was God's provision.

So we replied that we would be willing to attend on Sunday mornings. I would do the preaching and teaching for a modest stipend.

They agreed.

We had no idea that this was the beginning of something new, a life-changing decision engineered by the divine mind and hand of God.

Fifteen

ON THE FIRST Sunday morning that our family travelled to Aurora, my hands trembled as I held the steering wheel. I prayed the whole time, asking and imploring God to give me strength and courage.

I tried to garner the stoicism to push through, but every mile closer made me feel more and more aware that this was one of those times when I needed God to show up in a big way, for his grace to compensate for my weakness.

We arrived at the school where the church met to be greeted by a handful of people, all wishing to be introduced. We entered a classroom and sat behind desks, under which we tucked our knees as best we could.

I felt an immediate comfort. When I got up to preach, it was more like getting up in front of a classroom of students to teach a lesson. It took me back to my days of teaching school. The people were few in number, but they were all eager to learn. I don't think I could have stepped behind a pulpit in a more formal setting. The Holy Spirit was edging me closer and closer to something I dreaded, but doing it in such a way that I felt a degree of ease and reassurance. Grace steps. The Holy Spirit was clearly coming alongside and saying, "This is a new beginning."

We continued travelling to Aurora every Sunday morning for the next few months. After each service, we were invited into a home for dinner. We got to know the people and felt the warmth of their acceptance. This small group quickly became our church family and soon I actually enjoyed teaching the scriptures and connecting with them as a pastor. I still had nagging doubts and fears, but the Holy Spirit continued to draw me slowly with the tenderness of a Shepherd. And the congregation grew.

It became common for people to pull us aside and encourage us to come live in the community as their pastor and family. And I felt more and more like this was where we were meant to be. The Holy Spirit was gently nudging and resurrecting within me a faint yearning to once again be a pastor.

He was also giving Diane and me an increased burden for Aurora. It was a town of sixteen thousand people, and after doing a little investigating we discovered that there were only two evangelical churches, ours being one of them. The other was a very small work in the centre of town which had been there for many years. There were several mainline churches, but we found it incredible for a town of that size to have only two evangelical churches. Further, the population was expected to grow to thirty thousand over the next five to ten years. In fact, we saw it grow to a population of just over sixty thousand.

I couldn't imagine that there would be any other towns in Canada of a similar size with so little gospel witness. That was probably the most significant thing that leaped out at us. This was a mission field ripe for harvest, and it was right at our doorstep.

The Holy Spirit wouldn't let that image weaken. It only strengthened as the days passed. The Spirit was sharpening within us a sense of call to Aurora—and as much as I tried to shake it, it wouldn't go away.

We wrote down three God-sized needs and spent a day in fasting and prayer laying these needs before him.

Firstly, we asked God for the certainty of a divine call, that he was actually calling us to Aurora. This was a basic requirement.

Secondly, we needed a place to live. The house prices in Aurora were very high, much higher than we could afford.

Thirdly, there was the need of financial resources to meet our essential needs. We knew the church didn't have the capacity to provide a salary to guarantee and provide even a most basic salary.

We believed, however, and had personally experienced in numerous ways that nothing was impossible with God. For the moment, we were living in a house at no cost to ourselves. That was something God had done. This house was up for sale now and our financial situation would change dramatically once it sold. We held on to the certainty that God would continue to provide one step, one need at a time.

We also believed that our prayers of faith needed to be accompanied by action, so that same week we travelled to Aurora to begin our search for a house. We initially thought we would need to rent, but it soon became evident that even renting would be too expensive. It seemed easier to purchase a house and pay a mortgage.

That very first week of searching, we found an ideal house for our family. We looked at other houses, too, but the Holy Spirit kept bringing us back to that one house. There was one obstacle: it already had a conditional offer on it. The conditional offer had been on the house for a month. There wasn't even a for-sale sign on the lawn at this point.

We wondered, was God keeping this house for us? A soft voice seemed to speak into our ears: "This is it. This is the house I am providing for you."

Interestingly, the house was owned by a couple whose surname was the same as ours... Payne. God whispered, "This is the Paynes' home."

We dared not put a firm offer on the house without an official confirmation of a call to the church, though, and that hadn't materialized yet. A lot seemed stacked against us. The market was moving quickly and we were in waiting mode. But we believed that God could earmark this particular house for us if it was his will.

Sixteen

THE VERY NEXT day, I received a phone call from Ron, one of the men who had originally come to speak with us. He told me that the church was close to taking the leap and trusting God for the resources to call me as their pastor. He added that the church had some money set aside from the sale of a previous building, and they could loan it to us as an interest-free loan for our new home until we could obtain permanent financing. He also committed the church to doing its best to give us about $2,000 a month to meet our basic needs.

We admitted that this would be a challenge on both sides, even a test of our faith, but that God was the most important factor in this decision. He would provide.

With the church preparing to take the leap of faith, we needed to prepare ourselves to take the same leap. We had little more than our faith. Even when one has faith, however, the circumstances can cast a shadow that reawakens old feelings of insecurity, doubt, and apprehension. We needed to hear from God in a sure, undeniable way.

We spent another day in prayer and fasting seeking God's clear direction.

It shouldn't amaze us, but it always does, how perfect is God's timing. Two days later, we received a note from a friend who knew nothing about the decision we were wrestling with. But God knew. The note encouraged us to live by faith and not feeling. It included a short handwritten poem:

> When doubt creeps in and we start to wonder,
>   And our thoughts about God are torn asunder,
>   It's then when our feelings and senses are reeling,
>   We realize clearly it's faith and not feeling.
>   Just exercise faith and patiently wait,
>   Believing God comes not too soon, nor too late.

Other pressures bore down upon us. Mr. Jennings was our real estate agent, working tirelessly on our behalf in our search for a home. One evening he phoned and informed us that the house we believed God had provided for us would probably have a sale finalized that night or the next day. It would be off the market.

Mr. Jennings was not a person of faith, but we had been witnessing to him all along regarding how God provides and his perfect timing. We had told him numerous times that we were leaving everything in God's hands. I told him that if the house sold, so be it; God would provide.

However, something was still stirring within us, a voice still whispering that this house was for us. I don't think Mr Jennings knew what to think about our faith. He told us that he admired it, but I'm sure that he smiled behind our backs.

We felt the pressure of looming deadlines. The church in Aurora was soon to make a decision and we would need to give a reply. Our furniture was still sitting in the manse of the previous church and needed to be moved out. Diane's parents were moving into a new apartment in two weeks and would need their furniture, the same furniture we were using. And the house where we lived presently had been sold.

We needed to hear from God *now*. We needed the green light to go forward with Aurora… or a red light.

So we looked up and prayed: "Lord, clearly show us what to do. If you are really in this, we are willing. But we need to know."

We did something we had never done before, and something we have never done since. We laid out a fleece. This notion comes from the story of Gideon in Judges 6. I had always wondered whether laying out a fleece showed a lack of faith, but Gideon had done it and God had spoken to him.

Gideon felt insecure and needed to determine whether or not God had truly called him to deliver Israel from her enemies. So he laid out a fleece of wool on the ground and asked God, if deliverance was certain, that in the morning the fleece would be drenched with dew while the ground around it remained dry.

And that's exactly what happened.

Then Gideon went a step further. This time he asked for the opposite—that in the morning the fleece would remain dry while the ground around it was wet with dew.

God did as Gideon asked, assuring him that God would deliver Israel through him.

Not sure whether it was faithful or faithless to do so, but needing an answer from God, we set out our proverbial fleece. It had to be something that provided certainty that God had spoken.

It was April 17, 1985 and the weather had been warm. The temperature was supposed to rise to seventy degrees Fahrenheit the next day.

We decided on our fleece. We determined that if God was calling us to Aurora, there would be a layer of white on the ground by morning. We didn't specify what the white should be but assumed it would be some sort of snow. We prayed and committed this to God.

Seconds later, with sudden intensity, we heard the sound of something beating the chimney and pelting against the windows. We thought it was a gust of wind and jumped up from our seats in the living room to look outside.

We could hardly believe what our eyes witnessed. It was hailing so heavily that we could barely see past the windowpanes. How did we feel? Shocked. Dumbfounded. Overwhelmed.

I grabbed our camera and rushed outside to snap a picture. The ground was covered with white, exactly as we had asked. At that moment, I was a little like Gideon and asked for a confirmation.

"Lord, if this really is you, then may the white remain until morning in the spot where I have just snapped this picture," I prayed. "But let it be melted and gone on the ground all around."

In the morning, it was again just as we had asked. I snapped another picture with the camera. We now have both of those pictures hanging on a wall in our home. More than once, people have stood looking at the pictures with a quizzical stare before gathering the nerve to ask, "What's that?" And we tell them what God did. The pictures are memory aids and serve as constant reminders that God is present in our lives, actively and providentially involved in everything that's happening.

We had the confirmation we needed that God was calling us to Aurora.

The next morning, I informed Ron of what had happened. He was intrigued by what we told him about the fleece and how God had spoken. He told us that the church would be happy to hear about God's leading. His plans were to ask the church to vote as soon as possible.

Two Sundays later, we had our answer from the church. The people had been informed of our history and departure from our previous church and asked to vote. They gave us one hundred percent support to extend to us a call. This was a second confirmation of God's calling and the answer to the first God-sized need for which we had prayed.

There would be many obstacles to overcome, but we knew we were on our way to Aurora.

Seventeen

SEVERAL WEEKS HAD passed since hearing from Mr. Jennings, so we were surprised when he called to inform us that the house we wanted was still on the market. The people who had offered to purchase it had instead purchased another home. It was as though "our" house had been preserved for us.

That was the good news.

The bad news was that the next day, Mr. Payne, the owner of "our" house, took the house off the market. He no longer wanted to sell.

We suddenly found ourselves back at square one, backed into a corner by the deadlines that had been looming. We needed to be out of the present house within three weeks, and we had nowhere to go.

We decided to respond to this news by thanking God that he had everything in his control. We acknowledged his sovereignty.

God then gave us the solace we needed from Psalm 131.

> Lord, my heart is not proud; my eyes are not haughty. I don't concern myself with matters too great or too awesome for me to grasp. Instead, I have calmed and quieted myself, like a weaned child who no longer cries for its mother's milk. Yes, like a weaned child is my soul within me. O Israel, put your hope in the Lord—now and always. (Psalm 131:1–3)

These words resonated with us. The circumstantial ups and downs, triumphs and setbacks, and joys and disappointments were too much for us to grasp and outside our control. They were the fuel for anxiety and unease. Instead we needed to lay our heads calmly on our heavenly Father and rest in quiet confidence and trust like young children in the arms of a loving and caring parent. This was a faith journey—and before us was one more reason to trust our heavenly Father.

It shouldn't surprise us that our heavenly Father is always at work engineering his purposes. The next day, Mr. Jennings happened to run into Mr. Payne, the owner of "our" house. I use the word *happened* as though it were a coincidence, but it's amazing how many coincidences we perceive when God is at work.

Mr. Jennings took the opportunity to ask Mr. Payne whether he would be interested in a firm offer on his home. To his astonishment, Mr. Payne told him to bring a firm offer to him in several days and he would consider it.

That night, Mr. Jennings phoned us in excited disbelief. He made some comments about our faith and that he had never seen anything quite like this in all his years selling real estate. He told us to come to Aurora in several days to put together an offer on the house.

We agreed, and several days later we were sitting in Mr. Jennings's office writing up an offer.

Mr. Payne left us hanging for the next day. And the next. We didn't know what he was thinking.

Soon a week went by. We were down to the wire, but all we could do was wait and trust. We didn't want to poke the bear but could feel the anxiety rising like floodwaters. Still we stayed on our knees, recognizing that the entire situation was in God's hands. He knew our need, and we knew he cared.

We spent another day in fasting and prayer, asking God to soften Mr. Payne's heart. Mr. Jennings spent the same day taking Mr. Payne to visit houses he hoped would interest him. None did.

Mr. Payne had promised to give us an answer that same day regarding the sale of his house to us. But by day's end, nothing had happened. In fact, Mr. Jennings called us that night to share that he had little hope of Mr. Payne ever signing our offer.

We continued to pray into the evening. We had such a strong sense that God wasn't finished with this matter, and it was an intense enough feeling to keep us resolute in prayer. We prayed for a miracle.

By the next day, we had still heard no news. So we travelled to Aurora to look at other houses. Maybe God was pointing us in another direction.

When we walked into Mr. Jennings's office, he greeted us with the disheartening advice to forget the house we were interested in. He said that the door had closed.

And so we began a new search. We looked. And looked. We looked all day and into the evening and found nothing that gave us any peace. God didn't seem to be putting his approval on any other house. We were houseless and almost homeless.

That evening, after a day of searching, we returned to the real estate office rather dejected and wondering just what God was saying. When we entered the door, the secretary handed us a note from her desk. It simply read: *Please call Mr. Payne.* This was the first time Mr. Payne had taken the initiative to connect with us.

Mr. Jennings picked up the telephone immediately and called. We watched his face for any optimistic signs. I saw a slight grin cross our agent's face, which gave us some grounds for hope.

When he put the phone down, he looked up at us and his grin widened into a broad smile. He gave a sudden cheer and exclaimed that Mr. Payne was interested in looking at a house he had visited the day prior, which at the time he had shown no interest in. Mr. Jennings would show him the house early the next morning.

We returned home that night praising God and filled with anticipation.

The next day was May 8, my birthday. The telephone rang and I picked it up to hear an enthusiastic voice on the other end.

"It's done!" Mr. Jennings blurted out. "I have a signed agreement for your offer in my hands as I speak! You have a new home."

I was speechless.

After a moment for the news to sink in, I finally spoke. "This is something God has done."

I could feel Mr. Jennings's gratifying smile beaming through the phone lines. I couldn't imagine a better birthday gift. We had prayed that the Holy Spirit would soften Mr. Payne's heart and God had done exactly that. In fact, God had so softened his heart that he seemed practically willing to grant any wish we might have. He was accommodating and welcomed us to come through the house anytime we wanted at our convenience.

The next day, we sat in Mr. Jennings's office, and the first thing to come out of his mouth was that he couldn't understand the change in Mr. Payne's attitude. He had gone from inflexibility and obstinance to warmth and compliance. How could someone change so quickly?

I spoke up. We had prayed that God would change him.

There was still one detail to resolve. We couldn't take possession of our new home until the end of August, more than three months away, and we needed to be out of our present house by month's end.

As you can imagine, we were relieved when Mr. Jennings made a few calls and found a townhouse we could rent for the intervening three months. Everything seemed to have fallen into place.

But not so fast!

Eighteen

EIGHT DAYS BEFORE we were to be out of our present home, we received a call informing us that the townhouse we had planned to rent wouldn't be available. We suddenly and unexpectedly found ourselves urgently needing a place to live. This period of our lives was uncomfortable, but it taught us to rely on God, who had set the path and was leading us along it one faith step at a time.

The immediate task seemed impossible. We needed to find a place to rent in one day and move there within one week. We needed to find a landlord who would agree to us living in their dwelling for a period of only three months. Mindful of the implausibility of all this, Diane and I drove to Aurora. We prayed the entire way there. All the while, the last line of the poem we had received one month earlier kept coming to mind: *Believe God comes not too soon, nor too late.*

We checked the newspaper and found only two houses advertised for rent. We inquired into both and struck out. One owner wouldn't rent for a period of time under a year. The second house was too great a distance from Aurora.

Honestly, I felt like a batter at the plate with two down, two strikes against, and needing a homerun.

Unexpectedly, the owner of the second house pitched me another ball. He called as we were returning to our car, having just remembered a notice that had been posted on the bulletin board at work by a friend of his who also wanted to rent a house.

I phoned this friend, who informed me that he was in real estate part-time and that a client of his, an elderly woman, had just purchased a small house. Her plans were to move into the house in the near future and rent it out for a few intervening months. While we sat in his office, he made a call to the lady.

When he put the phone down, he smiled. Her plans were to do some renovations in the house and move into it in September. She was hoping she could find the right renters for only three months from June 1 to August 31.

Our jaws dropped. We could have the house for exactly the time period we needed. Moreover, we could move in immediately. And it was $250 a month cheaper than the townhouse we had originally planned to rent.

We felt overwhelmed. It was a homerun! God had come not too soon, nor too late.

We quickly dubbed this place our miracle home and within several days we were moving in and filling it with our boxes. It was a pocket-sized house, with only one level, but it was sufficient. It was rundown and dirty, too, but we got to work cleaning it up. We couldn't have been happier. It was God's provision.

The basement was full of water, so we piled our boxes on the one level. We forged a network of paths through the boxes, somewhat like a maze, so we could navigate from room to room. Our generous landlady even renovated the kitchen and tiny bathroom. For the first week, while our kitchen and bathroom were out of order, we rounded up the kids and headed down to a local restaurant for hamburgers and bathroom breaks. It was an adventure.

That summer, I pastored our small church. My study was in that small home. It was our Brook Cherith—Cherith being the name of the brook where Elijah took refuge during a famine. It became his sanctuary, a place where God supplied daily bread brought to him by ravens and his source of water until the stream dried up. We drank from the waters of our Brook Cherith and watched God provide our daily bread in incredible ways.

The summer of '85 passed quickly. Before we knew it, August 31 had arrived and we moved into our new home in Aurora.

One week later, I happened to be driving past our little miracle home and noticed a for-sale sign on the lawn. I was surprised. I checked into it and discovered that the elderly lady had decided not to relocate and was instead trying to sell the house. We were in wonderment at God's sovereign hand. It was as though God had told her to purchase that house, renovate and refresh the kitchen and bathroom, rent it to our family for three months, and then sell it after we had moved out.

We will never forget that small dwelling. Every time we drive by it, we are freshly reminded of something God did, and of our need to wait on him and trust him. The exercise of waiting and trusting isn't easy, but it is gratifying and rewarding. The reward is God's faithful daily provision and sometimes miraculous intervention.

Nineteen

IT'S GOOD TO be moving forward with your life. But I didn't want to step into the future dragging a heavy emotional load of hurt, disappointment, and loss.

Someone asked me one day if I had ever grieved my losses. At the time, I actually hadn't thought about my losses as something to be grieved. I came to understand, however, that one cannot move forward with any degree of mental, emotional, and spiritual health while holding onto the psychological burden that stems from the failure to deal with one's losses in a wholesome way. Unlamented losses become an encumbrance around the neck of our lives and prevent us from thriving.

I had experienced significant losses. The loss of inner peace. The loss of my church family, the flock I loved and shepherded. The loss of my job, income, home, reputation, and self-worth all at once. The loss of friendships and relationships I cherished and needed.

One doesn't move on quickly from such losses.

Several years later, Diane created a study for a women's group on the subject of living with loss. We prepared the content together and began to rethink our losses all over again. I'm not sure we ever stop grieving completely. There are still times when we think back on the past, or feel triggered by something, and feel the loss all over again. But even though the sense of loss can linger, its degree of intensity and emotional weight can be greatly diminished.

It's critical not to rush the process, but to allow oneself sufficient time to grieve. Sometimes our theology is wrongly applied to our experience. As Christians we can feel the expectation to move quickly through our trauma because we're led to believe that prayer fixes everything, like a pill for a headache. When our damaged emotions don't mend fast enough, we regard it as a crisis of faith. We can wrongly believe that grieving for an extended period of time means we have inadequate faith. We're quick to say that we can do all things through Christ's strength and then interpret our inability as failure. We don't forget that we are Christ-followers; we forget that we are human.

And so we push our feelings to the furthest recesses of our minds and try to move forward as quickly as possible. We simply end up living in denial.

Yet the sense of loss remains with us, and the capacity to feel deeply about it persists. We only cheat ourselves when we fail to take the time necessary to address and grieve those losses. Time is a gift God uses to cultivate healing and transformation.

Twenty

ONE OF MY favourite stories in the Bible is the story of Joseph (Genesis 37–50). Take some time to read it. This remarkable account demonstrates how God's plan persists and overrules the most difficult experiences in life. Joseph endured treachery, betrayal, and injustice, but he trusted God and waited patiently for him to bring good out of a bad situation.

Later in his life, Joseph spoke poignant words to his brothers who had dealt so treacherously with him, words that both summed up his life and revealed his trust in the plan of a sovereign God: *"You intended to harm me, but God intended it all for good"* (Genesis 50:20).

The experiences of Joseph's life taught me that God takes all the dark threads in the fabric of our lives and sovereignly weaves them into something of beauty that reflects his good handiwork and purposes.

The apostle Paul wrote something very similar: *"And we know that God causes everything to work together for the good of those who love God and are called according to his purpose for them"* (Romans 8:28). This is a promise. We can be absolutely certain of it. God works *everything* for our good, not just random things.

This doesn't mean that everything that happens to us is good. Bad things happen. Evil happens. But God is at work in everything for our good. His plan is unfolding. He never abandons us. This certainty can be claimed by everyone who loves him and follows the path he has set out for them.

One day, a gentleman who had spent his life as a pioneer missionary in the Amazon rainforest shared a verse with me that God had given him many years previous. He knew that God's calling and purpose for his life had been to go to the unreached peoples of the Amazon River basin. But while he and his young wife were travelling by boat up the river, she was taken ill with a fever and died suddenly before ever reaching their destination. He was distraught and felt so alone.

But he kept going.

One night on the boat, when the loneliness and despair were pressing down upon him like a heavy spiritual darkness, the Holy Spirit spoke to him in a voice that almost seemed audible. He told him to open his Bible. When he did, his eyes fell upon this verse:

> I will go before you… and level the mountains. I will smash down gates of bronze and cut through bars of iron. And I will give you treasures hidden in the darkness—secret riches. I will do this so you may know that I am the Lord, the God of Israel, the one who calls you by name. (Isaiah 45:2–3)

These words were a prophecy regarding Cyrus the Great, whom God was calling to fulfill his purposes. But this missionary in the Amazon saw his name written into the words.

I saw my name written into those same words. God works to make a way through obstacles and barriers where there seems to be no way, levelling mountains and cutting through iron bars. And it's all for his glory.

We hadn't been in our new home in Aurora two weeks when I received an invitation from a gentleman to meet him for coffee. I had no idea who he was or why he wanted to meet, but I was curious.

We met at a local coffee shop. He was an elderly man who had lived in Aurora for many years. As I sipped my coffee, it didn't take him long to get to the reason for reaching out.

"So I hear you've come to pastor a small church here," he commented, looking over his glasses at me.

I nodded and recounted a little of the story of how God had led us to Aurora.

He looked down into his cup, then looked up at me again. "This town needs a strong evangelical church. A bright spiritual light. But you need to know that you will find the task extremely difficult."

I listened intently and asked what specifically he meant.

"This town has a reputation. Satan has a seat here. It's a stronghold. Churches have come to this town and left just as quickly. They have tried to get off the ground but soon folded and moved north to Newmarket or somewhere else."

He didn't have much more to say than that, but I could tell he wanted me to receive it as both a warning and an encouragement. A warning that a church would not be built without strong opposition and intense struggle, and an encouragement to persevere and fight the good fight.

Exactly two weeks later, I received another call from a second gentleman inviting me for coffee down at the same coffee shop. Again, I didn't know who he was or why he wanted to meet.

He was another elderly gentleman who had heard that we had arrived in town and why. I had a strong feeling of deja vu as I slowly drank my coffee and recounted the story of how we had arrived at this point.

The man took a sip from his coffee, put the mug down, and looked at me with penetrating eyes. He spoke calmly and thoughtfully in a way that was unmistakably a word from the Holy Spirit.

"This town needs an evangelical church. Aurora is a town of sixteen thousand people and yet does not have one strong, effective witness to the gospel of Christ. But you need to know that you'll be in for the struggle of your life. This valley is the devil's stronghold. There are people here who will pray against you and your family. It will not be easy. Churches have come here before, packed it in, and moved on to Newmarket or some other place."

Our eyes remained locked. I couldn't believe what I was hearing… for the second time, almost word for word.

"I want to encourage you to stick with it and persevere," he added.

My first thought was that these two gentlemen knew each other and had conspired to meet with me to deliver their message of warning and encouragement.

But it turned out that they didn't know each other. This was something the Holy Spirit had orchestrated. Through them, I listened and felt humbled that God would speak to me in this fashion.

I left that second meeting armed with a warning, encouragement, and strong sense of divine call.

That same month, I received a memorable letter in the mail, written on official letterhead from the president of a Bible college and seminary in western Canada. I had never met this man, but he somehow knew about Aurora and the spiritual condition of the town. I could scarcely believe what I read. As I scanned the letter, I realized it was the same warning. And the same encouragement.

The Holy Spirit could not have been clearer if he had hit me over the head with a two-by-four. The ministry in Aurora would not be easy. There would be intense struggle and opposition. But God was in this. His plan was unfolding. We knew that we had been called by God and that he would cause everything to work together for our good and for his glory.

We had the assurance that the Lord went before us. He would level mountains and cut through bars of iron. We carried a renewed determination to persevere. We were all-in.

Twenty-One

DURING THE FIRST five weeks of ministry, we welcomed the arrival of five new families to Community Bible Church. We continued to see new families attend the service each Sunday to check us out. Some of those families continued on with us, causing us to experience steady growth through the fall and winter. In fact, over the period of our first year, we were encouraged to see our congregation increase to eighty people.

Our Sunday morning Bible study groups were attended enthusiastically by people of all ages. In our adult Bible class, I began a series exploring the basics of the Christian faith that I expected to complete in twenty weeks. However, we often found ourselves barely into the lesson when questions began to be asked and discussion ensued. That first series of studies was still going strong one year later! The class was alive. People were learning and growing spiritually. It was a year of building relationships within the congregation and strengthening the foundation of the church. They were challenging and rewarding months.

I chose seven men whom I believed had leadership potential and arranged to meet with them every Saturday. We met in our home early in the morning for coffee and Bible study. These were men I wanted to pour myself into and with whom I desired to go deeper into God's Word. We studied the Bible in depth and discussed at length its truths as they related to our lives. We enjoyed a Bible survey, memorized lengthy passages of scripture, and spent time in prayer for ourselves, our families, and our church. We also became a book club, reading and discussing books that spiritually enriched our lives. Some of these men became good friends who supported and cared for me as a man and a pastor.

Life was busy. We began a midweek prayer and Bible study group that grew from just a few people to about thirty participants. Diane also taught a weekly women's Bible study. She had a passion to see women grow deep in their relationship with

Jesus. In addition to her weekly study group, she routinely met with women one on one. And of course our focus every week was the Sunday preaching, teaching, and worship service.

The school where we met began renovating their classrooms over the summer, so we were asked to meet in the gymnasium. By the time the renovations were completed, however, our numbers had increased to the point that we could no longer fit in a classroom. We had to remain in the gym. Each Sunday morning, our family arrived early to set up the gymnasium. We were the first to arrive and the last to leave. Then we were back at it again Sunday evening, holding a service at the local library.

Sundays were long, especially for the kids, so we began a practice that continued for several years. At day's end, as a reward for all their help, endurance, and patience, we took the kids to Charlie's, a coffee and bakery shop down the street. The kids would take a long time choosing which doughnuts they wanted, and Charlie, who happened to be the owner, delighted in guiding them through his display of delicacies, making recommendations as he went. Charlie got to know the kids quickly and the reason for our appearance each Sunday evening at about the same time. He began giving out free doughnuts, as many as we desired, and a free bag of doughnuts to go. He looked forward to seeing us and the kids were more than excited to see him.

God blessed us as a family in numerous small and memorable ways.

I determined to visit every street and home in Aurora to inform people about the presence of Community Bible Church. I laid out a large map of Aurora and drew a grid which I used as a plan of attack for my undertaking.

Two afternoons were set aside each week to faithfully walk up and down the streets, knocking on door after door. For the most part, people were curious about who we were and what we were doing. I was surprised at how many times I was able to engage people in conversation.

However, I discovered a definite coolness and disinterest from people living in the newer subdivisions where row upon row of gigantic homes were being built. These people, many of whom seemed wealthy, were moving into town from larger urban centres. It wasn't uncommon to walk past a very expensive vehicle sitting in the driveway. I would knock at the door and find either no one at home or no one wanting to come to the door. When I did find someone in the yard, or in the driveway washing the car, they would make it clear they weren't interested.

I also arrived at the recognition that, despite my goal to visit the entire town, the construction of new homes was so prolific that the growth was eclipsing and exceeding my best-intentioned but unrealistic objectives.

Twenty-Two

I HAPPENED TO be looking out from our bedroom window onto the street when I spotted something unusual. Or more precisely, *someone* unusual. A lady dressed in long black clothing was walking up and down the street, scrutinizing each house. She seemed to be looking for a specific house.

I called Diane to ask what she thought. She gave us an uneasy feeling.

Suddenly, the woman stopped in front of our house, turned to face us and began to rock back and forth in a swaying motion as though praying. We had a deep and discerning sense that she wasn't praying for us. She did so for just a minute and then walked away.

We felt disturbed but not alarmed. Our minds recalled the three identical warnings God had given us just a month earlier. Aurora was a stronghold for darkness. We were light. We needed never to fear, just be faithful.

We felt constrained in that moment to pray against the darkness and for the light of Christ and his gospel to pierce the darkness in this town. We prayed that God would help us be faithful to his call and that he would establish his powerful name in this place.

Several weeks after this event, we heard a knock on our door. I went to the door and found myself greeting a woman we had known several years earlier. She asked if she could come in to deliver a message of encouragement for me from the Lord.

No sooner had she sat down than she began to tell me that God had sent her to inform me that there was sin in my life, and that if I didn't repent and expunge it I would lose at least one of my children in a month's time. I immediately felt alarmed and fearful, if not a little repulsed. My immediate response was to ask her to identify the sin. She answered that she couldn't say. She implied that she knew but wouldn't disclose it.

Diane and I began to discern a different spirit than the one she had originally said she represented. This was not a message of encouragement. And I couldn't imagine the Holy Spirit informing me about sin in my life without enlightening me as to what that sin was.

We're all prone to harbour sin. None of us are sinless. If there was specific sin in my life for which I needed to repent, I was more than willing to repent of it.

But something was off in this conversation.

I insisted that the woman identify the sin, but she refused. And the threatening tone in her voice regarding my children didn't resonate in my spirit with the way I understood God to operate. The apostle Paul wrote to Timothy, *"God has not given us a spirit of fear and timidity, but of power, love, and self-discipline"* (2 Timothy 1:7). I kept replaying these words. The Holy Spirit doesn't intimidate with threats that create fear and timidity.

This was not from God.

I told her that I discerned a different spirit speaking through her and asked her to leave. She felt offended that I would think this, then got up and left abruptly.

After she had gone, I felt weak and unnerved. I asked God to reveal any sin in my heart. Was there sin? What was it? Were my children in danger? He gave us the quiet assurance that this was the attack of a different spirit than his. We didn't need to fear. Instead we should put this event behind us and move forward.

God always balanced these kinds of events with a sufficient supply of his grace. He said, *"My grace is all you need. My power works best in weakness"* (2 Corinthians 12:9)—and his grace was always sufficient. His power was always more than enough to compensate for my weakness. His provision always met our need.

Throughout our first few years in Aurora, God provided for our spiritual and physical needs in unexpected and extraordinary ways.

Finances were always a challenge. Sometimes the church was able to give us the weekly salary they had budgeted. Other times not. Either way, it was extremely difficult to make ends meet. We really had no budget for anything except basic food needs. We could never go to the store to purchase clothing, boots, or shoes for ourselves or the kids. We lived on hand-me-downs.

One time we desperately needed bedsheets but couldn't afford to purchase new ones. A friend of Diane's happened to see our thinly worn sheets and went out and bought us a pair.

Diane became efficient at managing a lot with very little. She learned to make meals go further. One-pot meals became the norm. We never bought new furniture. Never. We used what we were given or what we salvaged from the end of a driveway as giveaways. We would pick it up and take it home to strip or paint it. For years, we used an old sofa and chairs that we simply covered with blankets.

But we were okay with this. We were doing what God had called us to do and enjoying his provision on a day-to-day basis.

We were given the opportunity to teach the music program at a local Christian school for a modest stipend to help us financially. The principal attended our church and made the offer. We were grateful for this provision, and so we taught music much like the apostle Paul worked as a tentmaker. Our children were allowed to attend the school for free as an additional bonus. It seemed like a good plan.

These kinds of occurrences are humbling.

One day a gentleman rapped on the door of our home holding a cheque in his hand. He told us that the Lord had clearly prodded him to share with us out of his abundance. We thanked the Lord for his provision that month.

What we didn't expect was for the Holy Spirit to prompt this man *every* month. For a period of one year, the same man appeared at our door every month with a cheque. It was always for a different amount of money, but just the right amount to cover our expenses. Not more, and not less. Just enough. Some months when we had an unexpected expense, such as a dental bill or car repair, the cheque was increased just enough to cover it. We never once told the gentleman about our needs. But God knew.

We never ceased to be absolutely amazed at God's faithfulness and provision.

Twenty-Three

THE GYMNASIUM AT the school gave our congregation the space we needed, but one major need made its presence felt whenever we walked into the building laden down with guitars, music stands, sound equipment, books, and seemingly endless supplies: the need for our own facility, a facility we could call home and from which we could launch our ministry.

Setting up the gym was a lot of work each Sunday morning, and equipment was always breaking down due to the constant moving of things. We had also discovered that the gymnasium was hot in the summer and cold in the winter.

There was another incentive. The church had owned a building many years previous, but it had been sold to the local Lions Club. The church had about $100,000 sitting in a bank account from the sale of that building. Whenever there was a shortage of operating funds, which happened regularly, that account was accessed as a kind of slush fund to cover the deficit.

I didn't believe it was a good idea to rely on these funds. Rather, I felt we should put that money into property while we had it and trust God to meet our monthly needs going forward.

I approached the leadership regarding the matter and they agreed wholeheartedly. So the decision was made to use the money to purchase property upon which to one day build our own facility. It was a huge faith step, and everyone was on board.

Thus began the search for property. We looked everywhere in and around town and ran into challenges quickly.

Firstly, suitable land wasn't readily available. Secondly, much of the property for sale had limiting zoning and bylaw restrictions. Thirdly, land was selling for about $100,000 an acre. The math was unpromising. The money we had available would purchase only one acre—and we needed more acreage.

Since real estate seemed beyond our reach, we called upon the church to pray. Need serves as a great stimulator for God's people to pray. It puts suction in our prayers. Our people prayed earnestly. We needed a miracle for Community Bible Church. We needed a miracle for Aurora.

What is outside the realms of possibility for man is within the realms of possibility with God. We truly believed that God was leading us to purchase property. Armed with faith, we prayed with persistence that God would give us land before the close of the year. We eagerly watched to see what God would do.

We continued to search real estate for the next month, faithfully following up on all the leads we were given. At each day's end, however, we were blocked by at least one of the same three obstacles: too little acreage, too many restrictions, or too little cash.

One Saturday morning in early December, I received a call from Chuck, one of the individuals on the search committee. He asked me and the others to come see a piece of property on the southwest side of Aurora. He seemed excited.

We met at the property and found it to be a superb five acres, completely forested with pine trees. We walked the perimeter and realized this was exactly what we had been praying for. We were arrested by both the beautiful setting and potential for numerous ministry uses.

Not only was the property adequate for us, but the listed price was scarcely credible. It was $110,000. In an area where $100,000 would buy only one acre, we were standing on a piece of property where that dollar amount would buy us five acres. How could this be? Clearly, God must have had something to do with it. Was this the miracle we had been praying for?

After walking the length and width of the land, we stood in the middle of the property and discussed the next step. We were of one mind that God had led us here in direct answer to our prayers. We also agreed that we should submit an offer immediately. We prayed fervently that God's will be done.

We didn't have to wait long. We heard back the next day that the offer had been accepted.

The news spread through the church quickly. Everyone was excited. As the level of enthusiasm rose, so did the level of praise, for everyone recognized that this was something God had done. We recognized what Israel had recognized in the days of Ezra and Nehemiah—that the good hand of our God was upon us.

At the time, we had no idea that there was another group keenly interested in purchasing the property: a group of Seventh-Day Adventists. They gathered for their services on Saturday and intended to present an offer on the property on Sunday. Without knowing this, we had presented our offer on Saturday and it was accepted. There was no sense of competition, just following the leading of our God.

At the beginning of December 1985, we needed $110,385.68 to cover the purchase of the land and the lawyer's fees. We were about $8,000 short and asked God to provide. We also presented the need to his people. Being a small church, $8,000 was a lot of money in addition to our regular giving, but everyone gave generously over and above. By month's end, we had raised the full amount.

We entered the new year with new property, zero debt, and $35 in the bank account. As I said earlier, this was a gigantic faith step for our church, and certainly for our family. Now the monetary buffer was gone.

"We have taken a faith step," I said to the congregation. "And now we move forward in faith that God will provide for all of our needs."

Interestingly, now that we had our property, and no longer had our $100,000 cushion, our weekly giving increased steadily.

Twenty-Four

I CLEARLY RECALL the warm day in June when I walked upon our five acres, exactly one year after our family had arrived at Community Bible Church. Our church now had a mammoth challenge before us. We had property. We were debt-free. But we needed more than a piece of land; we needed a building sitting on it, a home base from which to launch our ministry in Aurora.

We didn't have the financial resources to climb that mountain. I had the faith, however, to believe that if God had given us the property, he would also supply the resources to build a facility on it. I believed that if we proceeded with faith and prayer, we would continue to see the good hand of our God upon us.

Our church began to pray in earnest about this next faith step. I personally felt compelled by the Holy Spirit to walk upon our property each week at the same time to bring the matter before God. I chose Tuesday mornings.

The first time I began my prayer exercise was a warm Tuesday morning in June 1986. I found a narrow overgrown path leading up through the middle of the trees that I could follow. It felt like a sanctuary. A gentle breeze blew through the pines. Patches of sunlight filtered through the heavily needled boughs, warming the ground wherever the sun's rays found a space. Overhead, a squirrel chattered its discontent at my presence. A bluejay swooped down onto a nearby branch to get a closer view of this intruder and satisfy its curiosity.

Each time I came to the property, I felt alone with God in his creation. It always felt special. I thanked him for loving me and showering me with his grace, and I told him how much I loved him and needed him. I unloaded my burdens upon him. I pleaded with him to keep me close to himself, to teach me his ways, to fill me and use me. I prayed for Diane and the family. I talked to him about the needs of our church. I prayed for vision to see where God was going and for the faith to believe him to take us there. I thanked him for this property and claimed it for his purposes. I asked him to crown this land with a facility that would honour him and be used by him. I admitted our inadequacy and acknowledged his adequacy.

The challenge of erecting a building was a Herculean mountain to climb. But rather than tell God how big the mountain was, I decided to tell the mountain how big God was.

I continued faithfully to meet with God on the property every Tuesday morning, walking and praying and claiming this ground for his purposes. The path became well-worn.

One particular winter morning, after a snowstorm had blown in about three feet of snow, I tried to convince God that this wasn't a good morning for my prayer walk. There was too much snow for easy walking. But he wouldn't give me a settled feeling about neglecting it that morning.

So off I trekked, cutting a trail through snow almost up to my waist. I thought to myself how silly I must look.

And that's when I spotted it: a small mound in the snow. I nudged it, and there under the blanket of snow lay a frozen grouse. It was a most beautiful bird, adorned in its deep red and tawny brown plumage. It seemed probable that it had struck a branch in the night as it flew through the thick pine brushwood, knocked itself out, fallen to the ground, and frozen. I took it home to show the kids its beautiful coloured feathers.

Because of what I'd been doing when I uncovered the bird, Diane suggested that I have it mounted and placed in a significant spot—as a reminder that God had answered my prayer. I liked her faith in using the word *answered,* a fait accompli, as though the building was as good as up and functioning before a tree as yet had been felled or a spade sliced the sod.

And so the grouse was mounted and perched over my desk. It sits over my desk even to this day, as a memory aid to remind us that God hears us when we call. He answers the prayer of faith. For years I had it mounted over my desk in my church office. Many times people asked about the meaning of the bird, giving me an opening to say, "Let me tell you a story of something God did…"

The church gathered on many occasions out on the property. It was important to have people stand and walk on the land to claim it for God's purposes and keep the vision alive for what God was doing. We carried our lawn chairs, Bibles, guitars, and sometimes umbrellas there in order to spend an hour worshipping, praying, and communicating the vision.

Twenty-Five

WHILE IT WAS true that we had little in terms of financial resources, we decided to begin making plans. We formed a building committee that launched the search for an architect and contractor. It didn't take long to find one who understood our needs. There was so much groundwork to be done. It wasn't just a matter of drawing up plans for construction. There were topographical maps that had to be drawn up. Surveys that needed to be conducted. Environmental studies that had to be completed. Zoning restrictions that needed to be addressed. Applications for minor variances that must be submitted.

Our plans needed to be worked and reworked under the watchful eye of, and in accordance with, the conservation authority, the region, the township, and the neighbours. We collaborated closely with the members of the township building and planning department. It was important to have their involvement and support when it came time to submit our site plan application and seek approval for a building permit. Hours and hours were spent multiple evenings poring over the plans, addressing town and regional demands, and trying to resolve the tension between physical need and budget.

Building programs are exciting undertakings for churches. But they are also fraught with peril.

It became needful to appease the various parties within our church. There was no shortage of opinions percolating through the congregation.

There were those who felt we needed to address our present and future needs and trust God to provide the finances. Their focus was on faith, trusting God to provide.

Then there were others who only wanted to address our basic needs and proceed by calculated steps "as God provided" and as finances were available. They touted fiscal responsibility.

Some emphasized the quality of construction. Still others wanted to just get the job done by the cheapest route possible.

I feared that some of these parties seemed to be on a collision course. I often found myself as pastor doing my best to keep it from becoming contentious.

We spent much time in prayer asking God to provide the financial resources needed to begin construction. I kept the vision in front of the church at all times. People needed to feel passionate about what was happening and why.

Faith steps can lead to fear and I wanted everyone to be reminded of the bigness of our God. Special building offerings were held and the church responded in an amazing way. Our congregation gave sacrificially, truly reflecting the grace of our God. This served as a confirmation that the hand of our God was upon us and going before us.

We also contacted adherents further afield, those whom we believed had an interest in what God was doing in Aurora. Money began to come in from outside our immediate church family.

Finally the day arrived when we, including our architect and contractor, believed we were ready to submit our building plans to the town council for initial approval. The planning department was on board and we expected to receive a relatively quick approval.

This was not to be. Getting the plans approved proved to be a marathon ordeal.

The town council met on the first Monday evening of every month, and we entered the meeting with strong expectations and high hopes. Our neighbours on either side had been silent up to that point, so we were caught unawares when both neighbours showed up with lawyers. They both owned large estate homes and didn't want a church next door. Each lawyer spoke in turn on behalf of his client, posting objection after objection. They were troubled about traffic in and out of the church. They were perturbed about potential noise. They complained about light pollution. They were concerned about any infringement upon their property.

The members of the town council listened intently to their concerns. We listened, too.

The council then debated the concerns for about a half-hour before deciding that we as a church needed to address the concerns with each neighbour and work things out between all parties.

This began more rounds of meetings. The lawyers seemed impossible to reason with as they laid out demand after demand. We would resolve one concern only for them to move on to another. We came to realize that they simply didn't want a church building next door.

Again, we called the church to prayer. God had brought us this far and we didn't believe that he would have given us this land only to be brought to a halt by man. God had opened a door that we believed no man could shut.

The church prayed. And prayed. I continued to meet with God every Tuesday morning, claiming this land for God's purposes. This was a faith journey and we believed that God was teaching us to lean upon him.

We continued to meet with our neighbours and their lawyers. There were many meetings, many difficult meetings, as we tried to hammer out a solution. And over time they began to understand that we weren't going anywhere. They recognized that we wanted to be good neighbours and work with them to address their concerns.

Their hearts began to soften. And then we reached a resolution. It wasn't one we were particularly happy about, but it was an agreement. We agreed to put artificial berms on the perimeter of our property adjacent to their properties. We agreed to plant mature trees all along the berms to prevent light penetration and to muffle noise. They seemed appeased. It would cost us thousands of additional dollars, but there was no other way.

We believed that God was in charge and he would provide. We were ready to proceed.

On a sunny Sunday morning, the church met on the property to give thanks to God. But this was different from all those many other times we had gathered. I carried a Bible in one hand and a spade in the other. The scene reminded me of Nehemiah's workers rebuilding Jerusalem's walls; they'd carried a sword in one hand and a trowel in the other.

We thanked God for the way he had led us to this land. We thanked him for his provision. We thanked him for bringing us to the point of proceeding with construction. We acknowledged our need of him going forward. This mountain was bigger than us, but it wasn't bigger than our God. We committed ourselves to be faithful and progress by faith and prayer.

Then I handed the spade to each of our leaders. Each put the spade into the ground and turned the sod. I did the same.

Only one week later, we began clearing land for a structure and parking lot. Every Saturday for numerous weeks, the property rang with the high-pitched whining buzz of chainsaws. Trees were felled and limbed, logs piled, and mountains of branches thrust into high stacks. We left as many trees standing as possible to add to the beauty of the property. And of course everything was done under the watchful eye of the conservation authority.

It seemed like a never-ending job, but the camaraderie was special as gangs of people hauled logs and dragged brush through brambles with breathless satisfaction.

By midmorning, someone always showed up with muffins or doughnuts. We would take a break from our work and enjoy a cup of coffee out of our thermoses while passing the doughnuts until they'd all been consumed. Then we'd get back to work.

Lunchtime came around quickly, and by then we'd worked up a substantial appetite. Someone often showed up with baking and sometimes hot chili or lasagna. Everyone, young and older, seemed happily engaged in cheerful conversation and laughter. There was nothing quite like a good morning's work and a hearty lunch to strengthen the bonds of community.

After adequate space had been cleared for a building and parking lot, we began to clear away the trees for a soccer and games field on a lower level section of land. Men and women of all ages worked hard with the same sense of synergy.

I remember the day when we laid the grass sod on our cleared field. It had poured with rain the night before and the ground was soaked and soft. We slogged away all that day with rakes and shovels in wet slippery clay up to our ankles. But the hard work and foresight of those days benefitted the ministry immensely in the years to follow.

Many times since then, I have looked down upon that field and watched children running about during our summer day camp or our youth playing soccer, and remembered that rainy day when we cleared the field and sodded it.

Twenty-Six

AS THE SUMMER of 1988 drew near, the land had been cleared and heavy equipment moved in on schedule. Construction began in earnest. Tree roots had to be excised. A heavy grader spent long hours levelling the areas for both the building and parking lot. Dirt was brought in for the perimeter berms. The grading seemed to go on forever!

Finally it was completed and cement was poured for the slab upon which the building would be constructed. I had always advocated to include a basement in the plans, even if it was left unfinished at first. That discussion went round and round, but it was finally decided by the building committee that we would proceed without a basement to save costs. It was my opinion that we would regret that decision—which we did a few years later—but I had also learned to monitor tension and relax my opinion, rightly or wrongly, to safeguard congregational unity. There is always a fine balance between tension and unity.

In order to help offset costs, the church had agreed with our contractor to provide labour from the congregation, supplying x number of hours per month to assist with the construction. Many of those hours went toward cleanup at the end of each day. Some of our congregants worked with hammer and saw alongside the framers. Others were tradespeople in their own right and freely offered their skills doing electrical and plumbing. Several of our women, including Diane, offered many hours making design decisions and choosing paint colours and lighting.

This was a good plan when it came to saving money. But it was also a source of friction.

Through the summer and into the fall, most of the construction went smoothly. By the time we reached November and December, however, we were feeling the strain. Some of the men on the building committee began to make decisions on their own with little appreciation or consideration for the time, decisions, and labour of others around them, namely women. I know of no other way to state it than to say that the women who were involved in the building decisions were treated in a dismissive manner.

I first became aware of it when I overheard a man rebuking one of our women on a particular matter. I could see she was hurt.

I felt convicted to speak with him later that day and ask him what had happened. He really didn't have a good answer. I was careful to tell him how much his work was appreciated—it's always beneficial in such situations to stroke a man's ego—and then I asked, in as tender a way as I could, to please work alongside people and appreciate their efforts regardless of how he felt about them. I felt immediate resistance from him. In fact, his response was surprisingly intense.

Unfortunately, another woman came to me that same week and informed me that this same man had openly rebuked her over a decision she had made regarding the women's washroom decor. I couldn't understand why he was concerning himself with the decor in the women's washroom.

I could feel the emotional temperature rising. I was also aware of how strife can escalate if it's not treated with wisdom.

Now I was faced with the decision as to whether to leave this second incident alone, so as not to stir things up, or address it. Either response could rid us of the problem, or it could escalate it.

I spoke with the church leadership regarding the matter. They made it clear that they didn't want to jeopardize their relationship with the offender and so decided to just leave the matter alone. That's what we did.

But I also came away from that meeting with the realization that addressing the matter meant jeopardizing friendships. Something I learned in my years as a pastor was that the power of friendship usually trumps principle.

That was not the end of it. It all boiled over one day when two of the women on our decor team stated their intention to resign from the team. The reason? They had been treated disparagingly by another man on our building committee. They felt there was a disturbing lack of respect for them as females and for the many hours of research and comparison shopping they had done. They complained of the men's consistent failure to appreciate the value of their input as women. They spent numerous hours travelling to various outlets and manufacturers to make decisions about colours or lighting only to have their suggestions and choices brushed off with an offhanded "We won't be doing that. We've chosen something else."

It became increasingly evident that a chauvinistic attitude was pervading the work effort and causing hurt.

I spoke gently to the second man in question and asked for a clarification regarding his behaviour. Was that how he had intended to come across? Had the two women misunderstood him? His response was disappointing. He felt attacked and responded with the same hostility as the first man.

Both of these men began to shun me and it became gradually more awkward to be on the construction site with them.

These kinds of issues rarely stay contained. Dissension spreads through the body like a disease. I tried to stay focused on the building program to bring it to completion and at the same time to extinguish the fires of dissension, recognizing the attack of the evil one who was clearly attempting to derail our progress.

We pushed on despite the fact that it was a bit of a bumpy ride. The building was completed in January of that year and we had our opening service on January 29, 1989.

The opening service was bittersweet. Just before the hour to begin, one of the gentlemen who had caused such grief during the construction burst into my office in tears. He sobbed as he told me he was sorry for his part in the events of the past weeks.

But he also told me that he and his family would be leaving the church. In the weeks that followed, I was unable to dissuade him.

I felt a little unnerved going into the service that morning immediately following this episode. I was aware of others who were unhappy and threatening to leave. I felt uncertain about what might be looming on the horizon.

At the same time, this was the opening service in our new facility. God's hand had been all over this endeavour. His faithfulness had prevailed. In less than four years, we had gone from a small group of people in a classroom to having property and a facility of our own. We couldn't help but be grateful and filled with praise. The God who had gone before us would continue to go before. He had warned me that it wouldn't be easy. I also knew that his warning had come with the encouragement to persevere and not forget his call upon Diane and me to Aurora. He would make Community Bible Church a lighthouse on a hill pointing people to Jesus. His promise would not fail.

Twenty-Seven

THE NEXT SIX years would prove to be some of our darkest and most difficult days. Satan's attack was unrelenting. My ministry was continually being undermined. The attacks seemed to be directed at both me and the elders leadership team.

Interestingly, we were growing as a church community during this period. From the spring of 1989 to the winter of 1990, many new people made Community Bible Church their home. Wonderful people were faithfully supporting the ministry with fresh vitality and excellence. As a pastor, I felt their prayers, encouragement, loyalty, and support.

But all the good seemed to be offset by an undercurrent of unrest percolating through the church. A continual hemorrhaging. People leaving or speaking of leaving, creating instability.

Our new arrivals brought new ideas and the new building was filling up. However, there were people who just didn't seem to want the church to grow or change. They liked things the way they were.

I have always been an advocate for change. Change is good and necessary. Why? Because healthy things grow. And growing things change. And changing things mean… change. That's true for a healthy tree. It's true for a healthy body. And it's true for a healthy church body.

I've heard it said that we shouldn't change just for the sake of change. On the contrary, I believed then—and I believe now—that change in a church is good just for the sake of it. Why? To cultivate a mindset or culture of change. Churches too often see change as a disruption. They fear and resist it, settling for a comfortable state of stagnation. Or they find themselves reacting and adjusting to the inevitability of change, scrambling to mitigate the disturbance and to minimize the angst that unfamiliarity introduces.

It is critical to a church's health and growth that we become comfortable with change, plan for it, and embrace it. But that threatens and aggravates the status quo, and those who stand guard to maintain it.

There were times when I really believed I could not go on. The attacks became personal.

Ministry can take a huge toll on one personally. I was told that I always seemed to look calm and strong. But inside, I personally felt like I was melting into a puddle, like ice under a relentless sun. There were times when I questioned my ability to lead.

All this instability took a toll on my family as well. Diane and I had been teaching the music program at a Christian school, but we had stopped doing so recently because of the workload at the church. Our children, however, still attended that school.

Our youngest daughter was in Grade One. We began to receive notes regularly from her teacher accusing her of bad behaviour. This seemed out of character for our daughter. We met with the teacher and principal about it, but they assured us that she was misbehaving. We talked to our daughter about these matters, too, but she seemed reluctant to say anything.

In later years, we learned that she had been quiet out of fear of getting me in trouble or even losing my job. This deeply disturbed me because her love and concern for me were stronger than her need to speak.

But we could see that she was increasingly unhappy. She would cry herself to sleep every night, and every morning she resisted our urgings to go to school.

That's when the "lunch bag issue" landed on our doorstep.

One day when I arrived at the school to pick our kids up, our daughter's teacher marched out to me with our daughter in tow and informed me that she had thrown her lunch in the wastebasket. Our daughter was crying and unyielding in her denial, but the teacher was just as adamant in her accusation. The incident itself seemed harmless; if true, it could even be seen as an opportunity to teach a young girl a lesson in wastefulness. What concerned me most was my daughter's tears and denials and the teacher's accusatory attitude toward such a young child.

I asked to check the lunch bag, since it was the key evidence of the crime. When I looked inside the bag, the evidence spoke for itself: it was not my daughter's lunch! She was right; they were wrong. I was appalled. To me, there was so much more going on than the incident of a discarded lunch.

The principal and teacher attended our church and we became increasingly suspicious that the problems we were having in the church were leaching into the lives of our children. We couldn't know for sure, but we were more and more of the opinion that our daughter's struggles in school originated in the church.

We decided to withdraw our children from the Christian school at the end of the academic year and place them in a public school in Aurora where we lived. Unfortunately, both the teacher and principal were influential members of our church, and we knew this dynamic would make for a difficult situation.

And it did. The meshing of church and family can be perilous.

But we couldn't risk the mental and emotional health of our kids. So we did it.

The disunity was wearing on Diane and me. We felt deeply saddened that the disunity frosted our relationship with people with whom we had worked so closely. I lost thirty pounds over a short period of time and my doctor told me that the stress was going to severely impact my health if I didn't find a way to handle it. He ordered me to begin a rigorous program at a fitness centre. I did so and faithfully went to the fitness centre every other day. It seemed to help and I began to slowly put weight back on. My health began to return.

But emotionally it was an uphill battle.

Twenty-Eight

AS I SAT in my office at the church one Tuesday morning, something suddenly hit the window. A crow. A dirty crow with wet mud all over its feathers and claws. It scratched its way up and down the window in a frenzy. I had never witnessed anything like it. I watched in disbelief as it left muddy scratch marks all over the pane.

After about a minute, it flew away and I went outside to wash the window. All I could think was how strange an occurrence this had been.

The next morning, the same event repeated itself. I had no sooner sat down when the crow flew up against the window again and scratched its way up and down the pane. The incident alarmed me this time. What was happening?

It happened again the next day. And the next. The same crow would be sitting up in the same tree, cackling at me. When I'd enter the office, I'd take note that the window was clean. And as soon as I sat down at my desk, the bird would fly down from its branched vantage and assault the window.

There could have been a natural explanation. It could have been that the bird saw its reflection in the window and believed it to be another bird and attacked it. Or was it something else? I couldn't understand why the same creature would wait until I arrived and entered my office. I couldn't understand why the bird was so filthy and left so much wet mud on the windowpane. I had no reasonable explanation.

It occurred to me that maybe there was more to this than a deranged crow. Could it be that these bizarre incidents had a spiritual component? Could this seemingly possessed bird be attacking my window under the influence of something more sinister, designed to unsettle me?

The thought came to my mind that if it happened the next morning, I should speak directly to the bird and address it as though there was a more diabolical component.

When I drove into the parking lot the next morning, the black crow was staring at me from the same tree. Berating me. As I entered my office, it again descended to pursue its strange behaviour.

I walked outside. Facing my nemesis squarely, I commanded it to be gone in the name of Jesus and never return. The bird squawked, then flew up and past the tree it had used as its resting place and into the pines beyond. It never returned.

One can deduce what one wants from this story. I merely share what happened. But it served me as a warning: *"Stay alert! Watch out for your great enemy, the devil. He prowls around like a roaring lion, looking for someone to devour"* (1 Peter 5:8). Whether he prowls like a lion ready to devour or pummels the windowpane like a demented crow wanting to unsettle us, we need to be alert to the presence of the enemy.

My inclination was to feel anxious. But the apostle Peter urges in the same passage to give all our worries and anxieties to God, because he cares for us (1 Peter 5:7). We were covered by the protective hand of God.

Twenty-Nine

WHILE I FELT trapped in the quagmire of growing discord, the Holy Spirit led me to read and study the Welsh Revival that had occurred in the early years of the twentieth century. I was particularly moved by the story of Rees Howells, one of the revival's spiritual leaders. Norman Grubb tells the story of this man of God in his book, *Intercessor*, a top-shelf book in my library.[5]

The primary message to me as a pastor was that intercessory prayer is critical to a Spirit-filled ministry. It's easy to get mired and entangled, even overwhelmed, by personal hurt, fear, and anxiety over what man can do. I discovered that God can use intercession to convert the negative drain on one's soul into positive Spirit-filled power and influence.

Rees Howells was born in 1879 in Wales. A coal miner, he became one of the influencers in the great Welsh Revival of 1904 and a prayer warrior who impacted lives and world events from his knees. As I read and studied his life, I developed a thirst to live life through intercessory prayer.

I was challenged in other areas of my life.

Howells emphasized the need for absolute surrender. The Holy Spirit intercedes through the life of a person whose heart is unconditionally and completely surrendered to him. I hungered daily for the filling of the Spirit. The Spirit opened my eyes to understand that his filling was not how much I had of him, for I possessed all of him, but how much he had of me. And I yearned for him to have all of me.

The matter of absolute surrender was reinforced in another book the Holy Spirit led me to read at that time. In his book *The Complete Green Letters*, Miles Stanford emphasized rich truths that would greatly influence my thinking going forward.[6]

---

[5] Norman Grubb, *Intercessor* (Fort Washington, PA: CLC Publications, 2016).

[6] Miles J. Stanford, *The Complete Green Letters* (Grand Rapids, MI: Zondervan, 1984).

As I read, truths that I had previously understood were reinforced, and impacted my thinking anew. The self-life is the enemy of surrender. The self-life cannot be repaired. It cannot be reinvented. It cannot be rehabilitated. It must be gotten rid of. It must die.

I was enlightened to the truth that not only were my sins nailed to the cross when Jesus died on it, but I was also nailed to it. The self-life, with all its selfish desires and control, was crucified with Christ by identification with him in his death.

And then, by identification with Christ in his resurrection, I was resurrected to new life. I became a new person in Christ. Jesus now lived his resurrection life in me.

But to know the full impact of this in my life, I would have to reckon these truths to be my reality and appropriate them in my daily life by faith and surrender.

In Galatians 2:20, the apostle Paul wrote, *"My old self has been crucified with Christ. It is no longer I who live, but Christ lives in me."* The phrase *"not I, but Christ"* reverberated in my heart. God doesn't help me to live the Spirit-filled life; Christ himself is my life.

Howells focused attention on the term *abiding* from John 15:1–8 to describe the condition for answered prayer. Jesus used the term in his analogy of the vine and the branches. He is the vine; we are the branches. A branch has no life in itself; on its own, it is no more than a dead stick. It possesses life and bears fruit only when it abides in and receives life from the life-giving vine. In other words, we possess life and bear fruit only when we abide in Christ. Jesus was speaking of absolute unconditional surrender. Then Jesus transitioned into the topic of prayer, saying, *"But if you remain in me and my words remain in you, you may ask for anything you want, and it will be granted!"* (John 15:7) The promise is unlimited, but the condition is abiding.

It follows that if we are abiding in Christ and deriving our life from him, we will know what to pray for because our hearts and minds are surrendered to and aligned with God's will and ways.

Howells believed that effective prayer must be guided by the Holy Spirit, not our own personal thoughts and feelings. We must pray what the Holy Spirit gives us to pray. It's critically important to listen attentively to the voice of the Holy Spirit. We never learn much when we're talking; we can learn a lot when we're listening.

When our prayers are in alignment with the will of God, we can believe God for the answer. Faith lays hold of the answer and allows one to pray in the face of insurmountable odds.

Howells experienced this kind of faith when praying for his personal needs. He never made his needs known to anyone except God. He prayed and believed God for the answer.

This resonated in my own life.

Howells prayed in faith for revival to break out in his home country of Wales, and witnessed a supernatural moving of God's Spirit there. During that revival, it was said that even the horses stopped working because they no longer heard the curses to which they were accustomed hurled their way from the mouths of drivers.

His prayers of faith impacted international affairs. He joined with many others—among them my mother, as I recounted earlier—to pray for the deliverance of Britain's troops trapped on the beaches of Dunkirk. God answered in a miraculous way by calming the normally treacherous waters of the English Channel to allow boats large and small to cross and rescue the soldiers. He united with others to pray against Hitler's impending invasion of Great Britain. The invasion never happened.

The prayer of faith moves the supernatural hand of God to accomplish infinitely more than we might ask or think.

If faith is one side of the coin, perseverance is the other. Howells emphasized that when God gives a prayer, we must prevail in faith. When the enemy oppresses, do battle and keep praying. Howells wrote that man's extremity is God's opportunity. There will be times when we seem to be hanging by a thread, but the persevering prayer of faith draws down supernatural power.

Thirty

I HAD JUST gotten home from the funeral of a friend named Cathy. My mind returned to a morning back in 1986 when I had led her and her husband Bob to Jesus. They were the first two people to come to faith in Jesus in our new church.

I remembered sharing a story with them to help illustrate what it meant to have faith in Jesus. It was the story of Charles Blondin, the first person to cross Niagara Falls on a tightrope. He crossed the falls on many occasions, and on one of those occasions he carried his manager, Harry Colcord, across with him.

There are several versions of the story, but the version I told was the one about the wheelbarrow. Blondin asked how many from the crowd of spectators believed he could cross to the other side of the falls while pushing a wheelbarrow. They all cheered in the affirmative. He then replied that if they truly believed, one of them should get into the wheelbarrow and let him push them across.

The crowd went uncomfortably silent. He urged them to act on their belief, but no one dared take that step.

So finally he told his manager to get into the wheelbarrow. Mr. Colcord did as he was asked and sat gingerly in the small single-wheeled cart. Blondin gave some simple instructions: "Harry, do not attempt to balance yourself. Just sit still and let me do the balancing."

Off they started and Blondin pushed his somewhat reluctant volunteer across the falls.

I explained to Bob and Cathy that this was what faith in Jesus looked like. It's more than just verbal assent or acceptance. It's more like getting into the wheelbarrow, putting one's life in the hands of the one who died on the cross and rose from the dead for us.

Over the next little while, the Holy Spirit continued to speak into both of their hearts.

Several weeks later, Cathy walked into the office where Bob was working and said, "I really believe that I'm ready to get into the wheelbarrow." Bob nodded in agreement. The Holy Spirit had brought him to the same place.

Of course, I didn't know about that conversation.

But that same morning, the Holy Spirit spoke clearly to me and told me to make a visit to the office where Bob and Cathy worked. They owned a small financial business, so I knew where to find them. I prayed fervently that the Holy Spirit would give me the opportunity to speak with Bob alone, as I believed that Bob was more ready than Cathy to receive Jesus.

I walked into the office and Cathy greeted me with a big smile inside the door. I asked if I could see Bob in his office and silently prayed again that I would have some time alone with him. Bob reached out his hand over his desk and pleasantly welcomed me to take a seat. I had no sooner sat down than Cathy walked back into the office with a cup of coffee in her hand and settled herself into the chair beside me. It was becoming apparent that the Holy Spirit wanted Cathy in on the conversation.

I told them why I had come and began to share the good news. They both wept, and through their tears they told me that they were more than ready to receive Jesus as their Saviour. God had clearly prepared their hearts to surrender, just as he had prepared my heart to share. Bob and Cathy began a faith journey that morning and never looked back.

When Bob was giving Cathy's eulogy, he spoke about the day when he and Cathy had gotten into the wheelbarrow. My heart leaped for joy as my thoughts raced back over the memory.

Returning from the funeral service, I felt saddened that cancer had claimed Cathy's physical life, but I rejoiced that God had claimed her as his daughter for eternity. There was no doubt that she had gotten into the wheelbarrow. I knew where she was: alive and in heaven with Jesus.

There is nothing more encouraging and gratifying than leading someone to Jesus. It renews and refreshes one's soul. It reminds one of why we are here on the earth: to be a light and witness for Jesus.

In the midst of the struggles we had been encountering in the church, the new faith shared by Bob and Cathy was fresh air and it restored our vigour. Over the years, many people came to faith in Jesus, and every time it brought renewal and joy into our souls. It lifted our eyes toward our God and reminded us that he is at work, even in the difficult times.

When the apostle Paul arrived in the city of Corinth in Greece, he wrote that he came to them *"in weakness—timid and trembling"* (1 Corinthians 2:3). This might be because he had just arrived from Athens where he'd debated with the intellectuals of that city, leaving him discouraged and deflated. Athens was one of the few places where Paul visited but never established a new church. Maybe it was the combination of that and seeing the corruption and immorality of the seaport of Corinth, a great urban and cultural melting pot with a reputation for decadence. Whatever the reason, the apostle Paul arrived in Corinth feeling weak and timid.

This resonated with me, reminding me of how I had come to Aurora—weak, apprehensive, and timid. What an encouragement it must have been to Paul when he ran into Aquila and Priscilla, a couple who were already believers and tentmakers like Paul. They invited him into their shop and home.

One passage in particular stood out to me about Paul's stay in Corinth:

> One night the Lord spoke to Paul in a vision and told him, "Don't be afraid! Speak out! Don't be silent! For I am with you, and no one will attack and harm you, for many people in this city belong to me." (Acts 18:9–10)

At the time, Paul was experiencing a strong dose of intense opposition and insult. And so Jesus appeared to him in a vision to encourage him to persevere in doing the Lord's work despite the gravity of the resistance.

Resistance can cause a lot of anxiety and fear. Jesus countered Paul's anxiety and fear with the assurance of his personal presence and protection. He also reminded Paul of the reason the Holy Spirit had led him to this city; there were many people in Corinth who belonged to him. They were not yet his people at this point in the story, but they soon would be as Paul persevered in sharing the good news. Jesus was inspiring Paul to go out and find them.

Jesus conveyed to me the words he spoke to the apostle Paul. A striking remedy to discouragement is engaging oneself in the priority of heaven—sharing the good news with people. Jesus was calling many people in Aurora to himself. I needed to concern myself with going out and finding them.

Diane and I made it our passion to share the good news with anyone who would listen. This passion lifted us above adversity and helped us to persevere in the work to which God had called us. I can think of a multitude of people whom God gave us the privilege to lead to himself: Paul, Cedric, Elizabeth, Tom, Gail, Jeff, Bruce… and on and on the list goes.

One day, my daughters came home from school with the news that their principal had cancer. I had never met their principal, but the next day I felt convicted to call him and invite him to lunch. I thought he would be hesitant, but to my surprise, after only a slight pause, he answered in the affirmative.

We met for lunch that same week, and thus began a friendship and bond of trust between us.

Over the next seven months, we had many good conversations about life, death, and dying. I listened to Bruce as he talked about his fear and apprehension. He had many questions. I just tried to walk alongside him and be there for him as he faced his mortality and prepared for his departure from this life into what was at the time, for him, a great unknown. I shared with him how much God loved him. We talked about what the Bible said regarding the afterlife. I communicated with him why Jesus had come to earth and shared the gospel as clearly as I could. He always listened intently. I didn't pretend to fully appreciate his internal thoughts and struggles, but I affirmed him and encouraged him to receive Jesus into his life. I reassured him that when that time came, he could call me and I would come.

The phone rang late one night. It was Bruce's wife. She told me that Bruce was asking for me.

Knowing that the time had come, I responded without hesitation and drove to Bruce's home, a big farmhouse in the countryside about a half-hour from our home.

He was very weak and his breathing was shallow and irregular. It was evident that the end was near. He motioned to me to draw closer. I took him by the hand and leaned down. He whispered in my ear that he was ready and asked me to pray with him. I prayed and he repeated the words, though barely audible.

It is amazing grace that God will hear the faint cry of a man at the very end of his life and welcome him into his family and into heaven. I spent a few minutes with Bruce before leaving. The next morning, his wife called me and told me that he had passed away only an hour after I'd left his bedside.

I was asked by the family to officiate at Bruce's funeral. It was the first funeral service to be held in our new church. The building was packed, with standing room only. I had been warned ahead of time that the whole regional board of education would be present, along with principals and many teachers with whom Bruce had worked. I knew that most were not people of faith, many of them agnostic.

As I scanned my audience, I felt overwhelmed at the opportunity the Holy Spirit had given me to communicate the gospel beyond Bruce. I recounted some of Bruce's spiritual journey and shared the story of Jesus and the eternal hope that every person present could experience in him. Everyone listened intently. Some even came to me after the service and commented that I had given them something to think about. I prayed that the Holy Spirit would water the seed that had been planted and cause it to take root.

When our church was built, one of the first things I did was hang a sign over the door at the exit that read, "You are now entering the mission field." For years, the idea has persisted that the mission field is a distant place—across a border, over an ocean, or in a culture other than our own.

But the truth is that the non-believing world exists all around us, right outside the doors of the church. I wanted our church to understand that message and be continually reminded of it. Even many years later, people told me that that sign had been indelibly fixed in their minds.

I have always been convinced that a sign of a healthy church is an increasing number of new believers. They are living proof that the gospel works. They inspire with new life. They bring passion. They carry no coercive spirit, preconceived opinion, or prejudiced agenda about how church should be done. Rather, they bring fresh perspective because they see everything with new eyes. Their hearts are filled with gratitude for what God has done in their lives. They are enthusiastic about their faith and eager to learn. They are motivated to share their faith with friends. They possess a contagious love for Jesus.

Thirty-One

I WOULD LIKE to say that I enjoyed my time as a pastor. The word *enjoy*, however, is not really befitting. The experience was extremely gratifying, and it was rewarding to follow God's call and partner with him in doing what he called me to do. It was amazing to witness him accomplish things that only he could do in a city without any strong and effective witness.

But the pain and stress associated with pastoring this church were personally exhausting. The words and warnings of those two elderly men several years earlier over a cup of coffee had proven true.

It seemed to come out of the blue one day when a woman took it upon herself to challenge my calling as a pastor. She postulated that I hadn't been called by God to be a pastor, that I had felt exceptional pressure from my father to choose pastoral ministry as a career. I have no idea where she came up with that theory. She knew nothing about my father or my upbringing. She even phoned Diane one day and told her that her defence of me was misguided. And she followed the phone call up with a letter in the mail that reiterated her doubts.

As usually happens, the discontent of a few people flows downhill. Sometimes this kind of hostility lurked behind a supportive façade, with people pretending to have my best interests in mind. Sometimes it was less disguised. One person communicated that he was asking God to remove the scales from my eyes, as he had done for the apostle Paul. I wasn't completely sure what that meant. Another counselled that I should go away for a period of time and discern the will of God for my life. I think that person meant for me to just go away. It was also suggested that I consider leaving the church for the well-being of myself and my family. The undercurrent of malice could not be concealed.

Thankfully, there were strong and discerning people who came around to remind us of the spiritual source of these accusations, reassure us, and lift us up.

It all came to a head one Sunday just after the morning service. A man handed me a sheet of folded paper and just walked away. It was a handwritten list of grievances. As I ran my eyes over the list, I couldn't believe what I read. It was a record of random unfounded complaints going back several years. They seemed so absurd that I thought they would just stay on the piece of paper and go no further.

I had no idea just how things would escalate.

This man also asked to speak with the church's board of elders—I prefer the term "leadership team"—regarding his concerns, and a meeting was arranged.

I sat motionless in the meeting as this man read aloud from his list of complaints. Everyone listened attentively. The expectations placed upon me as a pastor seemed unrealistic and extreme. Much of what he said boiled down to the expectation that a pastor should give every ounce of energy and time to the church. I was already giving everything I could.

He believed I should keep the congregation more informed about my private life, because of my accountability to the church. For instance, I should be more open with information, such as where I was going on vacation and how I could be contacted if necessary. And as the pastor, I should be in attendance at every church event. The reality was that I already did attend pretty much every event.

He brought up the occasion of a church corn roast that my family and I hadn't attended. I brought it to his attention that the corn roast in question had occurred on the same day as my brother's wedding. And I had been the best man.

"Well," he said, "you could have at least made a brief appearance."

I was dumbfounded.

More so, I was shocked at the response of the leadership team. I expected support, but instead I got an assignment. I was asked to personally reflect on these matters and respond back to the board.

I did reflect. And, upon reflection, I responded that these grievances were unjustified. My reply resulted in another meeting in my office with two board members to discuss with me the issues at hand.

I asked Diane to join me this time. Again, we sat and listened. They didn't like our position on the matter and told us that the accuser was their friend and someone with whom they often golfed. They welcomed and appreciated his concerns and encouraged us to do the same.

My issue, however, was not the character of the man, or who he golfed with, but only what he was saying about me.

At that point, the meeting seemed to take a sinister turn. One of the men stood up, looked me directly in the eye, and pointed his finger at me.

"Examine your heart!" he charged.

He then hurled an insult, accusing me of not receiving adequate support from Diane. This was supposedly impacting me negatively. Clearly the attention had shifted away from my accuser's behaviour and obvious discontent with me… it had shifted *to* me.

As the two individuals moved toward the office door, I stood up and asked that we talk until we had the matter resolved in an agreeable way. I felt very uncomfortable with the way things had been left. The one who was particularly angry walked up to me with a threatening scowl and suddenly pulled his fist back as though to strike me. I decided in that instant to just take the blow.

It didn't come. He just pushed past me and stormed out the door. The other man sheepishly followed.

Diane and I looked at each other in stunned silence at what had just transpired.

The church was associated with a denomination called the Associated Gospel Churches of Canada, and some of the AGC denominational leaders were called in by the board to adjudicate the matter. I was informed about the meeting on the night before it was scheduled. At the time, I was exhausted from being run off my feet going from meeting to meeting to meeting. Every other evening seemed to bring another meeting that seemed to resolve nothing. I felt blindsided time after time.

That evening with the AGC, I sat in a tense room and once again listened to the criticisms levelled against me. My hope was that the denominational representatives would discern what was happening and provide some objective clarity and direction to the issues.

They didn't. They just listened, mentioned something about their concern for the church, and closed the meeting in prayer.

Thirty-Two

DISUNITY IS THE great enemy of the church. It has existed since the church's inception. The Bible warns against it. Pastors can teach about it, preach against it, admonish and rebuke because of it, and everyone will agree with what is said. And yet it continues to poison the body.

Everyone has their own perspective, opinion, and truth. Everyone also has their own friend group. Friendships are wonderful, but they can cause one to turn a blind eye to facts. The bonds of friendship are often strong and serve to strengthen alliances and draw dividing lines. Friends are typically loyal and lend support to each other, even if it means compromising or ignoring the objective truth of a matter.

When the apostle Paul wrote to the church in Philippi, he addressed a disagreement that existed between two women, Euodia and Syntyche. I'll assume that others were taking sides. He urged the two women to settle the dispute and reminded them on a personal note that they had worked hard with him in telling others the good news (Philippians 4:3). Other versions of scripture translate the idea of working hard as *contending* at his side and *sharing* his struggle.

Paul used a metaphor. He referred to gladiators fighting alongside each other in the arena, struggling against a threat such as wild animals. Can you imagine gladiators fighting back to back against hungry tigers or wild dogs? Now imagine that one gladiator suddenly trips over his comrade in arms. He whirls around and strikes his fellow gladiator. In a startling turn of events, the two begin to attack each other. The crowd roars with laughter, mocking the two combatants for their foolishness. The consequence of fighting each other and ignoring the real enemy is that the gladiators get torn to pieces.

Satan is the enemy. But we forget to watch out for the devouring lion. We fail to recognize the true enemy and real danger. A fatal error is made when we focus rather on the actions, words, and even wrongdoings of our Christian sisters and brothers. We turn against each other. The crowd outside our circle observes us. They witness the debacle and find reason to question and even mock what they see. It's a lose-lose situation. The body of Christ suffers distress and injury. It's reputation is damaged. The name of Christ is disgraced. The good news of Jesus's love is discredited. The lion devours.

Encouraging things were happening at Community Bible Church. We elected a new leadership team that was discerning, supportive, and prayerful. The new leaders seemed not easily swayed by friendships or relationships that would compromise or influence their decision-making. The church community was still growing and people were coming to faith in Christ.

The growth of the church made it necessary to review and evaluate the existing ministries. We decided to recast two of our ministries that had become increasingly ineffective and were having minimal impact. We had been conducting a Sunday school every Sunday morning preceding the worship service. It made for a long and tiring morning and the people's enthusiasm for it had waned. So we replaced it with a new and exciting program on Sunday evenings called Awana.

Awana was extremely successful from the get-go. We adapted the program to include all ages so it became an event for the whole family. Every corner and crevice of our facility filled wall to wall with people who clearly loved participating. There was laughter, singing, games, contests, and crafts. When one walked through the door, one immediately felt the energy and enthusiasm. The Bible was the focus of the program. Children, teens, and adults were all involved in learning, applying, and memorizing the scriptures.

We also recognized the need to begin breaking our growing community into smaller segments. We called them home groups. These groups were critical to cultivating deeper relationships and more intimate time for prayer, discussion, and applying scriptures to daily life.

They also became an integral part of our caring ministry. People began to relate to one another in their group as one would to a family. They got to know and trust each other and genuinely care for each other. They met in the warm, welcoming, relaxed atmosphere of homes. They had the flexibility of meeting on any evening or at any time during the week, giving everyone better access. The groups were amazingly successful.

But a few people who represented the status quo felt threatened. I never wanted us to have a status quo, but it seems to be ingrained in human nature. People who introduced fresh new ideas were viewed as intruders, upsetting "the way we do things." They grumbled and resisted change, believing that what *was* was good enough. Some criticized the successful Awana ministry because there was no longer Sunday school, to which they had grown accustomed. Others disapproved of the home groups because they had replaced the traditional Wednesday night prayer meeting.

Interestingly, these same people were never in the practice of attending the Wednesday prayer meeting. In fact, the Wednesday night event had died down to only a half-dozen participants. But they perceived this change to be evidence of the church diminishing the importance and value of prayer. They failed to see, or maybe admit, that the home groups were drawing many more people and that much more prayer was occurring.

The disgruntlement of a few people, however, seemed enough to keep the exit door swinging open.

This small but influential minority found a voice in a person we least expected: the chairperson of our leadership team. I mentioned that we now had a new good-functioning leadership team—and we did. A growing trickle of people, however, began sharing some disturbing reports that our chairperson was circulating among the congregation and undermining my integrity and credibility. He was also telling people I was too busy to make time for them and they should come to him if they had problems or concerns. People were confused. On his part, it wasn't concern for my welfare or eagerness to help relieve my responsibilities; it was a classic Absalom and David scenario.

I have discovered over the years that sometimes men change when they're placed in a position of responsibility and authority. I'm sure there are psychological reasons for this. It should cause a person to feel humbled before God. Instead something crawls out of the woodwork of their old nature, something that craves attention, affirmation, and power to feed their need of self-importance.

The leadership team was very concerned. It was also discovered that he was divulging confidential information from the board meetings and disclosing sensitive matters to others accompanied by his own personal analysis and point of view. This clearly amounted to a breach of trust. It was a serious matter, and unfortunately the seeds of suspicion and distrust began to germinate and grow.

He went further and covertly approached the leadership of our denomination to fill them in on the details of our church from his misguided frame of reference.

The church's leadership team called a leaders' meeting and took the chairman to task for the breach. Interestingly, he didn't deny his actions and words, but he couldn't understand why they were wrong. After all, in his opinion, he was only "protecting" the church.

It was an extremely difficult and convoluted encounter in which he vehemently resisted any attempts to resolve the issue. The board asked for his resignation. He refused. The board then wrestled with the dilemma of how to cause the least amount of disruption in the church.

Unfortunately, the board was forced to make the difficult decision to hold a membership meeting to have the man removed from his position.

I will never forget that church meeting. The room was full. The denominational representatives sat quietly at the back of the room, observing. The board carefully and sensitively reviewed the issues leading up to that night and explained the reason for the disciplinary measures. While they were asking the church to make a difficult decision, they emphasized the need for healing and restoration going forward. They affirmed their absolute confidence and support for me as pastor of Community Bible Church.

You could have heard a pin drop. The person in question was then given opportunity to speak. He did so.

It was then my turn to speak to the congregation. A profound sense of humility swept over me, for I recognized that only the Holy Spirit was adequate for this moment. Trembling inside, I paused for a second. I looked out at the people in front of me. Most of them supported me, while others were unashamedly antagonistic. The difficulty I faced was that one cannot adequately justify oneself against personal accusations. One cannot defend one's reputation without looking defensive.

So I chose not to. I chose to let the Lord vindicate me.

I addressed the negative impact of dissension upon our church, especially upon our youth and new believers. I entreated the church to strive for unity, for the sake of Christ's name and our witness in the outside community. I inwardly pleaded that the Holy Spirit would give me the right words and approach, knowing that everything I said and projected would be dissected and judged. I prayed openly that this upheaval would lead to self-examination on the part of us all.

And yet, deep within, I feared that this crisis was not over.

The church voted and the decision was made to remove the individual from office. There was an awkward silence afterward. The two denominational representatives said nothing. Their actions came one week later when they organized a meeting with the dissenting group.

Once our leadership board became aware of this meeting, they asked that it be cancelled, but it went ahead against the board's will. The dissenters were encouraged to remain in the church to try and work things out. I understood the principle of reconciliation that lay at the root of this advice, but the lack of wisdom and discernment simply gave the group renewed support and a sense of justification for their actions.

The next morning, I prayed through every room in our building and rebuked the evil in Jesus's name. I urged the Holy Spirit to root out the sin, sweep everything clean, and fill the space. I earnestly prayed for God's protection around his church. I prayed for a deep spiritual breakthrough.

The dissension and unrest, however, continued. The pain continued. I had no more answers. Only a feeling of betrayal, distrust, and deep sadness.

Thirty-Three

I WONDERED, WHAT is burnout? Was I there? I had read an article written by a psychiatrist about a pattern in leaders who burn out. It stated that the first warning sign is weariness. Then there is a progression downward to cynicism about things ever getting better. This is quickly followed by bitterness, depression, and finally burnout. I didn't know if I was burnt out. But to be honest, I felt a lot of the symptoms. If I wasn't burnt out, I was close.

God led me to two passages of scripture, both from the book of Isaiah. The first was Isaiah 51:12–13.

> I, yes I, am the one who comforts you. So why are you afraid of mere humans, who wither like the grass and disappear? Yet you have forgotten the Lord, your Creator, the one who stretched out the sky like a canopy and laid the foundations of the earth. Will you remain in constant dread of human oppressors? Will you continue to fear the anger of your enemies? Where is their fury and anger now? It is gone!

The passage was written for the exiled people of Israel, who feared their Babylonian oppressors. But the meaning struck close to home. To be honest, I was feeling more of an escalating fear for what my oppressors could do to me and the ministry than an increasing awe and wonder for the one who stretched out the sky and laid the foundation of the earth. But this was his fight. His work. His church. His kingdom. And I was his child. My accusers would one day be out of my life. Gone! But God, my Comforter, was always with me.

God continued to reaffirm in Isaiah 51:16: *"I have put my words in your mouth and hidden you safely in my hand."* Those words drove strength into my heart. He had laid his call on my life. The Creator of the universe had given me the words to say and was holding me safely in his hand. What more could I ask for?

The other passage of scripture was from Isaiah 40, where the prophet laid down the same foundational image of God's greatness as the Creator and the Sustainer of all things. He held the rulers and all the peoples of the world in his hands. He was all-powerful and sovereign. This being true, if he could be all of that in his world, surely he could look after everything in my world.

Isaiah wrote, *"But those who trust in the Lord will find new strength. They will soar high on wings like eagles. They will run and not grow weary. They will walk and not faint"* (Isaiah 40:31).

He promised to restore the weary and exhausted soul. I needed to be reminded of that. But the condition for restoration was trusting. Trusting was believing that my God, the Creator, is bigger than everything and everyone. To be confident that while I cannot, God can. It meant acting on the assumption that this is true. It meant giving him everything, exposing to him every circumstance I encountered, entrusting to him every need and challenge I faced, for him to do what I could not but what he, and only he, could. It meant to stop trying so hard and let God be God. It meant to begin living supernaturally.

I felt tension between my desire to serve God and people as a pastor with my personal need to find time alone with God and enlarge my capacity for him. I felt the same tension that Henri Nouwen expressed in the introduction to his book, *The Genesee Diary*.[7]

How could I prevent my calling from God from becoming a tiring job? How could I prevent myself from talking to people about God more than talking to him? How could I guard myself from speaking and writing about prayer, while failing to embrace a personal and meaningful prayerful life? How could I prevent the fickle praise or hostility of people from crowding my mind and heart more than abiding and resting in the constant love of God? How could I guard against the compulsion to be run off my feet with the expectations and demands of people becoming stronger than concerning myself with God's priorities and calling?

I began a concerted effort to open up more room in my life for God and for my own personal emotional and spiritual health. The latter need was closely linked to and interlocked with the first. There were obvious disciplines, like devoting myself to more prayer, scripture, and meditation. I renewed my commitment to scripture memorization. I listened to inspiring worship music in our home and while driving. I became more intentional about things like healthy play. Reading good books and

---

[7] Henri Nouwen, *The Genesee Diary* (New York, NY: Doubleday, 1981).

biographies. Hiking and cross-country skiing. Running. Writing. Rest. Hobbies like painting and sketching. Gardening and landscaping. I also practiced the discipline of "nothingness" without feeling guilty about it.

Thirty-Four

EVERY TUESDAY MORNING, I continued to carve out space for God on what I called my prayer walk.

I have always found a refuge in nature, whether walking through a field, into a forest, or along a stream. The psalmist David found the same solace in nature and experienced God in those away places. He often referred to it in his writings.

> He lets me rest in green meadows; he leads me beside peaceful streams. He renews my strength. (Psalm 23:2–3)

God restored David's soul by sitting him down in a green field or beside a quiet stream. We need to let God lead us into these spaces where we just sit surrounded by his bounty and beauty. Just to sit and listen.

> As the deer longs for streams of water, so I long for you, O God. (Psalm 42:1)

The psalmist watched a deer refreshing itself at a bubbling stream and saw in that image his own need of restoration, drinking at the stream of God's healing faithfulness and unfailing love.

> The heavens proclaim the glory of God. The skies display his craftsmanship. Day after day they continue to speak; night after night they make him known. They speak without a sound or word; their voice is never heard. (Psalm 19:1–3)

The heavens are wordless and soundless to the human ear, yet they speak volumes to the soul about God's glory and nature.

Gaze into a stunning starlit sky. Lay on your back and just observe the movement of the heavens. What are they saying to you? Walk through leaves and wildflowers. Look up through the green canopy of a forest, the home of countless songbirds, into an azure sky, and feel yourself strolling through God's sanctuary. It is healing. The experience is soothing. It provides life to restore the soul.

One experiences the same thing when contemplating a breathtaking view, or peering up at a magnificent waterfall, or when one's eyes follow an eagle soaring and circling higher as it rides thermal air currents. God has ways of speaking into your life at moments like that.

Take the time to stare at snowflakes drifting silently and effortlessly to the earth. Study the beautiful patterns of frost decorating the window on a cold winter's day. Listen closely to the sound of birds chirping, the breeze gently blowing, the thud of an acorn dropping to the ground, or a tree creaking. The forest is alive with the sound of nature and the music of God. And it all restores the soul. It calms. It puts one's problems, stresses, worries, and fears in perspective. Nature is God's craftsmanship and teaches us about his nature, glory, power, provision, and care.

Jesus used nature as an example of God's care and provision and a reason not to be filled with anxiety. He turned people's attention to birds and wildflowers growing in the fields:

> That is why I tell you not to worry about everyday life… Look at the birds. They don't plant or harvest or store food in barns, for your heavenly Father feeds them. And aren't you far more valuable to him than they are?
>
> …Look at the lilies of the field and how they grow… And if God cares so wonderfully for wildflowers… he will certainly care for you. (Matthew 6:25–26, 28, 30)

I usually began my prayer walk carrying concerns and anxiety. But I used the time to just be alone with God in his sanctuary. I prayed for my family. I prayed for my personal life. I brought up with God the needs of the church and expressed my fears, doubts, and concerns. I prayed for wisdom, discernment, strength, and guidance. I thanked him for his unfailing love, care, and provision.

Sometimes I worshipped and sang, hoping no one was nearby to hear me other than God. Other times I worshipped in silence. Sometimes I just walked or stood silently in a state of nothingness.

But I always ended my prayer walk and returned to my work with a fresh perspective, sharpened focus, renewed strength, revitalized commitment to persevere, and fortified sense of God's presence and power.

The Payne family in front of the '56 Chevy that carried so many people to the Yearly schoolhouse. David is standing next to his father.

Sunday school at the Yearly schoolhouse (1956).

*The old farmhouse where we lived in northern Ontario.
We called it the "little house on the prairie."*

Our "fleece," the answer to our prayer that there would be a layer of white on the ground.

Our miracle home at the corner of Gorham and Court Streets in Newmarket (1985).

The sod-turning ceremony to begin the new build.

"Our Bethesda," place of healing.

Our family on vacation at Pinecrest, our favourite spot.

The growth of the Campus Church.

The Campus Church's Bathurst site in Aurora.

Thirty-Five

TWO SIGNIFICANT THINGS were decided in those days that helped to bring change and relief. The first was a move to a new home.

We had been praying for several months that God would provide another home for us. We were extremely grateful for the home he had provided in Aurora, but now the time seemed right to move out into the countryside, away from the busy town. We wanted something a little removed from the church and all its activities. A location that would help us to decompress when we needed that. A refuge.

One day while driving home from the funeral of a relative, we passed a for-sale sign and stopped to look a little more closely. The house sat nestled in the trees just waiting for someone to love it. We did. It needed a lot of work and tender care, but we believed we could make it into a nice home.

To make a long story short, we ended up purchasing it.

The property was about fifteen minutes from the church along beautiful winding country roads, and it was surrounded by trees and backed onto three hundred acres of forest and trails. There was a farm across the road. It was perfect.

One of the first things we did after moving in was place a sign at the end of the driveway which read "Our Bethesda." Bethesda was a pool just outside the north wall of Jerusalem. It means "place of healing." God had led us to this location to provide healing. It's important to create space in one's life for God, and it's important to do the same for family. This place provided that space.

We were conscious of the impact that church ministry had on the family. The reality was that our three children lived under a lens. A world of often cruel jealousies, unfair judgments, and unrealistic expectations unwittingly placed upon them. They were sometimes accused of receiving "privileges" because they were the PKs (pastor's kids). They wore hurtful labels given to them by their friends which implied the ideal family or the perfect kid.

Our family often led worship on Sunday morning. We were all musical and this was something we enjoyed doing together. An amazing team accompanied us. Unfortunately, that drew jealousy from other worship teams, so we finally stopped doing it.

Church didn't always feel like a safe place for our children, despite the fact that it was a big part of their world. They learned to wear a mask and play a role. They were cautious not to show vulnerability but to keep their emotions and feelings buried — and to stay guarded about letting the outside world in.

Diane and I tried to remain vigilant to their emotional and mental needs, not to mention spiritual ramifications and challenges. We were deliberate about keeping our children Jesus-centred and helping them to understand their identity as children of God. We prayed earnestly that they would grow and thrive through and because of the challenges of living in a glass bowl.

I was mindful that anxiety could prevent me from being fully present when with my family, though I tried very hard. I felt torn and guilty when church demands pulled me away from them.

I previously related the story of the "lunch bag issue" to illustrate how the church could become entangled with family matters in a detrimental way. Soon after that time, we found out that one of our daughters had been sexually assaulted by a young man in our church. The fact that I was the pastor influenced how we responded to this. It also influenced the outcome, and this had ramifications for a long time.

Yes, pastoral ministry can be hazardous to a pastor's family. I'm not complaining. I'm just stating the reality as honestly as I can: the church impacted my family.

In addition to all that, our children could sense when their parents were carrying an emotional load. They also felt the weight of the church on our shoulders.

But I would be remiss not to say that the pastoral ministry did a lot of good for our children. We learned to serve together. Our kids learned to carry their responsibilities with grace and dependability, survive under the scrutiny of watchful eyes, exercise discernment, endure for the sake of Jesus despite difficult circumstances, be frugal, and sacrifice for the sake of the kingdom.

Our question was always, "How do we protect our kids from the trauma of ministry?" Our new home was, in part, a practical answer to that question. It wasn't the full solution, but it was a place where we could get a little more control back for our family. A sanctuary that felt like home. A shelter that felt safe. A space they would enjoy, where they could be themselves and not feel like they had to wear their "happy face."

As I said, the house needed a lot of work. First off, there had to be a major cleanup from the previous owners. Then, as winter set in, we set about doing a major renovation. We took down walls to open up our living quarters. We renovated the entire house, wall to wall, floor to ceiling, much of the work being done ourselves. We demolished, replaced, relocated, modified, reconstructed, sanded, painted, swept, and cleaned. We made it a family project. Everyone had responsibilities. It was actually fun.

Many nights there was no suitable room to sleep in, so we camped out around the living room's woodstove to keep warm. The smell of wood-burning permeated the whole house. We had someone deliver a load of firewood big enough to keep the woodfire burning during the winter. We split the wood with an axe and piled it into a shed we built for that purpose. And when it ran out, my son Jeremy and I spent many hours with a chainsaw cutting dead or dying trees behind the house for additional wood. More than once, we nearly dropped a tree on the top of the house. Thankfully we never succeeded.

Jeremy and I also spent much quality time just sitting on a log chilling and talking. It was great.

Diane was an amazing interior designer who believed you could always adapt what you presently had to fashion a new look. She planned and designed everything in the home, from layout to colours, and transformed it into a space with an ambiance of peace and calm.

Meanwhile, I took responsibility for the landscaping and gardens and spent hours outside. Gardening was wonderful and effective therapy.

The dinner table was the focal point of the day for our family, the time when we caught up with each other's lives. We frequently welcomed people from the church or immediate neighbourhood into our home to be part of our family. Having company over was a regular occurrence. Sometimes they came for a roast beef dinner, and at other times for hotdogs. Sometimes we provided a meal; at other times, a bed to sleep in.

We often gave hospitality to missionaries from Canada and around the world who were passing through on furlough. Our children were given the unique opportunity to listen and learn about other lands, cultures, and peoples, as well as what God was doing in those places.

We loved animals, so we built a shed—we called it "the barn"—and raised rabbits. The kids headed straight to the rabbits every afternoon when they got home from school.

We also adopted a beautiful husky/shepherd puppy who became a fantastic friend. We named her Timber. Over time she had three litters of pups and Jeremy got a small business going raising and selling them to good homes.

The night she gave birth to her first litter, Jeremy, Sarah, and Rebecca spent the whole night in the cage dog-sitting. It was an amazing experience.

We kept the first pup to be born and named him Dakota. He was full of vitality and warmth. Whether we were bedding down the dogs with lots of straw for warmth in their doghouse on subzero nights, taking them for walks, or pulling porcupine quills out of their mouths, it was a learning and growing experience for us all.

When I arrived home from work each evening, I enjoyed going behind the house to say hello to the dogs. Upon seeing me they ran in silly circles, barking with wild delight while jumping up to welcome me with loads of licks. Their carefree excitement rubbed off on me.

I was awakened each morning by the squawking of blue jays reverberating through the pines, chickadees chirping, and chipmunks chattering—a symphony of sound in nature. I was reminded every daybreak that God's faithful love never ends but begins afresh each morning (Lamentations 3:23).

At home in our Bethesda, I discovered anew the restorative power in things as simple as sunlight filtering down through the tree boughs, the reading of a good book in front of the woodfire, or a walk through the forest. These things led us outside the world of stress and expectations.

Thirty-Six

OBVIOUSLY, OUR NEW address did not give us immunity to the pressures of everyday life or the demands of the church. We weren't trying to hide; we were just doing what we needed to create a place of refuge. We worked hard at the church. It continued to grow and God blessed the ministry in numerous ways.

We still walked a thin line regarding our finances. We had come to Aurora with nothing but a strong faith that God had called us and therefore would provide for our needs. And he always had. However, our salary that the church was responsible for was inadequate for covering even our basic necessities—and as the kids grew, so did our expenses. We were just scraping by, managing to pay the bills and put food on the table, but there was little to nothing left over each month for anything else.

We will never forget the annual membership meetings when it came to the new budget and discussing our salary for the coming year. Diane and I were always asked to leave the room while the congregation deliberated and often debated about our salary, whether it should be increased, by how much, or not at all. We thought it odd that no one ever asked us about our needs.

And yes, there were those times when there was no increase.

When the discussion was finished, we would be called to return to the meeting. We'd enter the room and everything would go silent, with every eye following us uncomfortably to our seats.

On one occasion, I remember sharing our financial need with the leadership team. This is something which, rightly or wrongly, I otherwise never did. We had consistently followed what the apostle Paul wrote when ministering to the Corinthian church. Even when he didn't have enough to live on, he didn't become a financial burden to anyone—and God provided him with what he needed (2 Corinthians 11:9).

But this time I asked them to consider three requests, any one of which would help us financially.

The first was obvious: a salary increase. I was told that there just weren't enough funds in the budget.

Second, I asked that they consider hiring Diane as a children's ministry director to compensate for the many hours she volunteered for the church each week. She worked at least twenty to twenty-five hours weekly doing children's ministry, worship ministry, the women's study group, and numerous other church-related tasks. She also had a strong mentoring ministry to women who were struggling. I was told, however, that hiring my wife would be considered a conflict of interest and inadvisable. Hugely disappointing.

My third request was that the church contribute to an employee health and dental plan. We had a young family and were paying drug and dental expenses out of our own pocket. It was a significant financial drain. A health plan would be an enormous help. They responded that it would be considered. That sounded hopeful.

However, I raised the possibility of this several times over the next half year, and nothing transpired. It was finally realized and offered about three years later.

So, yes, we struggled financially.

But struggle didn't mean quitting; it meant adapting. Diane began to teach piano lessons to help boost our income. Her hours filled every week as she managed a busy household, continued with much of her church ministry, and taught piano to twenty-two students. A few years later, she became an interior designer and set up a small business called iRedesign.

The problem she encountered, as the pastor's wife, was that people appreciated her giftedness and asked for her expertise to help in designing their homes, but they expected it to be gratis. Not everyone expected this. Some treated it for what it was—a business. But it failed to provide the income we had hoped.

We learned to shop with flyers and coupons. We had to do this to make the dollars stretch as far as possible. We continued to wear hand-me-down clothing. Diane sewed, mended, and made alterations. All of our furniture was secondhand. We still did our best shopping along the roadside, too. Our eyes were always on the alert for a piece of furniture someone no longer needed. Many times, there it was at the end of someone's driveway, just waiting to be picked up. I would pull our van over, jump out, lift the furniture into the back, and bring it home. We learned to refinish and reupholster old furniture to make it look new. We outfitted our home this way, and it felt good.

I mentioned a van. We had been driving a vehicle that was on its last legs and needed something to replace it. We also needed something larger for carrying loads of kids to church activities. Our own three kids invited their friends to Awana and youth events, and we picked these friends up.

We needed a van.

But clearly we couldn't afford a van. We prayed much about it.

At this time, I happened to be doing some counselling at a local missions centre. As I left one day, the director of the mission began chatting with me. In the course of our conversation, I mentioned that we were going camping for a few weeks. Out of the blue, he pointed to a full-sized van sitting in the parking lot and told me that it was available for the next few weeks. We were welcome to use it for our vacation.

I was taken back and extremely grateful.

He then added that it was for sale. If we liked it, he would sell it to us at a very reasonable price. I knew that God was in this conversation. We vacationed with it and fell in love, and the purchase price was such that we were able to buy it. God had provided.

Our van was used to carry more than people. One summer, Diane and I were conducting a weeklong kids' vacation Bible school (VBS) with a farm theme. I was always grateful for the five acres God had led the church to purchase several years previous. It was perfect for holding outdoor summer events and activities.

For this particular VBS, we featured a different kind of farm animal each day, everything from pigs to sheep to chickens. The kids loved it.

I used the big blue van to transport the animals. One day I transported a young calf to the church; it had been loaned to us by a local farmer. When I opened the back door, it was immediately evident that my distressed passenger had splattered the contents of an upset bowel in every direction from floor to ceiling. I spent the afternoon cleaning and sanitizing, though the odour lingered for many weeks. I had to explain the embarrassing odour to anyone riding in the van.

There came a day when good friends of ours were moving back to their home in the United States and wanted to offload their vehicle. They came by my office and dropped a set of keys on my desk.

"These are yours," my friend said.

I wasn't sure what he meant at first. I was speechless.

He smiled widely. "We want you to have our car."

My heart pounded with gratitude.

When I told Diane the news, we wept tears of astonishment and joy. We had reached the point of needing a second vehicle. Only God knew and he had provided—again.

Some people misjudged us. The first Sunday that we drove it into the church parking lot, we parked it in the furthest corner of the lot so people wouldn't notice.

They did. One gentleman asked how we could afford such a nice vehicle. Another commented that it must be nice to be able to own such a car.

Our initial feeling was awkwardness and embarrassment, and I must admit that we had been conditioned to feel some guilt. But we didn't feel that we needed to explain anything. We knew in our hearts that even if we were judged, this car was God's provision. We were extremely grateful.

Years later, when the life of this miracle car came to an end, God provided again. Indeed, the ongoing miracle didn't seem to have an expiry date. A businessman in our church generously outfitted us with another car to use. And after that, another.

We were stunned by God's faithful provision. He supplied our needs in ways that were infinitely greater than we could have asked or even thought (Ephesians 3:20).

Thirty-Seven

IT WOULD PROBABLY be true to say that one of the lasting themes of my teaching ministry was the subject of memory aids. Many times I taught their meaning and importance from the scriptures and encouraged our people to place memory aids in their homes and lives. I included a whole chapter on this subject at the end of my previous book, *Hitting the Wall*, writing,

> Memory is a wonderful gift. It connects the dots of your life. It connects us to one another, to familiar places, to where we have come from, to our past. It connects us to what God has done. God wants us to keep our memory green. Alive.

Memory is foundational to learning to talk, doing simple math, making decisions, relating to faces, and knowing how we fit into the story of our lives. Memory affixes us to who we are, who we were, and who we know. It can give us wings to fly away to a happier place. It can help us process grief.

It also holds a significant place in prayer. The Bible tells us that when we need to petition God, we are to do so with thanksgiving. Thanksgiving is released when the memory takes us back to how God has helped, provided, and protected us in the past. In prayer, we feel reassured that he will do the same now and in the future.

One of the principal things memory does is remind us of divine encounters and, as I said, what God has done in our lives.

When the Israelites first entered the Promised Land, God performed an astonishing miracle and held back the flow of the Jordan River so that two and a half million people could cross in safety with all their gear.

After they had crossed, they built two memorials. They picked up twelve stones from the middle of the river and used them to construct a monument at the location of their first encampment in Canaan. Joshua also constructed a second memorial of twelve stones in the middle of the riverbed before the waters surged back.

These monuments stood for years and served as memory aids to the Israelite people of the astonishing miracle God had performed. For generations afterward, when children saw the stones standing in the middle of the Jordan River and inquired after the meaning, their parents would reply, "Let me tell you what God did."

The Bible is filled with memory aids, probably because we are so prone to forget. God set aside special days and established festivals to bring to mind significant memorable events. He established the rainbow in the sky. The faithful built altars in specific locations where they had encountered God in some way. People erected standing stones to remind them of what God had accomplished in a particular spot. The bread and wine of the Lord's table serve as a reminder of Jesus's broken body and shed blood. There are many others, all of which are memory aids of encounters with God or reminders of what he has done.

Once, upon returning from Israel after leading a tour there, I brought back small stones from the dry creek bed in the Valley of Elah where David killed Goliath. I gave each of my grandkids one of those stones as a memory aid, to remind them that when a person gives their life to God and puts themself out there for God to use, as David did, they will be amazed at what God does. Some of them believed they might have been holding the actual stone that brought the giant down!

On another occasion, I told my grandkids the story of the Ebenezer stone from 1 Samuel 7. The prophet Samuel raised a standing stone on the spot where God had given the Israelites a victory over their enemies. The Bible says, *"He named it Ebenezer (which means 'the stone of help'), for he said, 'Up to this point the Lord has helped us!'"* (1 Samuel 7:12) I instructed each of my grandkids to go out and find an Ebenezer stone they could place in their bedroom as a reminder that God is their helper in every struggle.

Diane and I filled our home with memory aids, including pictures that hung on the walls. We had a memory wall on which we displayed photos of all the homes in which our family had lived. Each one had a God story and our kids could tell the stories. Our Bethesda home was an aide memoire itself, for it told a story of what God had done; the "Our Bethesda" sign posted at the end of our driveway has hung in every home since as a reminder that God provides, heals, and restores. A mounted grouse hung on the wall of my office and served as a reminder of the story I recounted earlier in this book that faith and prayer change things.

And of course this book in itself serves as a memory aid for what God has done.

Thirty-Eight

MUCH OF CHURCH life and ministry is routine in nature, though it's never boring or preditable. Preparing messages and Bible studies. Planning. Counselling. Visiting the sick and hurting. Attending committee meetings. Handling administration. Going to staff meetings. Making arrangements for the upcoming Sunday. The list could go on.

There are other times when something significant happens to alter the whole direction and focus of the week. It can be something distressing, like the news of a serious illness, a death, or a car accident. It can be a special event, such as a missions focus or marriage retreat weekend. It can be Christmas. Or Passion Week.

And then there are those times when something happens so unexpected and earth-shattering that the whole church goes into shock. The church collectively pushes the pause button on everything and everyone has to take a breath.

That's how it was with the news of Karyn.

Karyn was a gifted artist. She called herself a visual missionary. She was a fairly new Christian and passionate about sharing her faith journey through painting. Her art pieces moved and touched something in everyone.

The previous Sunday morning, Karyn had stood before the church and explained her plans to transform the side windows in our worship centre into a stained-glass window illustrating Jesus as the Good Shepherd. Each person was asked to choose a small piece of coloured glass; their name was documented on their particular fragment. Each piece was a different shape and size and would be incorporated into the larger picture. The concept was that we are all individual, unique parts of the beautiful whole. Everyone loved the idea and looked forward to the following Sunday when a draft of the finished product would be displayed. That's also when everyone would see exactly where their piece of glass fit into the big picture.

The following Friday, Diane and I were packing our suitcases to leave by plane early the next morning for Vancouver. We planned to travel across the country to watch our son Jeremy compete in the Canadian nationals for track and field. He was a triple jumper.

We were busy packing a few last-minute things when the phone rang. Diane answered. I could tell by her changing countenance and quiet, sombre demeanour that something was wrong.

She handed the phone to me and I took it with a sense of apprehension. Karyn's husband was on the other end.

I heard just three words: "Karyn is dead."

They had been hiking in Algonquin Park on a trail that skirted the side of a high precipice. Somehow Karyn had fallen over the cliff onto the jagged rocks below. He informed me that he would be spending most of the night with the police as they tried to determine what had happened.

I felt numb. Everything in me wanted to deny that it was true.

He then made a request. Would I be willing to go to his youngest son, Ian, and break the tragic news to him? And would I stay with him for the night until he got home?

I hesitated. Nobody could be prepared to receive this kind of news. I had no appetite for this assignment. It was one of those grim moments when something unwelcome disrupts your life, shattering the peace. My mind tried to convince me that Karyn's husband should wait until he was home to inform Ian. But my pastor's heart told me that the young man needed to know and begin processing the news as soon as possible.

How does one tell a sixteen-year-old boy that his mother has fallen to her death and will not be coming home? I had no idea, but I was certain that God had placed me here in this moment and time to step into the crisis.

I agreed to do it and immediately drove to the church to reach Ian, who was attending youth group that night.

I started by telling our youth pastor the distressing news. He just stood there and looked at me with tears and a blank stare. When he had gathered himself, we made a plan: I would take Ian outdoors alone while he gathered the youth together to notify them and pray.

Looking into the gymnasium, I called to Ian, who was running around excitedly playing a game. He looked over at me but kept running.

I called out his name again.

Finally, he came over to me with a quizzical look on his face. I told him that I had something to speak with him about and asked that he come with me.

Now he looked even more puzzled, but I walked outside and he followed.

I wanted to bring him down to the gravity of the moment, so I asked him to walk with me around to the back of the building. He wore a rather odd expression on his face.

"Is everything okay?" he asked.

"No, it's not," I replied.

As he followed me around the building, he looked concerned.

When we got to the back, where we could be alone with some privacy among the trees, I asked him to sit with me on the grass. I told him that I had something to tell him that would fracture his life. Something crushing.

He went pale.

I quickly but gently broke the news to him. At first he just looked at me with an empty, confused stare. His face drained of its colour and his eyes glazed over. Then came an awful guttural cry from deep within and the tears exploded.

I just held him in my arms as he shook uncontrollably. I held on tightly.

As I said, it was one of those moments I wouldn't have wished for, but one in which I was thankful I was present—just to be the arms and heart of Jesus to a young man drowning in the deepest throbbing grief and anguish of his young life.

The whole church went into shock. No one knew what to say. The previous Sunday seemed so fresh in everyone's mind.

When the next Sunday arrived, the church gathered as usual. But nothing was usual. Few spoke. All one could hear was the weeping of many hearts. This was not the time to sing. It was not the appropriate time to preach the scheduled message.

I got up to face the congregation, fearing that I wouldn't be able to hold it together emotionally. And was it even necessary to hold it together?

I began with my honest thoughts, although I cannot remember exactly what I said. I allowed lots of time to reflect, grieve, and process as a church community. We prayed together. We spent long periods in silence, feeling the saturating warmth of the Holy Spirit's comfort and healing pour over us like sweet-smelling oil.

I prolonged the time together and we never officially closed off the meeting. We allowed people to remain for as long as they wanted to sit, mourn, comfort one another, and pray.

When the memorial service arrived, the building was packed to capacity. People came from all over since Karyn was well-known and loved. Her paintings had touched many lives. Every room, corner, and crevice of our church building was filled with mourners. We set up a TV monitor and speakers outside for the more than one hundred people who attended but were unable to get inside. We were thankful that it was a clear, sunny day!

I shared Karyn's faith story and the good news of Jesus's salvation. Everyone listened intently. These are the kind of times when even the most hardened heart is tender. Everyone pauses to think about life in such a crisis.

Everything came to a standstill for this—routine schedules, regular responsibilities, immediate tasks, usual programs, and set plans. But in the midst of it, the Holy Spirit moved in a mysterious way. The light of the gospel and unfailing love of God penetrated this darkest of times.

Thirty-Nine

I MENTIONED IN Chapter Thirty-Five that there was a second consequential decision that brought change to our lives, the first being our move to a new home in the country.

A very close friend of mine, one I had grown up with through my teen years in northern Ontario, had begun to attend our church. He was a huge support to Diane and me. Bruce and his wife, Denise, met with us every Friday morning for breakfast to encourage and support one another.

Bruce had recently accepted the position of president at Tyndale College and Seminary in Toronto. The institution was in a deep financial crisis and Bruce found himself preoccupied.

One day he asked whether I would consider accepting a full-time position at the seminary as executive assistant to the president, to help him with human resources and anything else he needed help with. Although I was busy at the church, he knew the emotional toll it was taking on me. This would bring some needed relief to both of us and be a win-win.

Diane and I prayed much about this proposal to discern whether it was from God. Over the next couple of weeks, we came to believe that this had originated with God, but that I should only pursue it on a part-time basis. God's calling was still upon us to lead Community Bible Church. I needed to continue on as the pastor, though this provision allowed me to do so in a more limited role.

Bruce agreed. We decided to speak to the church leadership as soon as possible regarding the idea. Clearly the decision would impact the church and my leadership in it.

I had no idea how the church leaders would respond. I asked God to prepare their hearts. For this idea to fly, I needed their support and blessing.

They listened to my presentation and, to my relief, were open to the idea. They understood the pressure Diane and I had been under and could see the beneficial aspects of such a pastoral adjustment. They agreed it should be temporary and requested that I plan to return to full-time ministry in one year.

The following Sunday, I read my proposal to the church and asked the people to pray earnestly. Ten days later, we held a membership meeting for the congregation to come together and discuss the proposal. There was the usual pushback from a few attendees, but for the most part there was acceptance.

The decision was made: I would accept a one-year contract as executive assistant to the president at Tyndale College and Seminary. We believed that God had provided a much-needed break from concentrated pastoral ministry. God is faithful.

It was a busy year. Every day was packed. In reality, I was holding down three jobs: Tyndale Theological Seminary, the church, and co-manager of our house renovations. Each morning I left the house early and drove into the city to the seminary for a day filled with responsibilities in administration and personnel. In meetings with Bruce, I was given the high-priority task and challenge of, among other responsibilities, managing staff, resolving conflict, and working on pay equity issues. I was also given the opportunity to teach a course in pastoral theology and really enjoyed that. Other professors often asked me to relieve them when they needed someone to substitute.

Part of each day was spent preparing for Sunday's teaching and preaching at the church. Even though I had limited my pastoral responsibilities, issues still often came across my plate. I attended leadership meetings, and of course Sundays were full days with the sermon in the morning and teaching the adult class at the Awana program in the evening.

When I arrived home at night, I had dinner with the family and then started into my third job. We were up to our ears with renovations to our Bethesda. Something always needed to get done. It wasn't uncommon to drop into bed around 1:00 a.m. Thankfully, Diane took on the role as contractor and manager for the renovations, a sometimes stressful and involved task.

Then I'd be up again early to do the whole thing over again.

It was tiring but regenerating. The year rolled by rapidly. Tyndale was a refreshing experience, the church was peaceful, and the house was almost completely renovated.

It was soon time to return to the church. I finished up my season at Tyndale and prepared to resume my full pastoral responsibilities at Community Bible Church as previously planned.

Forty

WHEN THE CHURCH leadership announced the news to the congregation, it was decided that a membership meeting should be held to affirm the original plan. No one suspected any problem and chose to ask for a two-thirds confirmation vote.

To most, the news was welcomed. To some, however, it was not. The same faction of dissenters remaining in the church seemed to have not expected my return, having believed I would continue at Tyndale Seminary. Not only did they feel that my full-time return was regrettable, they felt it should be opposed.

Immediately, this group went into overdrive. They connected with everyone, both long-standing members and new members—we had welcomed thirteen new members into the church just one week prior—to solicit a negative vote. They worked the phones night and day to convince people that I shouldn't be allowed to return. They also castigated the leadership team for chicanery and having misled the church. They made strong unfounded statements about my managerial style, calling it dictatorial. They questioned my motives, circulating the lie that the reason for my return was that I had been denied the opportunity to continue at Tyndale by the seminary's board. This just wasn't true.

They invented every argument necessary to persuade people that change was needed. Initially, neither the leadership nor I were aware of any of this activity. They circumvented us completely.

But we began to catch wind that something was happening.

I have always believed in friendship. However, I have discovered, as a pastor, that having a close friend inside the church can be fraught with problems. Nonetheless, I thought I had found just the right friend. It has been said that a good friend can talk with you about any struggle, but a best friend experiences the struggle with you. This friend of mine had experienced much of the conflict and strife alongside me in ministry. He understood. He was also in Christian ministry and had recently joined our leadership team. We met every Friday morning for breakfast to pray and discuss the needs of the church. He was a huge support and encouragement to me. We shared our hearts with each other.

Most of all, I trusted him. Whenever there was trouble brewing, he offered to meet with the instigators to attempt to resolve the matter. His purpose as a friend was to protect me from becoming personally entangled in any issues and from becoming the target of criticism. It freed me to focus my time on teaching and pastoral care.

Just a few days before the membership meeting, my friend asked to meet. I expected his usual encouragement and looked forward to the opportunity to pray together about the outcome of the meeting.

On this occasion, however, he caught me off-guard. His encouragement this time was to persuade me not to return to the church or take a negative decision by the church personally. I found his comments disconcerting and tried to process where they were coming from.

A few days later, on the same day as the membership meeting, I received a letter from him. In it, he acknowledged that I was a "victim of abuse." But then he went on to say that I had not resolved the inner struggles that result from abuse. He felt that my re-entry into pastoral ministry was premature and a big mistake. His letter encouraged me to step back for a longer period of time to renew my strength. Apparently I needed a longer break from the church, and the church needed a longer break from me. He affirmed that I had laid a good foundation at Community Bible Church, but now he believed it was time for someone else to build upon that foundation.

I was dumbfounded. And somewhat confused.

Forty-One

IT WAS A most memorable meeting. I was first up on the agenda and given the chance to offer a brief summation regarding the damage that had been done within our church in the years prior. My family and I had endured emotional abuse that I would have never dreamed possible from individuals who claimed to identify with the name of Christ. My credibility and integrity had been questioned and judged, and my character maligned. I spoke with gentleness yet boldness, warning that such actions and words grieved the Holy Spirit. I encouraged the church to unity and to spend our energy building up the body of believers. I emphasized the need to keep an outward focus and reach into our community with the good news. I reminded everyone that we lived in a mission field like few others in Canada. We had a harvest to reap.

The chairman of our leadership team continued with a statement of support for me and my leadership. He spoke to my character, gifts, strengths, and qualifications for pastoral ministry and gave a strong recommendation for my continuing on as the church's full-time pastor.

He then opened up the floor for questions.

Immediately it became clear that some didn't feel it was appropriate for me to be present for the discussion. The chair ruled that I should be present, though, and an exchange of views went back and forth for about a half-hour.

Many stated their love for our family and endorsed their support for me, affirming my character, leadership, and ministry. Some attested to the fact that my teaching was always centred on the scriptures and had resulted in transformation in their lives. Others testified that they had come to know Jesus under my pastoral ministry. One lady reminded the church about the unique satanic stronghold in this area and how Satan desired to extinguish the work God was doing. As I sat quietly and listened, I felt very uncomfortable with this discussion that focused on me.

The obvious and adulatory support for me as their pastor drew the ire of the other party. A cacophony of protest arose that almost seemed choreographed. They accused and admonished the leadership of everything from cowardice and duplicity to being unapproachable and failing to listen.

As I listened, I heard what I knew was a misrepresentation of facts, but I felt that I should stay out of the debate. The chairman was doing a good job. He was composed, wise, and discerning in his responses. Other leaders also responded to correct facts and misinformation.

My supporters continued to make their voices heard. One woman gave witness that my ministry had given her the encouragement and inspiration to talk to others about Jesus and become involved in community ministry. Another woman encouraged the church to look forward and not backward.

And so it went, on and on, back and forth.

Finally the chairman called for the vote. Fifty-eight votes were cast. We needed thirty-nine of those votes to affirm my continuation.

We got thirty-eight.

It was declared that the pastor would not therefore be reinstated. The leadership team had underestimated the depth of animosity of a minority of people and the power of this factious group to dissuade unsuspecting listeners from the desires of the board.

There was a shocked stillness. A hushed quiet, like the oxygen had been sucked from the room. There seemed no air to breathe.

Diane and I had put heart and soul into birthing and growing this church for seven years. It wasn't supposed to end this way. There had been so many blessings and successes along the way, but it had been a battle. And now it seemed like we had been dealt a defining defeat.

Everyone was speechless. Someone began to weep. Another got up and walked out.

Finally, an elderly lady who had been with us in the church since its inception spoke in a quivering voice that my friendship and pastoral ministry had blessed her immensely. She was devastated. Others stood in protest. There were even some loud and angry outbursts.

Diane and I returned home to our Bethesda. Not a word was spoken. Just silence. I was out of a job and didn't know where to go from here. We felt beaten up and helpless but securely in the hands of God. He knew.

I could not accept that it was over, but it *was* over. We were shaken. Numb.

We began to mourn the loss of something we deeply loved.

Next came the dilemma of communicating to the kids what had just transpired: the challenge of how to help them understand the decision of the church without feeling insecure, fearful, hurt, and even angry... the challenge of guarding them from becoming ministry casualties.

The whole week to follow was extraordinarily distressing. There were numerous phone calls and visits to our home. At any given moment, there could be a knock on the door. It was like a weeklong wake. Anguish and tears. Mourning. Questions. Anxiety. Anger. We felt the acute pain of our flock and were unable to offer much comfort to them. They were shepherd-less, and we were flock-less.

Some asked whether we would consider starting a new church that they and many others would support. I gave no encouragement to go in that direction.

The outcry grew as the week dragged on. In the meantime, the dissenting faction was also busy telephoning and visiting people to reassure them that everything would be okay, that the church would go on. The difference this time, however, was that the congregation was beginning to finally speak up and answer back. People were beginning to discern these spirits at work.

Deep in my heart, I believed that God was going to use this traumatic experience to break the power of darkness that had besieged the church for such a long time. For many years, it seemed that only I discerned the powers that lurked in the shadows and pulled the strings of the unsuspecting, exploiting their weaknesses.

Then the leadership team became fully convinced of it.

Now the whole church was enlightened, and I believed this new awareness would break the bondage. When the light arises, darkness flees.

Forty-Two

LATER THAT WEEK, one of our leaders spent time searching through the church constitution to clarify its position regarding the dismissal of a pastor. The constitution was a document I had put together seven years earlier laying out the rules and regulations for the church's governance. It wasn't relaxing or enjoyable reading!

A church constitution can sometimes seem like an encumbrance; at other times, it can be a lifesaver. This leader simply wanted to know what the constitution said regarding the issue at hand.

And he discovered something: a pastor could be dismissed *only* by a majority vote of the membership. I had been dismissed with only one-third of the total votes cast.

He immediately brought this to the attention of the leadership team.

I received a phone call from the chairman of our leadership team that same day asking me to meet with them for prayer and to decide what steps to take next.

We met early on Saturday and prayed silently. Some of the best prayer occurs when no words are spoken. The Holy Spirit prays with groanings that cannot be expressed in words. There were sincere tears. The sweet presence of the Holy Spirit filled the room and was keenly felt by everyone. We were on holy ground.

Later I was asked by two of the men's wives what had happened at the meeting because their husbands had returned home with a different countenance.

Two moving letters had been received earlier that week, both written by new believers in the church. They were read to the leadership team. Both were heartwarming and emotional appeals to "keep our pastor."

Significant time was given to a discussion about the constitutional matter.

After much prayer, the group decided to hold another membership meeting. They would take responsibility for having been negligent to the constitution's stipulations and resolve to rectify the wrong. That meeting was called for the following Wednesday evening.

I felt like I was in the midst of a gruelling spiritual battle. And I was.

Wednesday came and it was another memorable meeting. The chairman addressed some of the misleading information that had been circulating over the past week. He then referred to the section in the constitution that governed the dismissal of a pastor. He admitted that the leadership team had failed to follow these guidelines, and they now had to correct that oversight and right the wrong: based on the previous week's vote, the pastor would be returning to full-time ministry in the church. A loud cheer and clapping erupted.

The chairman then asked everyone, including those who had voted against my return, to throw their full support behind me and the church leadership. He exhorted those who were unwilling to let go of their grievances to take the ethical step of finding another church they could support.

Some vehemently questioned the leadership's actions and motives, but most gave their full support. The decision was carried.

Most of the dissenters left Community Bible Church over the next few weeks and began attending another church in the next town. It was particularly grievous to watch some families leave that hadn't originally been part of the factious group. Some left because they had been influenced negatively. Some left because of friendship loyalty. Others withdrew because they couldn't cope with the constant emotional drain and stress of disunity; they just couldn't weather the storm.

I was dismayed to witness new believers leave the church, believers whom I had led to Jesus and who had become friends of ours. It felt like my insides were being ripped out. But I understood. I had always wondered how long they could hang on.

A few disgruntled people stayed on a little longer, but they made it clear that they didn't support the pastor or the church leadership. They just weren't going to be told to leave. They also stated that they would withdraw their financial support from the church. The chairman of our leadership team met personally with each one and challenged them to test their actions against the principles of scripture. His response was loving but firm. I was so grateful for this man who was wise in the handling both of people and God's Word.

It was encouraging to see the many families that did stay. Some of them were new families who had begun attending only in recent months. These families had a strong resolve to support the church and help to make a difference.

Actually, it felt like the dawning of a new day for Community Bible Church—and I looked forward with anticipation to what God was going to do.

Some still had a last kick at the can, so to speak. One Sunday at the end of a morning worship service, a man stood and asked for the opportunity to share a testimony of God's blessing. It sounded safe to me, so I took him at face value and invited him to do so.

When he began to speak, he quickly seized upon the opportunity to launch into a diatribe against me and the leadership team. I immediately realized I had been misled. As he continued, I saw a deflating spirit sweep over the congregation. Again, that feeling of the air being sucked out of the room. He spoke very emotionally about how his heart was breaking because of the "unacceptable" actions of the church leaders.

Wisdom dictated that I should allow him to finish. All the while, I wondered how to respond. When he was done, I thought for a moment, asking the Holy Spirit to give me the right words. I gently rebuked him for having spoken under false pretences.

I then quickly turned the congregation's attention to the good things God was doing in our church. I spoke for only one minute, until I could see the life returning to the eyes of the congregation. Their emotions were lifting again.

Afterward, many thanked me for my response. People seemed to be feeling a new and refreshing sense of security and relief.

Not everyone was happy with me that morning, however. My one-time friend, of whom I spoke earlier, brushed past me as he headed for the exit without looking at me. He was clearly angry.

Forty-Three

THE RELATIONSHIP BETWEEN my former friend and the leadership team disintegrated over the next three months. He and his family didn't move on right away. It had become clear that our friendship had ended. It was a huge loss for me.

One day the leadership team received a letter from him expressing both blame and pity for the "misguided" direction they had taken the church. He wrote about troubling inconsistencies in their conduct as leaders. He accused them of compromising their integrity, of hypocrisy and divisiveness. He accused me of having made negative comments about some of them. This was particularly disturbing since it could potentially drive a wedge of suspicion between the leadership team and me. And it just wasn't true.

He pressed on, denouncing them for demonstrating a "mean spirit of vindictiveness," manipulative behaviour, a severe lack of forgiving spirit, and irresponsible leadership. He scolded them for not insisting that the pastor leave the church when they had the opportunity to do so, and for not calling a new pastor to lead the church out of its "miserable patterns." He rebuked them for having "blind allegiance" to a pastor. He encouraged them to have the integrity to demand my immediate resignation.

He then cast judgment and doubt on my motives and the reason for my desire to return after my one-year contract at Tyndale. He was convinced that it was "more a desperate career move than a call from on high." He felt they should have doubted my version of events and consulted my bosses at the seminary.

In fact, they could have done that with my blessing; I had nothing to hide.

At last, this former friend warned that it was only a matter of time before disaster struck.

One afternoon while I was sitting in my office preparing a Bible study, I received a similar personal letter from this same man. I opened it and began to read. He started with a comment regarding his grief at what had happened to our relationship. As I read on, however, it was like following a bewildering serpentine path deeper into the shadows, calling into question everything about me. He believed I was unqualified to shepherd God's flock. He charged that I was hindered by pride hiding behind a mask of humility. My forgiveness was selective, self-serving, and hypocritical.

He made some very serious and unfounded charges regarding my moral uprightness that disqualified me from pastoral leadership. He also called me to immediately get out of the ministry. He threatened to publicly defend or pursue any issues referred to in his letter if need be.

For a second time, he urged me to resign from pastoral ministry. He then closed by warning that if I didn't allow God to change my heart, he feared a terrible disaster would fall upon me and others around me in the very near future.

This wasn't the first time I had received such a disquieting warning. My memory went back to the very beginning of our ministry in Aurora. Seven years previous, a lady had sat across from me at our kitchen table and warned me to repent or else I would face the disaster of losing one of my children.

The leadership didn't respond to this man's letter. I didn't reply either. But I felt betrayed and sorrowful. My emotions were like heat mingled with ice. Most of all, I mourned the loss of what I had believed to be a good and trusted friend. I grieved that loss for a long time.

There were occasions when I listened to the wrong voices and doubted myself. And yes, there were things I would do differently. To some degree, my estranged friend was right in that I wasn't fully able to process my pain in a healthy way. This was due in large part to the unrelenting and intense barrage of criticism, blame, and abuse inflicted upon me over such a long period of time. It had clouded my mind with anxiety and paranoia, making me feel anxious over what might be coming next—worried about how a leadership meeting might turn out, who might be on the other end of the phone when it rang, and why some individual wanted to meet me for coffee.

And yes, I felt anger. In fact, I dreaded becoming everything my accusers said I was. I knew that I must not allow extreme negative emotions to embitter me and further scar my soul. I needed to nurture a tender heart.

It felt like I was hanging on by a thread, but I knew who was holding the other end of the thread. I couldn't remove all the anxiety from my life, but I could trust in my Shepherd who held and loved me more than I could ever comprehend.

I remembered the truth: God is able, through his mighty power at work within me, to accomplish infinitely more than I might ask or think (Ephesians 3:20). In the verses immediately preceding that passage, the apostle Paul prays that our roots will grow down into God's love and keep us strong. This is a love so wide, long, high, and deep that it is impossible to fully understand.

We will experience God's fullness of life and power when we sink our spiritual roots deep to draw from the well of his unfathomable love, a well that never runs dry, never fails, always holds us, constantly heals us, relentlessly pursues us, and reaches the depths of our discouragement and disappointment. We will flourish in every adversity. We will navigate resistance. Our hearts will remain tender and not harden. We will be totally secure in his love.

I prayed for strength and courage, a gritty faith, and a steadfast hope that is rooted in the Shepherd's unfailing love.

Forty-Four

WE HAD OPPORTUNITIES to escape our situation. We were contacted by a wonderful church in Burnaby, British Columbia, that invited Diane and me to visit and consider the possibility of their lead pastoral position. At first we turned the invitation down. But after persistence on their part, we gave in and flew to Vancouver.

This trip was an amazing breath of fresh air. I taught and preached several times. We shared about who we were and enjoyed an interactive Q&A. It was inspiring to witness their existing ministries flourishing effectively and with vitality. We were invited into many homes where the people were extremely warm and welcoming. We received so much encouragement to come to Burnaby. To be honest, we began to think that this was God's provision and calling.

We boarded the plane for the return trip with a sense of anticipation as to what this all might mean. We talked a little about the possibilities, but mainly we were silent. We did a lot of thinking. A lot of reflection. A lot of introspection. A lot of soul-searching.

And by the time the plane landed in Toronto, we looked at each other and knew the answer: "It's not to be, is it?"

We both agreed that our call to Community Bible Church wasn't over. We would only be running away.

Shortly after we arrived home, our church's denominational superintendent asked for a meeting with me and the leadership team. We met, and once again were admonished for not preserving the unity of the church. He stated that we should have gone after the dissidents and encouraged them to return.

The leaders answered him well. Despite the accusation that we hadn't adequately attempted to resolve the grievances, we believed we had done everything we could. While we were strong believers in forgiveness and reconciliation, there comes a time when dissension must be dealt with firmness for the sake of unity. The apostle

Paul was very firm when it came to dissension: He wrote in Romans 16:17-18, *"And now I make one more appeal, my dear brothers and sisters. Watch out for people who cause divisions… Stay away from them"* (Romans 16:17).

I met with him two days later for breakfast in an attempt to clarify any misunderstanding. He sounded supportive, but there were definite walls and disinformation. The denomination hadn't mediated our situation well. I admitted to him that discernment is extremely difficult in situations that are so complex, confusing, and loaded with ambiguity. But neither I nor the leadership team, nor the majority of the church, felt any support from our denominational leadership. Rather, they had caused distrust and alienation. And to add fuel to the fire, they had given justification and affirmation to the people who had caused so much damage.

I tried to explain the unique spiritual warfare we were engaged in in Aurora. We were combating spiritual demonic powers, not flesh and blood.

Since the problem had been exposed, a load had been lifted. We were able to breathe again in a way we had not done for a long time. We could once again invest our time and energy in kingdom work—and God was pouring down blessings on our church.

The superintendent listened politely but didn't give me any confidence or assurance that he either understood or was in agreement. We parted on friendly terms, but the relationship was undeniably strained.

A couple in the church wrote a letter to him a little while later and copied me. They affirmed that since they'd been attending Community Bible Church, they had benefitted much from sound, relevant, biblical, Spirit-filled teaching. The recent difficult times in the church had deepened their faith and they testified that the church was experiencing healthy growth. There was a new and refreshing warmth and fellowship. They wrote about a husband and wife who had recently given their lives to Christ.

The letter beautifully affirmed that the church leadership had handled the recent conflict with discernment, gentleness, and firmness. They appealed to the denominational leadership to pray for Community Bible Church as it sought to do God's kingdom work while contending with an intense struggle against spiritual powers. It was an inspiring and challenging letter.

I don't know how the letter was received. But I do know that just one year later, the same man and his wife slipped into one of our Sunday morning services. Later that same week, he wrote me an encouraging letter regarding their Sunday morning experience.

> It seemed to us that the Holy Spirit was in fact pulling everything together into an integrated whole. Your message was a fine example

of the kind of Bible teaching that I long would come from all of our pulpits. There is evidence of growth among the people. We were greeted warmly and sincerely. There seems to be a genuine spiritual concern on the part of everyone. Please stay encouraged, David.

The people who left Community Bible Church moved on to other churches. Most followed each other to a "sister" church in the next town. I feared for this particular church that over the next few years it would encounter similar controversy because of some of the contentious people it had welcomed in.

One day I received a letter from the pastor of that church, requesting a letter of reference for three of our families who had been attending there. I was able to give a positive reference for one of the families named. I related my deep sadness at losing this particular family and told the pastor that I believed his church would benefit from their presence and ministry.

Regrettably, I was unable to give a positive reference for the other two families because of the responsibility they bore for their part in the upheaval and injury inflicted upon our church.

My warning went unheeded by the pastor. These families were received into the other church's membership. There seemed little cohesiveness between sister churches and no sense of accountability for people's actions. I was disturbed when I learned that one of these individuals was also offered the position of treasurer for the denominational head office.

I received a disturbing phone call a few years later. When I answered, I was puzzled by what I heard on the other end—no words, only the pitiful sound of an individual sobbing. I had no idea who it was.

After a long period of silence, the person spoke in a weak and broken voice. "I wish I had listened to you. I wish I had listened."

It was, in fact, the pastor from our sister church. I listened as he related an upsetting, sorrowful story. Some of the same people who had caused such damage in our church had done the identical thing in his church. The attack had been particularly vicious upon him as the pastor.

I understood and empathized completely.

He told me that the stress and struggle had been too much for him. He had resigned as pastor and would be leaving the pastoral ministry.

Forty-Five

AT THE END of those intense times, it's probably not surprising that our emotional tanks were low. That summer, we decided to take a trip westward to the Rocky Mountains. This would be a fun time for our family, and getting away would be good for us all. We looked forward to it with great anticipation.

Lots of planning went into the trip. We got the maps out on the floor and charted our route. We planned to follow the Trans-Canada Highway overtop Lake Superior, across the prairies, wind our way through the mountains, and pay a visit to Vancouver Island. We would then make our way home following a route through the United States.

God had provided us with a full-sized van. We could load it up with all the food, apparatus, and gear we needed as well as haul a small camper behind us.

I remember the day we headed off for a full month of travel and family time. How exciting! Each family member had their role to play. We had setup and takedown to a science. As dinner was being prepared on the camp stove, the camper was erected, firewood gathered, and drinking water hauled from a central tap. After supper, we explored the vicinity around our campsite.

We weren't too many kilometres down the road before I had left the problems behind. Well, sort of. It was hard to shake everything. But I was determined to just enjoy my family.

This trip was a time of unwinding, disentangling, escape—not from God, but from people. From church. From problems. From anything. I didn't want to think about coming back. I just needed to be away, following a ribbon of highway wherever it took us. Lake Huron. Lake Superior. The black spruce forests of northern Ontario. The prairies. The foothills. The Rockies. The Pacific.

It was everything we expected and more.

On the return trip, there was a particular place I wanted to visit in Montana: the historical site of the Battle of the Little Bighorn, where George Armstrong Custer and his famed Seventh Cavalry attacked a large Sioux encampment one hot June day in 1876. Custer's pride blinded him to foolishly underestimate the strength of those he planned to destroy. This battle served as the bloody climax to one of the most ruthless sagas in American history. More than 260 soldiers, including Custer, met stunning defeat and death at the hands of several thousand Sioux and Cheyenne warriors under the outstanding leadership of Chiefs Sitting Bull and Crazy Horse.

On the way there, we travelled through the spectacular Glacier International Park. Elk and deer wandered across the road and regal bighorn sheep and white woolly mountain goats peered down from their lofty peaks. We hiked along a threadlike path on the steep mountainside of the Continental Divide. Here we encountered some of the most breathtaking scenery we had ever seen.

Then we descended into the rolling hills of Montana with miles and miles of endless prairie grass and boundless sky. Antelope played on the ridges. A graceful doe followed a stream deep in a hollow with three—yes, three—fawns trailing along behind her. She and her triplets took time to stop and give us a long, curious gaze.

On a Sunday while travelling through Montana, Diane shared how nice it would be to attend a church somewhere as a family. This was the first time she had mentioned anything like that on the trip. I gave a polite nod but felt a cold chill run through me. Her innocent comment brought back a flood of feelings that were just too painful. Personally, I just wanted more time away from church.

I gave no affirmation. She turned her head toward the side window and stared in the other direction. An awkward silence passed between us.

We drove all day until the sun was low in the west. Its rays cast a blinding glare over the roadside sign indicating our nearness to the Little Bighorn Battlefield National Monument. We had only a few miles to go. The next sign indicated the boundary of the Crow Native Reserve.

We kept our eyes peeled for a suitable place to camp for the night. The plan was to tour the battlefield the next morning.

Over to the left in the middle of a wide field, we spotted a large domelike structure with flashing, revolving lights and a sign that could be seen a hundred miles away. A casino. You couldn't miss it. It stood out unabashedly like a giant Goliath, its armour glistening in the rays of the setting sun.

Just a quarter-mile farther, in the shadow of this bombastic behemoth, stood a tent. It was much smaller than the casino, but it was still large enough to hold a hundred or so people. And there was no doubt about the purpose of the tent; above it was a large banner with the words *REVIVAL MEETINGS*.

The tent stood next to the casino with the humble defiance of David, lowly slingshot in hand but armed with the name of the living God.

"There's our church!" Diane blurted out.

I remained quiet.

We found our campsite, and after setting up it was decided that we would investigate the tent meeting. I didn't have much choice, although I must admit I was drawn by a strong curiosity.

So off we set. The tent was encircled by dozens of beat-up half-ton trucks. People were seated inside the truck cabs, posted like sentinels on the roofs, crowded into the trailer boxes, and perched on the bumpers. The sound of guitars, drums, and lively singing reverberated from under the canvas ceiling. The tent was filled with the commotion of people crammed into a confined space and the constant clamour of children talking and crying.

I looked for an inconspicuous place to sit down. The only chairs I could spot were along the back row against the rear wall. We tried to slip in as unnoticeably as we could. Actually, in a crowded tent of dark-tanned Indigenous Crow, we were about as inconspicuous as lightbulbs in a dark room.

We sat down. Everyone knew we were there.

From what I could tell, the meeting was being led by four Indigenous pastors. They led the worship, played the instruments, prayed, testified, and preached with passion and fervency. There were several messages preached in succession, each with increased zeal. We had arrived about 8:30 p.m. and the tent meeting had been going on for three or four hours before that.

Several hours after our arrival, it still seemed like things were just warming up. It was a sultry summer night and the temperature in the tent was rising. Little did I realize just how warm it was going to get!

"We are standing on holy ground," everyone began to sing, as if on cue. "And we know that there are angels all around. Let us praise Jesus now. We are standing in His presence on holy ground." Their voices made a beautiful, melodic, and moving sound that resonated heavenward and filled every corner of the canvas sanctuary.

I was thinking we should get going because of the time. We had to be up early the next morning to visit the battlefield.

As the song began to wind down, one of the pastors jumped up onto the makeshift platform and opened his Bible. Another sermon was about to begin.

We thought this might be the best time to make our exit, before he got started.

Just as I leaned forward to signal to the kids that we should go, the preacher bellowed, "I don't know what you're running from!"

Have you ever known a time when someone pressed the pause button on your life? When words spoken publicly seemed to be aimed directly at you personally? When you felt like you were under surveillance on the end of someone's telescope? I looked up and realized he was pointing straight at me.

The colour drained from my face.

He stepped down off the platform and started to walk toward me, his long finger still pointed at me like an arrow. I sat upright in my chair, the back of my head pressed against the back of the canvas. I had nowhere to go.

Trapped, my heart pounded. It felt like I was being pursued by God. I had come to the Little Bighorn to explore the site of the last great battle of the American West, not to fight my own battles, not to be engaged in a spiritual conflict boiling inside me. I seemed to be in the middle of nowhere, far from home. And now to be confronted by God?

When the preacher was only several feet away, he spoke again in a passionate but penetrating voice: "I don't know what you're running from."

By now every eye was focused on me. Diane and the kids watched me too with frantic looks in their eyes.

I could read the questions on everyone's faces. "What has he done? Who is he?"

"I'm innocent!" I wanted to shout out. "I've done nothing!"

But I was paralyzed. I felt like a serial killer. At least, I imagined that that's what everyone was envisioning.

The preacher pointed at me with his one hand and gripped his Bible with the other. He glanced from me to his Bible for a brief instant and I felt a split second of relief from his focused stare. The relief dissipated just as quickly, as his eyes rebounded back to me.

He embarked on a series of questions, all straight out of Romans 8. "If God is for you, who can ever be against you?"

I shook my head to signify my answer: no one. I knew that was the answer he wanted. I had decided that my best plan of retreat would be agreement. It was the karate technique: go with the throw.

He continued his pursuit. He looked at his Bible again and then straight back at me. The back of my head was pressed as hard as it could be against the tent wall. Diane's eyes were as big as saucers. My kids looked traumatized.

"If God did not spare even his own son but gave him up for you, won't he meet every other need you have?" the pastor demanded.

"Yes, he can... or, er, w–will."

"Do you feel accused by people?"

"Yes, I do," I answered rather timidly.

Since the preacher had entered my space uninvited, I decided to enter his space and dialogue with this messenger from heaven. My heart began to open up.

"Yes, I do feel accused," I said more boldly. "In fact, I have been maliciously and unjustly accused! Maligned! Abused! Beat up! I'm tired! Done!"

"Who dares accuse you whom God has chosen for his own?" the pastor questioned. I didn't have time to get my answer in. "No one. For God has given you right standing with himself. So what if men accuse you? Let them! What matters is that you belong to God. What matters is that you are in right standing with God. Who will condemn you?"

"No one!" I said with more passion than I had felt in a long time.

"That's right," he replied. "Because Jesus died for you, was raised for you, and prays in heaven for you. Just think of that!" His voice then lowered and softened, as though reaching right down to my soul. "Now tell me… think of everything Christ has done for you because he loves you. When you experience trouble and accusation and threat, does that mean Jesus has stopped loving you?"

The room was packed beyond capacity and every eye was glued to the preacher and his prey. But it was as though he and I were alone in the room—just this preacher and me. Or maybe I should say, just God and me.

Tears began to fill my eyes. The face in front of me glazed over and his auburn-skinned countenance appeared as the face of an angel. The tears washed my eyes—but even more, my heart.

The preacher leaned down and placed his smooth, high cheekbone near the side of my head. "Can anything ever separate you from Christ's love?" he whispered in my ear.

"No… nothing."

"Then there is nothing and no one to run from, only Someone to run to. You are in his hands, his care, and his love. Be strong and courageous."

There was no doubt that this was a divine appointment—in a most unplanned way, in a most unexpected place, by a most extraordinary messenger. I was standing in God's presence. On holy ground.

Forty-Six

WE RETURNED HOME and felt rejuvenated from the time away. Personally, I went back to work renewed in spirit and with a restored vigour after my unusual and unanticipated encounter at the Little Bighorn.

The church entered a new era of freedom and growth. We were welcoming new people every week. It soon became apparent that our present facility was inadequate for the number of people attending and the number of ministries happening throughout the week.

The church understood the need and everyone was enthusiastic to pursue the prospects of a major expansion. I was also eager, although this would be my fourth time to pastor a church through a building campaign. I was very much aware of both the personal and corporate blessings and perils of building programs. They are exhausting and demand a lot of time-consuming hard work. There are needs to assess. Plans to draw up. Proposals to consider. Decisions to make. Committee meetings, and more committee meetings. Finances to raise. Arrangements to make for alternate facilities for all the various ministries, including the Sunday morning worship service. Changes to negotiate. Disagreements to settle or evade, if possible.

Building campaigns are a highlight in a church's story, but they can also be the devil's playground. As the lead pastor, it was critical for me to intentionally pursue a strong spiritual focus and not let the building and construction monopolize all the church's energy and attention.

I communicated regularly the vision God had given for our church. I kept the vision before the people... the who, why, and what we would be going into the future. I continually reminded them that the church was not a building. The building was a home base for a church family, a tool or resource that belonged to the church to help establish a witness for Jesus in the community. It was a launching pad for ministry and outreach.

The plan was to significantly enlarge the size of our worship centre to accommodate and welcome larger numbers of people. At the rear of the new worship centre, we planned a gymnasium that would serve several purposes. On Sundays, it would be our gathering and meeting room with café tables and chairs for conversation and coffee. Our people were avid coffee drinkers and loved to gather around the coffee stations that we called "Solid Grounds." This large area would also serve as an overflow when needed. People could sit behind a wall of glass with a large screen TV and still see and feel part of the worship service.

During the rest of the week, this versatile space would serve as a gym and community room. It would have basketball nets, a volleyball court, and be equipped for almost any possible event. One of the things I advocated for was a climbing wall. The gym, along with our beautiful multiuse outdoor property, would facilitate an extensive range of activities. We also added a large, fully equipped kitchen so we could host breakfasts, socials, weddings, funerals, and any gathering where food or refreshments were required.

I wanted a space that would have the potential to attract both church families and families from the surrounding community. Both Diane and I, and the staff serving alongside me, envisioned a building that would act as a community centre—a safe environment to provide healthy activities for neighbourhood youth, a location that could serve as an emergency centre for the city in times of crisis, a depot from which to distribute food and clothing to people in need, and even a site for blood donor clinics.

I expected hesitation on the part of some to the church facility being used for these kinds of activities. Some people have a limited view of what a church should do. They fail to appreciate the possibilities, seeing only obstacles. Legal risks. Insurance liability. Financial challenges. Scuffed walls. Broken chairs. Disruption. Inconvenience.

But I could see a resource that opened a window of opportunity.

Above the gymnasium, we proposed a large room for the youth to make their own. We had a thriving youth ministry, with many teens attending every week for Bible studies and social events.

The plans also called for sizeable rooms below the gymnasium, on a lower walkout level, to facilitate our vibrant children's ministry. We had many young families and therefore our kids' ministry was a priority. It needed its own designated area. A good portion of this lower level was also earmarked for new office space for our increasing staff.

A building expansion meant holding many meetings to pore over the plans, make alterations, and accommodate various ministry needs, all the while trying to stay within a budget. We also needed to regularly consult with our architect and contractor. And it soon meant endless rounds of meetings with the town council, the building department, the conservation authority, the regional authority, and anyone else with their spoon in the pot.

Then there were the neighbours—again. I will come back to them.

Raising the finances is a huge part of any building expansion. It was huge because we were challenging people to give significant financial gifts over and above their regular giving for the daily operation of the church. That was a big ask.

Although it was considered, we never entered into any capital campaign with intense fundraising efforts. We didn't engage in special events such as large galas with special speakers, auctions, or walkathons. We didn't conduct dollar-matching challenges where donors were to raise certain numbers of dollars to be matched by a major donor. We didn't feel led to hire a consultant to do campaign planning, solicitation, or assessments. We didn't even do pledges.

I'm not saying it's wrong to do these things. There are some definite benefits to these strategies. Rather, our strategy was elementary and uncomplicated: I consistently preached and taught biblical principles of giving to God's kingdom and the joy of sacrificial giving. I taught that we cannot all give equal amounts of money but emphasized the principle of equal sacrifice. I taught the principle of sowing and reaping. We held special building fund offerings and the people responded with overwhelming generosity.

We encountered challenges. There were some who wanted to donate large sums of money, but I learned there were conditions attached. Some wanted recognition, which I found difficult to believe. So I conducted some teaching on the discipline of secrecy. Jesus taught, *"But when you give... don't let your left hand know what your right hand is doing. Give your gifts in private, and your Father, who sees everything, will reward you"* (Matthew 6:3–4).

Others stipulated that a portion of the money they donated should be designated for a particular purpose or end they personally prioritized. We simply couldn't open that Pandora's box. I was extremely grateful for such gifts, but as a pastor I couldn't expose myself to someone else's control, and I certainly couldn't give the wealthy the power to use their money to manipulate the outcome or enjoy special privileges.

And yes, we lost some potential significant gifts.

Mostly, however, everyone just gave cheerfully, the best they could, out of generous and sacrificial hearts and a sincere desire to see God's kingdom in Aurora expand and grow. It was a remarkable, exemplary, and happy time in the history of Community Bible Church.

Forty-Seven

OH YES, I said that I would return to the neighbours. They were the same ones who had lived on either side of our property during our first building program. At that time, they had put up considerable roadblocks and caused so much delay. We hoped and prayed they wouldn't do the same this time.

Interestingly, the neighbour who lived on the south side of our property knocked on my office door one day and sheepishly requested something of me. His face was a little flushed and, sensing his awkwardness, I asked him to come in and sit down. He did so and got to the point rather quickly. He wanted to get married and wanted a pastor to officiate, so he wondered whether I would be willing to do that. I was a bit taken back, not having expected this. He admitted that he hadn't been a very good neighbour but was asking me because he didn't know any other pastor.

I agreed to do so and he seemed relieved and extremely grateful. I saw this as an opportunity to build a bit of a relationship with him.

On the day of the wedding, after a short ceremony in my office, he asked what he could give me for officiating the event. I assumed that he meant a financial gift and answered that he owed me nothing... except perhaps one thing.

"Certainly," he replied. "What would that be?"

I informed him about our plans for our upcoming building expansion. I reassured him that it wouldn't impact him at all. With a teasing grin on my face, I boldly asked that he not offer any resistance. He smiled back, shook my hand heartily, and agreed.

True to his word, we never heard from him.

The neighbour on our north side was a different story. When he heard about our new plans, he also showed up at my office door. He had lots of questions, which I answered. I then tried to reassure him that the impact on his property would be minimal, if anything at all. I asked that we work together and stay in communication.

Instead he left the office and hired a lawyer who became a thorn in our side. Whatever we did to resolve problems, he came back with another roadblock. He insisted on more berms. We agreed to do more berms. He demanded more trees to ensure privacy, as well as to reduce light and noise intrusion. We agreed to more trees. He wanted guarantees as to the future use of the property. We did what we could, but not to his satisfaction. This lawyer was obnoxious, disagreeable, and intimidating.

We finally decided that the only way to resolve the matter was to go to the ombudsman to get a final decision on our expansion plans and what was required of us.

It seemed a long wait for the day when the meeting was scheduled. The church prayed fervently, since so much rested on the impending decision. Our faith was strong that God was in control of all things, but our humanity felt growing anxiety as the time approached.

Finally the day arrived. We had done our due diligence and submitted our case as required a week prior to the meeting. We sat awkwardly in a boardroom along with the neighbour's lawyer, waiting for the ombudsman to show. When she finally arrived, she sat and immediately reprimanded the lawyer for not having submitted his case to her office ahead of time for her deliberation. I glanced across the table to one of our team with an optimistic and favourable nod.

She then asked to see his documented concerns. The lawyer looked uneasy and stated that he had been away on the weekend previous and hadn't had the time to collect all the papers and review and prepare them. He boldly asked for further time and to reschedule the meeting. Clearly perturbed, the ombudswoman replied that he had been given as much time as she was prepared to give and that she would give him ten minutes to organize his thoughts.

When those ten minutes ended, we were abruptly called back into session. The lawyer was noticeably and uncharacteristically flustered. He stammered on for a few minutes, betraying how ill-prepared he truly was. It was like a scene out of a movie God had scripted.

After he finished, the judge looked at him with steely eyes. She spoke pointedly and concisely as to the unreasonableness of his arguments. With one stroke of her pen, she then granted us everything we wanted. It was over in five minutes.

It was so apparent that God had choreographed every sequence of this meeting for his purposes. There are times when the hand of God is so obvious. This was one of those times.

The following week, the neighbour came knocking at my door again. I wasn't sure of the reason for his visit, and it never really did become apparent. I reassured him that we would do what we had promised. Out of the blue, he announced that he was also a Christian and we were all on the same side. I made no comment. We may have been on the same side—I was not the judge of the man's salvation—but this whole issue had cost the church thousands of dollars and it had seemed like we were on very different sides.

The construction began and continued through a long winter. Meanwhile, the church gathered for Sunday worship services in the local high school. It made us appreciate the building God had given us.

When we finally returned to our new and enlarged home, we found it beautiful, welcoming, basic, and functional. It was what I had envisioned, what I had dreamed, planned, and prayed for. But it was something God had done. We were so grateful.

Forty-Eight

THE CHURCH ENJOYED amazing times of worship, with our hearts and voices rising in united praise to God. There is no greater or more profound way to bring people together than worship, but more so to bring them into God's presence as one. The body, emotions, heart, and soul unite in each individual worshipper and the body of worshippers as a whole. To worship is to encounter our living God. It is as close to heaven as one can get on earth.

We placed our emphasis on contemporary songs. Our worship pastor worked with me weekly to design and facilitate a worship experience for believers that was Jesus-centred, relevant, engaging, and life-changing. We also planned that it should be an experience that was relevant to anyone unfamiliar with the spiritual practices of the church, an encounter in which they could find meaning and be awakened to the presence of God.

We still sang some of the traditional hymns. These hymns were new in their day, and some were enriched with melodies and lyrics that transcended time and gripped the heart. Others were revised to a more contemporary arrangement. Still others belonged to a time past.

The melodies and lyrics of much of the new music expressed the same faith and unchanging, time-proven truth as the old, but in ways relevant to the current times. The psalmist David wrote, *"Sing a new song to the Lord!"* (Psalm 96:1) and *"He has given me a new song to sing…"* (Psalm 40:3) New songs are essential because God is making his presence known in new ways all the time.

It is not my purpose here to get into a debate about traditionalism versus tradition. Many traditions uphold values and practices that are critically important and meaningful. But it is important to keep them meaningful and relevant.

Traditionalism is different. Traditionalists uphold certain practices only because that's the way they've always been done. They mindlessly go through the motions of a particular custom or procedure because that's what they're familiar and comfortable with. They resist any change, feeling threatened by it. They emphasize the practice of the outward and minimize the condition of the inward. What's worse, they often view the practice of these traditions, or the failure to do so, as the standard by which to assess another's faith and spirituality. They sinfully stand in judgment of other worshippers.

We wanted our worship to be contemporary and connected to the times. The truth never changes. But styles change, and language changes. The faith of our fathers needed to be sung in the language and style of today's worshippers.

In earlier years, we proceeded slowly. We didn't want to upset the whole wagon over how many hymns were sung per worship service or where the piano should be positioned. We introduced new instruments and new ideas over time.

This process wasn't without some resistance and pain, but we got there. The organ and piano were slowly replaced by a keyboard, guitars, and a drumkit. We used a worship team with vocalists and band so as to cultivate the gifts and talents of as many people as possible. I loved any opportunity I got to play the guitar and harmonica. Our collective goal was to ascend as one voice to God. We did our best to be sensitive to the tastes, preferences, and sensitivities of a multigenerational congregation, but mostly we were sensitive to how we as a church might best and most meaningfully worship the Lord as one body.

It's sad when worship, the very thing that should unite us to honour God, becomes the source of discord. Sometimes we focus on the style of a song rather than its message, our taste in music over our thirst for worship.

A few people complained that certain songs were too repetitive or too shallow. A song was too long. The music was too loud. We were warned of hearing loss and headaches. We were often caught in the crosshairs of traditionalists who were determined to preserve the status quo.

I was amused—or saddened, I'm not sure which—by some of the objections that surfaced. A small oak table from which we served the Lord's Table sat at the front centre of our auditorium. A large Bible sat in the centre of it. The positioning of the table in the room, and the positioning of the Bible on the table, altered from time to time.

One gentleman took it upon himself to guard the table and the Bible rigidly and would predictably inform me whenever there was a rearrangement in the placement of either. He was adamant that the table should remain in the very centre of the room, and the Bible should remain in the very centre of the table in the centre of the room. He argued that any change to that signified the Lord's Table was no longer a core value, or that the Bible was no longer central in our church. I reminded him that the Lord's Table was practiced regularly; and more important than placing the Bible in the centre of the table was to have it central in one's heart.

That mattered little to him. In the end, the solution was to remove the table and Bible altogether.

One day, I built a wooden cross out of old cedar posts and had it erected centrally on the wall at the back of the platform. It was rustic and realistic, a weekly reminder to everyone about the cost of our salvation.

The problem came when we needed that same space to position a screen so everyone could view the lyrics of the songs we sang. So we moved the cross to the side of the platform and hung the screen.

The following Sunday, someone commented that we wouldn't need a screen if we went back to singing out of hymnbooks. Then we could keep the cross where it belonged. Several individuals complained that the change was evidence that the cross was no longer central in our faith. I explained that it was no longer central in the room, but it was still central in our faith and teaching.

But that's traditionalism. It accentuates the proper positioning of an artifact and overlooks the heart. And it's a joy killer.

Fortunately, traditionalism didn't afflict most people. Just a mighty few. Most of our church readily embraced our times of worship. They sang the celebratory songs with enthusiasm and passion, and they sang the contemplative songs with meaning and heart. Sometimes they just listened with heads bent down or lifted up. They felt free to worship as they pleased with hands lifted or not, whether standing or sitting. Some swayed with the music; others stood still and silent. Sometimes the sound of guitars and the rhythmic beat of drums filled the space; other times these instruments fell silent and gave way to the voices of the worshippers. It was the heart that mattered.

Worship was the highlight of every week. It was holy ground.

Forty-Nine

BUSYNESS IS PART of a pastor's life. It was certainly part of my life. The challenge was to devise and prioritize plans and schedules that would be fruitful and purposeful and not drift into the tangle of barren routine.

In the earlier days of our young growing church, both Diane and I were involved in everything. There were regular weekly responsibilities. Sunday was always coming and I needed to be ready to preach two sermons and lead an adult Bible study. We were involved in Awana, men's and women's ministries, youth ministry, worship, and home groups.

We planned and launched additional events every year. Missions weekends. A Christmas cantata. We always had a float in the Christmas parade, advertising the church and highlighting the birth of Jesus. We held a Good Friday service in conjunction with other like-minded churches in neighbouring towns. Every year, we also planned and led a successful marriage retreat called Couples Connection. For kids, our summer vacation Bible school was always a wonderful outreach into the community, and over time it evolved into a summer-long day camp.

I took our leadership team away for weekend prayer retreats where the agenda was focused solely on prayer. Most years, I planned a weekend canoe trip with the men. Our men also became involved in Promise Keepers, and for many of them this annual event became a life-changing experience. Every year the church participated in the town's street festival too, one of the largest street festivals in Canada. It was an amazing opportunity to participate in something the town was doing and let people know who we were, and why we were.

One of the most compelling things we did was organize block parties in the community. We had bouncy castles, games, food, and live music. The whole church was engaged in hosting and serving at these events.

Initially we had no idea how successful they would be. I'll never forget the first one. We visited up and down the streets, inviting families. We expected three or four hundred people to attend, but by day's end about 2,500 people had shown up. These events were extremely successful and accomplished two things: they gave our church great visibility and brought the community together.

Every year, we sent out teams on missions trips. Many times we sent a team to Zambia to serve with Faith's Orphans Fund, a dynamic ministry to 4,500 orphans. Most years we sent a youth team to serve on an Indigenous reserve in northern Ontario, giving any teen who desired the opportunity to participate in an affordable cross-cultural experience serving the Lord. These trips inspired many of our young people to consider further ministry. God called a good number of them into full-time missions at home and abroad.

Of course, Diane and I weren't doing all these things on our own, especially as the church increased in size. New ministries were initiated and expanded and we worked hard to develop leaders and equip ministry teams. As time went on and the church was large enough to hire staff, my role morphed to managing a team that carried much of the ministry responsibility alongside me. Building a team of staff was a lot of work on my part as the lead pastor with staff meetings, one-on-one meetings, offering encouragement, praying, listening, teaching, motivating, guiding, holding each one accountable, resolving tensions, and sometimes correcting.

We had some amazing staff—spiritual, servant-minded, self-motivated, loyal, hard-working, highly productive, visionary, and mature. They were a rich blessing to me personally and to the church.

There were others who were a challenge and drain on the ministry. You really couldn't know what kind of person a staff member was until you had worked with them for a while. Resumes and references didn't always reflect the truth.

There were times when it was necessary to let a staff member go. No one ever wanted that. Those times were very painful and difficult. Some didn't vacate graciously and their exits caused some disruption in the church body.

One of the challenges I personally faced daily was having to transition abruptly from one task to another, usually a distinctly different kind of task. I've watched with fascination the whirling dervishes in Istanbul, Turkey. In their long white skirts, they spin round and round in hypnotic circles, remaining in one spot for long periods of time. They experience no dizziness, though one feels dizzy watching them!

At times I felt like a whirling dervish myself, spinning from one thing to the next with dizzying speed. In the morning before the school bus arrived, I might be encouraging one of my children regarding a particular challenge at school, and the next moment I'd be scheduling a meeting with a staff member. I would receive a disconcerting phone call from a parishioner, then circle around to congratulate another parishioner about a job promotion. I'd shift into another gear and close my study door to spend dedicated time preparing the Sunday morning message, immediately after which I would jump into lunch with someone who had asked to meet with me but really only wanted to get my ear on a particular church matter. At least that day I wouldn't skip lunch! After an uncomfortable lunch, I'd whirl off to counsel and comfort a grieving family. Following that, I would sit with a sick patient on a hospital bed, struggling with the uncertainty in his life. After whirling home for dinner with my family, I would clean up and spend time with them, often helping with homework. I might then spring into a three-hour leadership meeting, taking on the role of the church CEO. All the while, I would be trying to look like I had it together.

Sometimes my mind was strained, stretched, squeezed, and sucked, all in one day. I rarely got sufficient time to refresh and reboot between tasks. Some days weren't too bad, especially those that I set aside to study and prepare for teaching. Those days placed me in my sweet spot.

But too many days I felt dizzy by the time I fell into bed.

All kinds of people will give all kinds of counsel on how I should have handled my level of busyness. Yes, there are things I would do differently. And yes, sometimes we learn lessons the hard way. But the reality was that I was pastoring a growing church. There was lots happening. At that time, expectations of me as the pastor were high. And on top of it all, I experienced persistent resistance, adversity, and personal spiritual attacks.

Excuses? Maybe.

As mentioned earlier, I built disciplines into my life to help relieve the whirling. I purposefully cultivated and practiced those disciplines as best I could. I implemented ways to be less available, drew on strategies to slow down and take control of my time, learned to say no, and carved out time just for me to relax and practice some mindfulness.

The term *crickets* is used to describe silence, and I tried to protect time where it was just crickets—nothing happening except nothing.

I pursued something I called the discipline of distraction. Amongst other leisurely interests and diversions, I combined my love for history, reading, and exploring to study the lives of particular historical characters and the events surrounding their lives. With backpack and boots on the ground, I'd then go in search of the places where X marked the spot. This recreational hobby led to many absorbing experiences and the discovery of captivating places. I found myself crossing a farmer's field to find an old burial site, climbing down over a rocky ravine to explore the site of a frontier skirmish, or following a path along a stream to locate the ruins of an old fort. It was another world to lose myself in.

I was accustomed to reading and studying the scriptures for the purpose of preparing and teaching lessons and sermons. It was difficult to read and study just to feed my soul. When I read the Bible for my own personal spiritual nourishment and growth, I often found myself detouring into work mode, unearthing points and applications for an upcoming message or group study. So I became more conscious and deliberate about meditating on scripture for myself, asking God what he was saying to me. In order to feed others, I needed to feed myself.

I determined to meet regularly with one or more of my pastor friends, whom God had placed in my life for mutual support. Sometimes we just chatted and enjoyed the moment. I gathered with these friends as a group for prayer. We fully trusted each other and our sense of brotherhood ran deep. They always understood. They were a wonderful gift from the Lord.

But the tyranny of demands and expectations kept biting at my heels.

I intentionally tried to move the church in a less-is-better direction—encouraging fewer programs and ministries so as to open up more time for family and community. I encouraged less emphasis on *doing* and more emphasis on *being*.

In churches, serving Jesus is often equated with involvement at church events, and much effort is spent getting people into church-sponsored programs. Now, I'm not saying that church ministries aren't important. They are. But they need to be purposeful and prioritized. We must purposefully cull the good from the best.

Each church needs to know its essential needs and limitations. No one church can be everything to everyone. People can become so busy with church activities that they have little meaningful time to spend alone with God and in his word and prayer. They have little time to be present in the home, enjoying quality moments with their spouse and feeding into the lives of their children. They have little time to be present in the neighbourhood as a hockey coach, to have a neighbour over for coffee, or just to hang out at the park with other parents. They have little time to be the presence and likeness of Jesus to those around them in their sphere of influence.

It was a constant struggle to hold back the tide of church-related activities and ministries that people seemed to want and need. Clearly, people found benefit and enjoyment in them.

Fifty

WE WERE DELIBERATE in carving out meaningful time for family and making plans for fun ventures. We maximized time at our Bethesda, hiking, working around the yard, gardening, biking, exploring, playing, looking after pets, enjoying campfires, building forts, and having friends over. Our home became a haven and gathering place for our kids' friends. We seemed to always have someone at the dinner table with us. One couldn't really call them visitors, as they were regulars at our table.

A favourite activity for our family was going to the farmer's market most Saturday mornings. We looked for bargains and always ended the morning with a large hotdog topped with mustard and relish, along with French fries and gravy.

Every summer, we took our family on vacation to the same place in northern Ontario. It was called Pinecrest, a family campground on the north shore of Lake Huron. We set up camp at our favourite spot beside the blue lake that spanned as far as the eye could see. The white sandy beach circled the whole bay. We swam, baked in the sun, ran in the sand, played badminton, and enjoyed lunch on the beach. We canoed to Seagull Island and explored an old sunken ship. Every evening we sat around the campfire munching on s'mores and watching the stunning sunsets. When it was bedtime, we had to bundle up to keep warm through the cold northern nights. And every morning, it was bacon and eggs. After breakfast, the kids would race up to the candy store, money in hand, to purchase their treats for the day from Bob and Heather, the warm and easygoing owners. They would come racing back to the campsite to show us what they had purchased.

Pinecrest was a refuge for our family. Our favourite place. When you invest yourself in a particular place over time, you write a book of rich memories that remain etched in your mind forever. This was that place for us. Every summer we painted our names and the particular year on the rocks out on a craggy point, leaving a record of our times there. Every year we returned to Pinecrest and added more memories.

One of our leaders, a man I had led to Jesus, asked me one day whether I thought I could benefit from a prolonged study sabbatical. He believed I was overdue for one. I didn't need to think long. Does the rain refresh the earth? Does oxygen fill our lungs with life? *Benefit* was an understatement. I hadn't expected such a question but replied that I would most definitely benefit, as would Diane and the whole family.

This was the beginning of a discussion that led to an eight-month sabbatical to study, rest, relax, reboot, and recharge. I put together a plan, along with the leadership team, for how to spend the months. Primarily it became a period when I could be free from obligations and responsibilities. I read books, reflected, journaled, wrote, and spent time with Diane and the family.

One of the most intriguing and thought-provoking activities we did was visit a different church every Sunday for the eight-month sabbatical—not just a different church, but different kinds of churches. Our purpose was to observe and learn. We visited both contemporary and traditional liturgical churches. Churches that were free-spirited and dynamic, where people swayed with the music, and others that seemed emotionless and dispassionate, where people sat like wooden effigies. The churches were conventional and unconventional, large and small, urban and rural. We visited places of worship that were totally unfamiliar and atypical for us. For example, a Quaker meetinghouse where the attendees sat in a circle for more than an hour in silence, every so often someone getting up to share something. We were invited to attend an old order Mennonite meeting where the men sat on one side in their black suits while the women, clothed in long dresses, sat on the other. We had many conversations about what we experienced, discussing the reasons why some churches seemed to flourish while others were declining and dying.

It was an interesting time. We learned something unique from every place we visited and brought back what we had learned to our own church.

The study sabbatical quickly came to a close, and we so appreciated the opportunity for rich learning, spiritual growth, and refreshment. Our family enjoyed this period of normality and unhurried connectedness. We were deeply grateful for God's provision.

Fifty-One

OUR SOCIETY GIVES attention and admiration to the wealthy and the celebrity. The rich and powerful are the standard of success, valued and rated highly. But while Jesus loved and died for everyone, he paid special notice to the marginalized and shunned. He considered the lost and least in society as worthy of his attention. These people were defined by their neediness and destitution.

Compassion for these kinds of people was instilled in me from my earliest years.

There are people whom God brings into your life who penetrate your heart. Their needs kindle your compassion. I often think of the words spoken about Jesus, that he was filled with compassion for the crowds because they were like sheep without a shepherd. Shepherdless sheep are in grave danger. They cannot help themselves.

Chris was one of those shepherdless sheep. When I first met him, his body was thin and emaciated from years of alcohol abuse. He looked at me with gaunt, sunken eyes and shyly held out a trembling hand to shake mine.

We sat down. He opened his mouth and spoke in a quivering but earnest voice. "Pastor, I really need help."

Chris had made a decision of faith in Jesus many years before, but life had been difficult. And just one drink of liquor had opened him up to a life of alcohol addiction. It was all downhill from there. He was unable to hold a job. He'd suffered a failed marriage, experienced incarceration, endured depression and loneliness, lost first his health and then his driver's license, and developed a debilitating sense of worthlessness.

I met with Chris many times after that first encounter. Sometimes it was a mayday call because he was drinking. At other times, he was seeking support and encouragement to not pick up the bottle. He had tried every method of recovery, including

Alcoholics Anonymous and the twelve steps, but nothing seemed to work long-term. He just kept falling off the wagon into weeks of binge-drinking, sometimes leading to hospitalization.

I couldn't give Chris everything he needed, but I offered what I could: friendship, counsel, and the path to a stronger spiritual foundation of faith in a God who loved him, cared for him, and was his help in time of trouble. This was an opportunity to be part of a supportive community at the church. The church embraced him and became a family to him.

I also offered him my example of abstinence. I could manage and enjoy my life without alcohol. He often asked me if I drank, and my example offered him hope. I have been asked this question more than a few times by people who struggle with alcohol addiction. Some of these people took ownership of their problem. Many others did not. Some were self-confessed alcoholics. Most were social drinkers who, in fact, were functioning alcoholics in denial. The latter rarely confessed it to be a problem, yet they couldn't arrive home, go to a social gathering, or go out for dinner without a glass or more of alcohol. Drinking gave them a sense of calm after a hectic day. It helped them with conversation and camaraderie at a party. It helped them to loosen up and feel comfortable.

But the fact is that they needed it. They needed whatever the alcohol gave them.

Early on in my life, I chose to abstain from alcohol to extend hope to people who struggled.

I made the decision because of the biblical law of love for the weaker brother and sister. Paul wrote that it is better not to drink wine or do anything else if it might cause another believer to stumble (Romans 14:21). Everything we do affects others, for good or bad. It affects one's spouse, children, friends, and church family. If ever there was the possibility of causing another sister or brother to stumble because of what I was doing, I should voluntarily abstain from that activity.

I keenly recognized from my work as a pastor that there was no other drug in society more destructive to lives, marriages, and families than alcohol. So I chose abstinence. It wasn't something I expected of others but a personal decision I made to be honest with my convictions and my understanding of a biblical principle.

Chris lived in a small rundown house. A team of men in the church decided to fix up the house and began the task of repairing and renovating his place. We went out to his house most Saturdays for several months. We put a new roof on, repaired the plumbing, reinforced the foundation, cleaned the floors, replaced broken furniture, and filled his refrigerator weekly with healthy nourishing food.

Chris was always grateful. The love the church showed him was powerful and produced meaningful change in his life. He never won complete mastery over the bottle, though. There were setbacks and letdowns in his progress. Chris was incapable of helping himself. But with God's help, he greatly reduced alcohol's control and began to progressively live with greater freedom and quality of life. He walked with a lighter step. He looked at you with a smile. He was able to keep commitments. His memory returned. He read his Bible daily. He asked questions about the Bible. He attended church regularly. And he grew stronger in his faith.

Years of alcohol abuse, however, had wasted his body and caused his health to deteriorate. One sad day, he was found lying lifeless on the floor in his humble home. He died alone. And yet he was not alone. Jesus was with him. I have no doubt that Chris died knowing that Jesus was at his side and that he was loved by his Christian brothers and sisters.

It was always gratifying to speak into Chris's life—to love, support, and help someone who couldn't help himself. Jesus said, *"And if you give even a cup of cold water to one of the least of my followers, you will surely be rewarded"* (Matthew 10:42). There is reward today and for eternity for giving unselfishly and compassionately to those who are most incapable and vulnerable, those who are least able to return a favour. But do it in a way that only God sees.

Fifty-Two

AND THEN THERE was Big Joe. At least, that's what everyone called him. He called himself Hungarian Joe.

Joe showed up the first time one Sunday morning like a gatecrasher. I forget how he discovered us, how he arrived, or why he showed up—but when he made his appearance, everyone knew. He rolled in like a steam locomotive, panting and puffing as he walked along with a cumbersome limp.

One was always warned when Joe was nearby; he exuded a strong smell of garlic. Joe was larger than life in both physical size and presence. He only stood about five and a half feet tall but looked as big around as he was high. He always wore an old, stained T-shirt and loose flannel track pants that he had trouble keeping up around his waist.

He had no problem approaching a stranger and asking the person in his thick Hungarian accent to pull up his pants for him. I'm sure no one had ever been requested to do that before in church. More than one person showed acute red-faced embarrassment, not knowing just how to respond. I'm sure we lost more than one first-time visitor over an encounter with Joe.

When I came into the worship centre, Big Joe often beckoned me with his finger to come over. If I tried to ignore him, he'd call out to me with an increasingly determined voice that got louder and louder: "Pas-tor Day-veed! Pas-tor Day-veed!" When I approached, he would make the dreaded petition: "Pull up my pants!" So I would transition from pulling up Joe's pants to stepping up to the pulpit to preach, trying to stay focused on the immediate task at hand.

Big Joe had a voice as big as his size. Once he knew a particular song, he sang his lungs out with an operatic volume that filled the room. At one point, he began the awkward practice of getting up at the end of a service and addressing the congregation, even reprimanding them if he felt so inclined.

One Sunday he did this and I decided that I'd had enough of his disruption. I went up to him after the service and said in a quiet but stern voice, "Joe, don't ever do that again!"

"Why not?" he replied. "What will you do?"

"Try it and see!"

I had no idea what I would do. But he never did it again.

I remember the time Big Joe accompanied us on our annual men's camping weekend. It was dusk and we had to paddle canoes across a small lake to the campsite. No one else would take him in their canoe because of his awkwardness and size, so I was awarded the challenge.

I helped him onto the floor of the canoe, to sit in the very centre, and then packed all the gear around him. That seemed like the safest and most secure spot.

After he had fallen into place, there were only four inches between the canoe's gunwale and the water. It seemed like a precarious situation.

When we were out in the middle of the lake, he began to get restless and shifted his weight. The canoe rocked and a little water spilled in. When Joe felt the wetness, he panicked and attempted to get up. I could see us tipping over and losing everything, including Joe.

"Joe, sit down!" I yelled.

He continued to wriggle his way out of his seat. Without delay, I wielded my paddle and smacked him on the side of his shoulder, hard enough to startle him and arrest his movements.

He stopped, composed himself, and relaxed a little. I breathed some relief.

Later that night, we all settled into our sleeping bags. As I slept in my small tent, I was woken by what sounded like a large bear lumbering through the bushes. It seemed to be coming right toward me.

I slipped out of my sleeping bag, grabbed my flashlight, and beamed the light out through the screen opening. There he was—Joe! He had gotten up to relieve himself, became disoriented, and began frantically stumbling blindly through the underbrush. If I hadn't intercepted him, he would have kept going and we would probably still be looking for him today.

Big Joe came from a subsidized housing development. At home, he slept in the laundry room. The family was very dysfunctional and his wife wanted nothing to do with him. But since neither she nor he had anywhere else to live, Joe went to the laundry room to sleep. The neighbourhood was a breeding ground for drug trafficking and each day Joe sat at the entrance to the complex to guard against drug peddlers. Joe wanted his bigger-than-life presence to protect children from being victimized. His own kids, now adults, had suffered from harmful drug abuse, and he decided to do what he could to protect his community. This was indicative of what was in Joe's heart beneath his unceremonious, gruff exterior. He had a soft, protective spirit.

Joe attended everything that happened at the church. Two men faithfully took turns picking him up in their SUVs. A large vehicle was needed to transport Joe to and from, and it took several people to get him in and out of the vehicle.

Joe craved community, a place that was safe and accepting, and the church provided that.

The church attracts the Big Joes of life because it is a place, or should be a place, of love and acceptance for anyone.

Some people had difficulty loving Joe. At times he could be overbearing and hard to love. He could wear one down with compassion fatigue. Some even feared him. But the church became his family.

After several years, Joe became a Jesus-follower. From that point on, I could see a steady and progressive transformation in his life. He became more others-centred and less self-centred. We witnessed the blooming of a gentler, more tender spirit and the formation of a more courteous and respectful attitude.

I baptized him one Sunday morning. I remember lowering him into the water. As he went down, the water came up almost over the top of the baptistry tank. But when he came out of the water, his face shone with a huge smile that lit up the whole sanctuary.

Big Joe passed away one day when his heart gave out. I wasn't surprised, but I was saddened. Joe had entered our space as disruptive as a rhino in a rose garden, but he left it with a sense of loss and endearment in everyone. There were many tears.

Despite the trauma of his family life at home, we invited his wife and children to the church for a memorial service and time of refreshments. They attended. They felt the same warmth that Joe had felt, and a bridge began to be built into their lives.

The church learned much from Big Joe. I always believed that he had been placed in our midst by God to teach us how to love the seemingly unlovely, and to show grace and acceptance to the shunned and the misfit.

Jesus said in Matthew 25:34–40 that his followers should love the marginalized and serve the needy—the hungry, thirsty, homeless, poor, sick, and imprisoned. In other words, the Big Joes. These are the vulnerable, the hurting, and the mentally and physically disabled. Then Jesus added that when we do this to one of the least of these his brothers and sisters, we are doing it to him!

Fifty-Three

THE CHURCH GREW exponentially. We conducted two services every Sunday morning and were at capacity, especially in the children's ministry. By now, about six hundred people were being welcomed every Sunday morning and the building was being used most evenings during the week.

For several months we did a trial run to see whether we could hold a third service on Saturday evenings, but it was never very successful.

We needed to expand again. There was adequate property to enlarge our facility, and so we filed an application for expansion with the city, asking for a review and approval of our proposal.

We met several times with the city council. The process was slow and not very promising. Unfortunately, our building was located on a regional belt of land that had been designated a restricted zone and was subject to stringent limitations on the amount of construction that could be done. There were multiple roadblocks.

We prayed much about this perplexing problem and the uncertainty that lay before us, asking God to clear a path through it all, but for some reason our prayers didn't unblock the obstructions. Every avenue came to a halt.

One day while looking out through the windows of the worship centre, I envisioned the layout of a new facility and dreamed about the benefits it would mean for our ministries. I also prayed about the barriers in front of us.

Two words kept coming into my mind: *Tim Hortons. Tim Hortons.*

A coffee shop. It didn't seem to make much sense. I'd had my coffee for the morning, so it wasn't the insistent urgings of a craving.

Because the words persisted and I couldn't get them out of my mind, I decided to ponder them. It didn't seem like much of a spiritual exercise to ruminate on the words *Tim Hortons*, but I couldn't escape them.

Tim Hortons is a Canadian coffee shop started by a hockey player. It took on a life all its own, combining two Canadian passions, coffee and hockey.

On this day, it took on a new meaning for me.

The Holy Spirit seemed to be whispering something. There were churches with large buildings, much like a big box retail store. But there was another model of growth: the Tim Hortons model. A smaller facility or franchise on every major corner. We could go out into communities where the people were without expecting them to come to us. This way, we could be present in multiple communities at once.

While no model is perfect, this model was efficient, less costly, and met the immediate need for our growth.

Aurora continued to be a spiritually needy mission field with a growing population. The city was now home to more than fifty thousand people with still very minimal evangelical witness inside its boundaries. My eyes looked out over a map of the city to an area on the east side that we called the Bayview corridor. There were more than thirty thousand people living there and absolutely no gospel witness present. It seemed like a field ready for harvest.

The Holy Spirit was impressing on my mind and heart the idea of starting a new church in the Bayview corridor. I felt the thrill of something new—and the fear of something new.

It would mean a rethinking and reworking of plans. Change is difficult for some. But again, the reality is that healthy things grow, growing things change, and changing things change things. I had tried to create a culture of change in the church so people could adapt to revision with greater ease.

The first change we made was to adopt a new name for the church. We selected the name of the Campus Church. A campus is a place of learning. Discipleship is all about learning. As disciples of Jesus, we follow him by learning from him. That learning translates into obedience and transformation into his likeness.

The new name was embraced by the church quite quickly, and it facilitated the naming of new campuses. Each campus could bear the name Campus Church with the addition of its own identity. The Campus Church Bathurst, the Campus Church Bayview, etc.

But was the Bayview corridor the right location to plant a new site? And what facility would we use? We attacked both questions at the same time.

The obvious venue was the cinema. It stood out centrally and visibly, it had a large, cheerful, welcoming space, and it was a place that people outside the context of the church were familiar and comfortable with. We conducted a series of interviews in the community, walking up and down the streets to ask random people what they thought of a church in the theatre. The response was very positive. We recorded those interviews and showed the video to the church in a morning service. The church's response was also positive.

Having a campus on Bayview Avenue addressed a spiritual need in the city, and the cinema answered the need of a venue. It also augmented the vision of creating a strong and viable witness for Jesus in a city that had very little witness of him. There was an unexpected step of confirmation that this was the direction to go.

When we spoke to the cinema's management regarding our aspirations, they were agreeable but informed us that another church had recently reached out to them with the same proposal. We'd had no idea. The Meeting House was a rapidly expanding church in southern Ontario that reached into many regions. They were considering expanding into Aurora and had also looked at the cinema.

We decided to meet with their pastoral leadership to discuss both their plans and ours and discern our direction more fully.

When we met with them, we listened with openness to each other's plans and perspectives. I took time to explain what God was doing in our church and shared our vision for Aurora. They listened intently, interested to learn about our history and our plans.

After a meaningful time of discussion, the leadership of the Meeting House expressed their enthusiasm to defer their plans to the intentions of the Campus Church. I couldn't help but feel their response was another confirmation that this was the direction along which God was leading us. We prayed for each other and asked the Holy Spirit to bless each other's vision and dreams. We then parted ways, each organization to its own path.

Fifty-Four

THE PLANS WERE well received by the church, even eagerly received by many. As always, there were a few who resisted. We believed we could turn a cinema into a house of worship on Sunday mornings, but some felt that a cinema was not a place for a church to gather and worship. Ironically, these same people attended the theatre during the week. They saw a difference between watching a movie in a cinema on a Tuesday night and worshipping there on a Sunday morning. I could only see some hypocrisy in this view.

There were also those who propagated and circulated the erroneous idea that one doesn't grow a church by dividing it. I tried to explain that we weren't dividing the church but multiplying it. Most people could understand the difference.

There were still others who didn't want their comfort disturbed and were happy with the way things were.

Some others were concerned about losing their friends or family to the new campus. They wanted their social network to stay together and remain fixtures at the same campus site, at the same service time, sitting in the same row of seats.

I was diligent to keep before the church the big picture and vision of who and why we were. Jesus's command was to *build* his church, not just maintain it.

Preparations began and a start date was set in place. Our staff worked hard to make the new endeavour a success, each contributing their particular expertise to make it happen. We purchased a large trailer, with our Campus logo on the side, and it contained anything and everything we would need to operate our ministries on a Sunday morning in the theatre: sound equipment, lighting, platform planks and plywood, signage, curtains, bins full of toys, craft and administrative supplies, tables, and other furnishings. Everything needed to be rolled in and out on carts every Sunday morning.

We hired a new site pastor: my son-in-law, Pastor Ian, who had been serving in youth ministry in another city. The leadership team believed that he and Sarah had the gifting to help launch and lead a new campus, so they extended an invitation for them to join us. They agreed to accept the invitation and began serving at the Campus Church several months before the actual launch of the Bayview site to acclimatize themselves and prepare for the kickoff.

We asked for one hundred people to sign up to move from the Bathurst campus to the Bayview campus and become the core for the new site. It was a significant ask, but people had bought into the vision and responded positively.

It was a sacrifice for everyone who migrated over. They were stepping out in faith from something familiar to something unfamiliar. It required a solid commitment of time and energy, hard work, vision, a willingness to devote oneself to the challenges of growing something from the ground up, a kingdom-building perspective, and a missions-minded spirit. But they accepted the challenge and were committed to the task.

Aside from me, my whole family, including Diane, migrated over. This came at a personal cost, since we would no longer be together on Sunday mornings. I was still the primary pastor responsible for the Bathurst campus while being the lead pastor for the whole Campus Church and divided between the two sites.

We began on that first Sunday with just over one hundred people in attendance. They not only showed up but embraced the new endeavour. The energy was high. The spirit was strong.

Everyone was involved in one or more ways. Setup was a big job. The trailer arrived early and a team unloaded it, rolling the carts into their respective rooms. Another team set everything up. The worship team rehearsed. The children's ministry and nursery workers got their tables ready and prepared their rooms. Diane led the children's ministry and organized her well-motivated team. The coffee and refreshments were readied and another group prepared to welcome everyone who came through the front doors. And they all did it faithfully and enthusiastically week after week after week.

Pastor Ian conducted the pastoral responsibilities throughout the week. He was a young man with high energy, and he loved the Bayview campus. He had many novel ideas that his people welcomed and supported. He was the one who proposed and championed the block parties that were such a success.

Because the Bayview campus was in the cinema, it was important to get out into the community and be visible. It soon became noticed that there was a new player on the Bayview corridor.

For the first year and a half, I carried the responsibility for the teaching ministry each Sunday morning. It made for a busy morning. I preached at the first worship service at the Bathurst campus and then drove the fifteen minutes to the Bayview campus to do the same. I usually arrived just in time to run up onto the platform. At the conclusion of my sermon, I discreetly exited the building without lingering, and without making it look like I was making some kind of escape. I jumped into my vehicle and returned as expeditiously as possible back to the second service at the Bathurst campus site, just in time to preach for the third time. I would step onto the platform with the seeming energy of the Energizer Bunny.

One Sunday, as I was driving to the Bayview campus, I suddenly saw a flashing light behind me. My heart sank under a weight of anxious numbness. My expectation of a punctual arrival suddenly evaporated.

I pulled over to the side of the road and rolled down my window. The police officer leisurely approached my vehicle and informed me that I had been driving over the speed limit. I was aware of that, of course, but it had seemed safe since the streets were empty on a sleepy Sunday morning.

I deemed that the best approach to this problematic situation was to admit my guilt and offer up a contrite explanation without sounding like it was a lame excuse. I smiled awkwardly and apologized for my misdemeanour. I then went into a brief explanation that I was a pastor and on my way to speak at our campus on the Bayview side of town. I was under a time constraint, although I also admitted that this was no justification. The law was the law. I deserved a ticket but asked if he could write it up as quickly as possible so I could be on my way and arrive at my destination without further delay. I promised not to speed.

The officer asked me which church I pastored and I told him the name with awkward hesitation. I'm sure that my heightened colour betrayed my embarrassment.

He replied that he knew the church quite well, then grinned and assured me that he understood my time restraints. He informed me that I was free to go with only a warning.

Relief swept over me as I thanked him and drove away.

I wish that I could say that I learned from this situation, but it happened a second time. Again I admitted my guilt and explained my dilemma. Again the officer was empathetic and said that he understood. And again he let me go with a warning. Another lesson in grace.

Both campuses continued to grow. The new Bayview campus attracted many younger families. It was an exciting place to be involved. The numbers increased to more than two hundred people during the first year. The children's ministry flourished and our teens joined with the youth ministry at the Bathurst campus.

We still felt the need to have a more prominent presence in the community, so we began praying and looking for some type of storefront. God led us to a unit in the same plaza as the cinema. It was perfect. We signed a rental agreement, moved in, and raised our flag. The name, the Campus Church Bayview, was clearly noticeable. Inquisitive passersby would peer in the large windows. A welcome sign invited them to come inside if they wished, where they could learn about who we were and why. A notice pointed to the cinema next door as the location where the church gathered each Sunday morning. We utilized the facility throughout the week for offices and as space for lots of activities.

The storefront proved to be the ideal location to give the church the visible presence we were searching for. It was a significant provision from God.

The news was out: the Campus Church was on the Bayview corridor to stay.

Fifty-Five

MY SWEET SPOT and gifting was teaching. I see preaching more as a proclamation or declaration of truth. There is a definite purpose and need for preaching. When I preached, however, my natural bent was to proclaim truth through teaching.

Teaching is more than imparting knowledge. True teachers break down or simplify knowledge into understandable bites. They build one point upon another. They reinforce with illustration. They explain, engage, and inspire. I discovered throughout my schooling, from the earliest years to postgraduate studies, that there are teachers who know how to teach, and those who do not.

Many instructors possessed knowledge and could share knowledge, but not elucidate and clarify information. They lectured, but did not inspire. I sat under some of those so-called teachers and couldn't wait for the class to end. They gave me a distaste for the subject rather than a passion for it. My high school history teachers seemed to have no idea how to teach history and did their best to shatter my love for it. Fortunately, my amazing Grade Five teacher was such a wonderful history teacher and instilled in me such a love for the subject that no one could squelch it.

My church history professor in seminary and university was an inspirational teacher and motivated me to pursue my studies further. He made history more than an assemblage of facts, events, and interpretations. He was a great storyteller and I easily inserted myself into the story alongside the historical characters. He inspired me with the lives of the reformers of the sixteenth century Protestant Reformation, especially the stories of faith and sacrifice of the early Anabaptists. I wanted to be like them. That's a teacher!

I loved teaching. Always had. I loved charting out a series of sermons. I loved to learn and research a passage of scripture, its historical background, context, original meaning, and application for our day. I loved planning and mapping out a sermon or lesson. I loved pulling it together with illustrations and stories. I was inspired when teaching people who really loved learning. I loved the challenge of leaving people wanting to know more.

I developed an extensive filing system before the use of computerization. Over the years, I filed illustrations, quotes, anecdotes, and anything I thought I could use in my teaching. I always read with a pencil in hand, noting anything that I might want to retrieve, and then filed the source for future reference. Everything was cross-referenced in both topical and scriptural reference files. I could retrieve the relevant information or illustration I needed from either file in under a minute. When any material was used, I either discarded it or noted when and where it had been used. It was a homemade filing system, but it worked well for me. It was an indispensable resource.

In earlier years, I spoke from behind a mammoth pulpit and taught directly from my notes, not straying or deviating far from my manuscript. The large pulpit was replaced gradually by a smaller pulpit, which was exchanged for a small stand or lectern, which was in turn swapped out for a small table. As time went along, I decided to take everything away and just stand alone on a small peninsula that extended out from the front of the platform.

As I became more experienced with public speaking, I refined what I did to teaching with only a Bible in hand without copious notes. I kept a minimal sketch close by to keep me on point and prevent me from digressing down rabbit holes. This method was a stretch at first, but it worked well for me, giving me a greater sense of freedom and a better connection with my audience.

I must admit that I never once got up to speak without feeling butterflies in my stomach and asking the Holy Spirit to do through me what I could not do on my own.

I often allowed for an interactive time at the end of my teaching. I loved doing that but always felt some apprehension during this time as I didn't know what questions would be generated by the subject at hand. It always provoked thinking with respect to issues related to a particular scriptural passage. Some people sought clarification, others commented regarding how they had been enlightened or how the scripture had impacted them, while still others added a thought of personal application. Some questions, of course, were more confrontational. It was an engaging time and everyone looked forward to it.

I worked hard at cultivating my craft. Good teachers are good students, lifelong learners with an insatiable appetite for knowledge. They then work to perfect the skill of taking that knowledge and presenting it in a way that it can be grasped, understood, and digested by others. And they know how to motivate their students to think and research for themselves.

I wanted to be that kind of teacher.

My love was exegetical teaching, working my way through a book or biblical passage verse by verse, word by word, always careful of not getting bogged down and making it more than a cranial experience. My aspiration was threefold, to inform and shape the mind with truth, ignite the heart with love for the truth, and spur one to act on the truth. If genuine learning occurs, it results in action. The ultimate goal was transformation.

Everything I did as a pastor came from the frame of reference of a shepherd leading his flock. I wasn't a hireling doing a job for remuneration. I had been called to be a shepherd. I loved my flock immensely. I was aware of the perils and would do anything to protect my flock. I was very mindful that I walked the same dirt path as everyone else. A shepherd stands in the dust and scorching heat of life alongside his flock.

Teaching gave me a particular dynamic with my flock that was unique. There was something special, something one cannot adequately articulate about a shepherd leading his sheep into the green pastures of God's Word and watching them graze and find nourishment. It was much more than a teaching time or sermon. It was personal for me.

I had the privilege and responsibility of an uninterrupted time to address the spiritual needs of my flock. In order to do this effectively, it was critically important to both understand the needs of the flock and stay true to the text of scripture, thus providing good nourishment and a healthy diet. These two things dictated whether the purpose was to instruct, encourage, inspire, comfort, challenge, rebuke, or admonish.

From my vantage point, I often witnessed the Holy Spirit opening minds to what God was saying, and opening hearts to Jesus. It was energizing to see the glint in someone's eyes the first time they grasped the meaning of a particular truth.

Many Sundays, a group of women from a Christian organization called Teen Challenge sat in the first three rows directly in front of me. These women struggled from the debilitating effects of drug and alcohol addiction in their lives and had committed to a full year of rehab and treatment. Their hearts were filled with hurt and loss.

But I loved to watch their faces. They listened intently and responded readily with acknowledging smiles and nods. They came hungry and ready to receive, like baby birds in a nest with mouths opened wide to receive whatever God brought them. If I needed encouragement to go on, I just looked at them.

One never knows the full extent of what God is doing. I remember the day I received an email from someone living in Tasmania. The only thing I knew about Tasmania was what I had seen as a young kid watching the Tasmanian Devil, a cartoon character from Warner Bros., whirling its way across the screen grunting and snorting in a beastly manner. I knew that Tasmania was a very long way away on the other side of the planet.

The email revealed that a woman and her husband had been listening to my teaching online from Tasmania for about a year. They belonged to a small church that was struggling and didn't have a pastor. Somehow they'd discovered my sermons online and they and their church began gathering in their home each Sunday to listen in alongside our Campus Church. They felt like they were part of our congregation and considered me to be their pastor and teacher.

So here we had a little sister church down under and had no idea!

Over the next several years, we developed a close spiritual bond and friendship with this couple. You never have any idea how far God is reaching into every corner of his world with his word.

There were two things I paid particular attention to when preparing to teach. The first was a question. What did the original listeners hear when a specific passage was first spoken or written? What was the original intended meaning?

The second thing was storytelling. Jesus regularly taught using stories. People love a story, not a lecture. A story grabs people's attention. People remember a story. Stories make them think. People relate to a story; they identify with the characters.

So I worked on crafting the art.

Learn how to hook your audience at the beginning of a story. Manage details. Too many details confuse and lose the listener, but sufficient detail is needed to create interest and credibility.

Bring the story to life by using vocal inflection and animation. But don't become overly animated and risk distracting your listeners.

Practice the power of the pause to create suspense. Avail yourself of appropriate humour to shed light on your subject. Make the story imperfect and thus more authentic; anything that fits too perfectly into the subject matter will sound fabricated, like something that was pulled off the internet.

Ensure that your story is relevant and truly clarifies the lesson you're trying to teach. People may enjoy the story but feel confused as to what it has to do with the lesson. At the end of the story, the listeners should be thinking, "That really helped my understanding. I get the point."

Fifty-Six

I APPLIED MY love of storytelling to writing. My first book, *Hitting the Wall: Finding Perspective When Life Stops Working,* was filled with stories readers could relate to about finding hope in the midst of life's adversity. It was the same with my second book, *Run! The Amazing Race.* This book was about running the race of life that God has set for each of us. When researching for this book, I personally connected with many great ultramarathon runners and heard their stories. These stories enlightened me regarding the meaning of running my life's race for God—and their stories filled the pages of the book.

Writing books did many things for me. It provided an opportunity to put my thoughts and learnings into print for others to read and hopefully benefit. It was a distraction from the challenges and stresses of leadership. It was a soothing retreat from the rigorous routine of church life. It drew upon my creative juices, in addition to being exhilarating and therapeutic. Therapeutic, because it helped me understand myself as well as dissect and reflect upon the challenges I faced in life and pastoral ministry.

Most of all, the message in a book travels down many paths in many varied directions and touches lives one would never expect long after it has been written. I heard from people I had never met who told me my books had blessed them or spoken into their lives.

One morning I gathered around a table for brunch with a group of Christians to pray for the mayor of our city. When the mayor arrived, she happened to sit beside me. During the course of the meal, we got into an interesting conversation. She seemed quite transparent with me regarding some of the challenges and stresses she faced as mayor. I listened intently. As we chatted, she mentioned that when she had been walking into the gathering earlier she had squeezed past a car and noticed a book in the back seat that she wished she could read. I asked her the name of the book.

"*Hitting the Wall*," she replied.

I smiled. "That was my car. And the book is one that I wrote."

She stared at me in astonishment. I gave her a copy and she promised to read it.

Only one week later, she called and informed me that she had read the book. She shared what the book had meant to her.

Publishing my previous two books opened up many speaking engagements outside the Campus Church.

I was once invited to be the guest speaker at the annual mayor's prayer breakfast in the city next to ours. There were about four hundred businesspeople, politicians, and clergy present. I shared stories about running God's race for our lives. At the end of the breakfast, each person present was given a copy of *Run! The Amazing Race*. A deep sense of humility and gratitude swept over me as I signed books and pondered the amazing opportunity presented to me. This was something God had done.

I was also invited to speak and teach at various Bible conference centres—sometimes on weekends, but usually for whole weeks. I witnessed the Holy Spirit move in remarkable ways. I never dreamed that I would ever have such occasions of ministry.

Those weeks were exhausting, preparing and teaching two sessions per day for six consecutive days. But they were invigorating and rewarding. Diane would accompany me and involve herself in a full week of one-on-one ministry to women.

We saw broken lives begin the journey to wholeness and fragmented marriages restored. One day Diane and I ministered to a couple whose marriage was under terrible strain due to the tragic loss of their daughter in a vehicle accident.

Another time I spent a long evening with a pastor who had been under an incredible amount of stress in his church. In an attempt to drown his sorrows, he had made a foolish choice: surreptitiously entering the local liquor store to steal a bottle of hard liquor. He had dared not pay lest he be seen. But he was caught. The result? Not only was he fined, but he faced community service. And he was fired from his church. He was in such a state of anguish that he was on the edge of taking his life.

On a different occasion, a young man unexpectedly committed suicide just one week prior to beginning a summer ministry as the worship leader a summer Bible conference centre. He had spent past summers on the grounds with his family and was known by everyone. His family and friends fell into a state of shock. The matter could not be ignored and needed to be addressed for the work of healing to begin.

An uncle of the young man met with me and told me that he had read *Hitting the Wall*. He believed that I could speak into this delicate and tragic situation with the tenderness, understanding, and biblical perspective that was needed. I agreed to do so, though in all honesty I felt less than adequate for the task. I entreated the Holy Spirit to use me to be his voice and heart.

On the same weekend that this young man had previously intended to begin his summer ministry, I was present to speak into the lives of these hurting people with a message of comfort and hope.

I never knew who or what was going to unexpectedly materialize. But my family and I were available to be in any place where God could use us to intercept people on their journey and walk with them for a short distance.

Fifty-Seven

I COMMENTED EARLIER that when preparing to teach on a specific book or passage of scripture, I would always begin with a few questions. What did the original listeners hear when the words were first spoken or written? What was the original intended meaning?

I had known the stories of the Bible since I was a child. I studied the text extensively in seminary. I studied it daily for my own spiritual walk. There is no replacement for exploring the text. I had also conducted an intensive study of the biblical languages, Hebrew and Greek, and this effort offered me enormous advantage for understanding the way people thought and saw the world back then.

But as I grew in my knowledge of the Bible, I recognized that I needed to bridge the gap between western thinking and the eastern mind. The Bible was written in an eastern culture and mindset—and more specifically, its events are set in a Jewish context. To more fully comprehend the scriptures, I needed to research the nuances of thought and meanings behind the words as understood by the original audience. I needed to research the contextual setting.

I began a more vigorous study of biblical peoples, culture, history, geography, religious thought, and archaeology. The more I studied, the more I yearned to experience the lands where the biblical story occurred. I wanted to touch and taste it, to walk in the dust of Jesus's sandals, to encounter the land the biblical characters had called home. My appetite grew to visit the biblical lands with my Bible in hand—to breathe the air, hike the paths, walk the streets, camp in the desert, and explore the ruins.

My quest began with a trip to Israel sponsored by the Israeli government, all expenses paid for pastors who would potentially lead tour groups to Israel. That was me and I jumped at the opportunity.

It was a new experience for me. From the morning we landed to the night we departed, I absorbed everything. I followed directly behind our Israeli guide everywhere he went and listened intently to every word he spoke. I was like one of Jesus's disciples walking in the dust of the teacher, listening, asking, and learning. I asked question after question and took pictures of the sites, the flowers, the trees, the landscape, the people, everything.

I will never forget the night we slept at a kibbutz just north of the Sea of Galilee and under the shadow of the ancient tell of Hazor. Hazor had been the principal city in the northern region of Canaan in ancient times.

At daybreak, I set off alone, strolling up the steep hill and onto the ancient site. As I wandered amongst the timeworn stones, I came upon a marker that read something about Joshua, the Israelite leader who had led the Israelites into Canaan when they first conquered the land. The biblical account says that Joshua attacked Hazor and burned it to the ground with fire. Suddenly, there before me among the excavated remains were physical traces of soot and burned stone, evidence of a fiery destruction dating back to the time of Joshua—solid archaeological evidence of Israel's conquest as narrated in the Bible.

I stood and looked out over the surrounding countryside. My eyes followed the road winding through the hills, the same path Joshua's army would have followed. I imagined how foreboding it must have felt for Joshua to round the bend and be confronted by the massive walls of Hazor, rising to a threatening height on the precipitous tell.

Captivated, I made up my mind that day to bring others to these places to experience firsthand what I had just experienced.

I descended the sloping grassy hill of Tel Hazor and back to the kibbutz. There awaited me an authentic Israeli buffet breakfast of honey, numerous kinds of warm delicious breads, eggs, eggplant, cheeses, fish, fruit piled high on platters, danishes, yogurt, freshly pressed juices, and hot coffee. The day had just begun; my stomach was full and my spirit was stirred.

Fifty-Eight

MY BROTHER AND sister-in-law were living in the Kingdom of Jordan when they invited Diane and me to spend some time with them exploring the country. Jordan lies east of Israel across the Jordan River and played an integral role in the narrative of the Bible.

After arriving in Amman, the capital city, we stepped off the plane and into a very different and contrasting culture. The streets of Amman were crowded with people buying and selling in small booths and recesses lining the sidewalks. The sound of honking horns and smell of spices and baking bread filled the air.

That first morning, we were awakened early by the call to prayer from the minaret. Outside our open window, we heard the bleating of sheep and the shouts of young shepherds leading their flocks up the road.

We definitely stood out in our Western blue jeans and T-shirts. The Jordanian women wore long, loose-fitting black garments that covered the entire body except for the face and hands. Their heads were covered by the traditional hijab. Many wore a burqa that covered the entire face. They stared at us through a narrow slit that conveyed suspicion and wariness, and when they saw our cameras they immediately turned their faces.

Every man sported a black beard. They were robed in long-sleeved white cotton dishdashahs and their heads were covered by a white thagiyah. Many wore the traditional red and white checkered head scarf called a kuffiyeh.

On our first day of travel, we drove our jeep along the Dead Sea escarpment. It was a day never to be forgotten. The road sometimes led precariously along a high narrow ridge with both sides sloping steeply away. We steered with care around hairpin turns with no guardrails. We stood on Mount Nebo and enjoyed the same view Moses was given when God showed him the Promised Land. We scanned the Dead

Sea with the backdrop of the Judean wilderness, then looked north along the Jordan River and beyond. I wondered where God had buried Moses, for the Bible says that God buried him in this same vicinity but in a location no one knew.

Standing there was like going back in time thousands of years.

We sat in the hot springs of Herod the Great, the very place where the infamous king had soaked two thousand years earlier to relieve his intractable itching skin disease. We crawled back into the deep cave from which the hot water sprang.

We climbed up a high pointed hill to the ruins of the fortress of Machaerus where Herod Antipas, son of Herod the Great, had built a palace. This fortress was identified by the first-century historian Josephus as the place where Herod Antipas imprisoned and beheaded John the Baptizer. Machaerus had a reputation for being a hellish place of suffering for anyone imprisoned there. After entering, no political prisoner ever returned. Some of these prisoners were kept in an ancient cistern underneath the fortress. Was this the spot where John was imprisoned, where he sat cold and alone, wondering whether his work had been in vain? As I stood in that damp hole in the ground, I tried to imagine what it had been like for John on that fateful day when the executioner arrived. His head was thrust down onto a stone block and severed from his body by a bloody sword for the pleasure of the king's court.

We had lunch atop the escarpment, looking down from the high cliffs toward the dark turquoise water of the Dead Sea with its ever-present pale mist. The shores glittered white with crystallized salt. Beside us were some Bedouin tents with barefoot children running around. We hadn't seen any adults, but as we enjoyed our sandwiches several approached without our notice.

We were startled to turn our heads and see two Bedouin men and their wives, four or five women wearing brightly coloured garments. They smiled and seemed friendly, more inquisitive than anything. We called them over and before we knew it were engrossed in a happy conversation none of us understood but, with the help of facial expressions and hand signs, everyone seemed able to interpret. One man grabbed my hand and we stood together holding hands. It is common in their culture for men to hold hands. There was a definite awkwardness in me, but at least I knew I had been accepted as a guest.

Bedouin life fascinated me and took me back to biblical days. The entire extended family lived together in large black tents made of densely woven camel and goat hair, surrounded by flocks of goats and sheep. A donkey was always tethered to a post and several camels hobbled nearby; the Bedouin say to trust in God but tie your camel.

They are a rugged people but very hospitable. I was fascinated by how they were able to survive in such a hostile environment. Desert. Heat. Isolation. Barrenness.

We did a little hiking in the desert and discovered that without water and shade one could be overtaken by heat stroke in just a few moments. Somehow they not only survived in these conditions but flourished.

Two things were impressed upon me from observing the Bedouin. The first was the absolute, essential importance of water to sustain life. As we enjoyed our visit with that Bedouin family, I wondered how they survived in such a parched wasteland where the intense heat could shrivel a man into a bag of dry skin in such a short span of time. I knew, of course, that they couldn't survive without water. But where was it?

As we navigated our way down the escarpment later that day, I looked back up to where we had met the family and noted a patch of green hundreds of feet below their encampment. I scanned it with my binoculars and focused in on a few trees nestled into the side of the desolate cliffs—an oasis where fresh, life-giving water flowed out of the barren rock.

I perused the site further and there, winding its way down the side of the cliff to the oasis, was a narrow path with several children descending it carrying buckets. Life-giving water. In our homes, where we just turn on a tap and fill a glass with cold water, it's easy to forget that water is life.

When I led tours to Israel a few years later, I always chose the same Israeli guide to accompany me. We worked well together. Aharon often lifted his bottle of water above his head and reminded everyone in a loud voice, "Water is life." He reminded us that the most important factor for establishing a dwelling, village, or town in a particular location was a freshwater source.

I know of only one city that was built without any freshwater source. Herod the Great founded the Roman city of Caesarea Maritima on the Mediterranean coast in a location that had no reliable source of freshwater. Herod was a paranoid narcissistic psychopath, but he was also a masterful builder. Everywhere one goes in Israel, one can witness his genius in building. He probably built Caesarea on a coastal plain with no freshwater just to prove that he could.

But he still had to supply water in order to sustain life in the new city, so he built an aqueduct that extended for about fifteen kilometres from the foothills of Mount Carmel to the city. An amazing engineering feat.

During these travels, I was continually reminded about how Jesus referred to himself as the living water. He sat talking to a woman at a well one day and said to her, *"Anyone who drinks this water will soon become thirsty again. But those who drink the water I give will never be thirsty again. It becomes a fresh, bubbling spring within them, giving them eternal life"* (John 4:13–14). He drew an important analogy. He is as essential to spiritual and eternal life as water is to physical life. He is the water of life.

The second thing that was greatly impressed upon me was the life of the shepherd. My interest was probably amplified because the Bible is filled with stories of people who were shepherds. It often uses the analogy of a shepherd and sheep. The most well-known passage of scripture in the Bible begins, "The Lord is my Shepherd" (Psalm 23:1). I learned so much from observing the Bedouin shepherds. Lessons about the character and ways of God. Lessons about Jesus, the Good Shepherd. Lessons about leadership. Lessons about life.

One day we set up camp in the Wadi Rum, a desert in southern Jordan next to the border with Saudi Arabia. The Wadi Rum is known for being the pivotal backdrop for the escapades of Lawrence of Arabia. Mostly, it is the home of the Bedouin. It's a stunning desert landscape of red sandstone mountains, valleys, craters, and sand dunes beneath a cloudless cerulean blue sky. In my imagination, it bore a resemblance to the red planet Mars. Deep wadis cut their way through the red terrain, each year their dry beds swiftly filling with raging torrents from the rains spawned in far-off mountains during the rainy season, only to vanish as quickly under the intense and merciless heat of the sun.

As we prepared for dinner, we saw a herd of goats and sheep running toward us. We felt little concern, as we were positioned on a small plateau of rock about eight feet high. But then we realized they were goats and sheep. Eight feet of rock wouldn't be a problem for them.

Before we could throw everything back into our four-by-four vehicle, we were swarmed. The herd began to eat everything in sight.

Running along behind them was a shepherd, a young girl—most of the shepherds I saw were children, and most of them young girls. She was uttering strange clicking sounds which most of the animals seemed to understand; they responded by returning to her side. A few refused to obey. She bent down, picked up a few small stones, and hurled them with amazing precision at each disobedient target. One particular goat stood stubbornly about thirty feet from her, refusing to return to the flock. She picked up one more stone and forcefully tossed it at the delinquent, striking it on its rump. It jumped at the sting of the stone and hoofed it back at full speed.

When I witnessed that young shepherdess sling her stone, my mind carried me to the time when David, a young shepherd boy, walked out into the Valley of Elah to fight the giant Goliath. King Saul offered him his own personal armour, but David turned down the offer; instead he would go armed with his weapon of choice—a sling. He had spent hours in the fields around Bethlehem perfecting his skill. He was now an expert slinger, able to sling a stone with impressive accuracy.

And when David combined his skill with his faith in the living God, the result was miraculous. He sank that stone into Goliath's forehead and the giant fell headlong to the ground.

I was reminded that when we surrender to God all who we are and all that we do, and fuse that with faith in who he is and what he can do through a heart abandoned to him, the result is beyond anything we can imagine.

Any old rock will do. Throw it. That's the essence and message behind the story of this book.

Our excursion throughout Jordan was not without its perils. One evening, we set up camp atop a sandy hill under the welcomed shade of palm trees near the Gulf of Aqaba by the Israeli and Jordanian border. A gentle breeze refreshed us; it was peaceful and still.

That is, until we saw something driving madly in our direction. As it got closer, we realized that this was a military vehicle. We watched with consternation as it skidded to a halt at the base of our hill.

Five men jumped out and began shouting at us. We had no idea what the dramatic scene before us meant. Whatever was happening, though, it was clear that we were in the middle of it.

The men came no closer but gesticulated wildly, pointing to the ground and then throwing their hands up in the air, yelling, "Kaboom! Kaboom!"

It suddenly struck us: landmines. We were camped in the middle of a field of landmines.

Now what?

We delicately took down our campsite and carefully retraced our steps back to our vehicle. It was a little disconcerting when we saw the soldiers retreat from us. We figured that by stepping into the same footprints as before, we wouldn't trigger anything explosive.

We did it. And I lived to tell the story.

One of the most interesting days of our time in Jordan was the day my brother and I decided to explore the Jabbok River. The Jabbok, which flows into the Jordan River, is the stream that the patriarch Jacob followed upon returning home from his exile.

The closer Jacob got to home, the more fearful he became. Why? Because his brother Esau awaited him. Jacob had duped Esau out of his birthright years earlier. He was the reason for Jacob's quick exit in the first place.

Now Jacob was returning home with his two wives, a large family, and many possessions, including sprawling flocks and herds of animals.

As he got further down the Jabbok, he received news that Esau was coming to meet him with an army of four hundred men. The fear of Esau's revenge overwhelmed Jacob and he devised an elaborate plan to soften his brother's heart toward him.

In Genesis 32, the Bible records that Jacob crossed the ford of the Jabbok with his family to get them to a place of greater safety. He then returned across the ford to spend the night alone.

That night, a stranger attacked Jacob and a fight broke out that lasted until dawn. By daybreak, Jacob came to the realization that he was wrestling with none other than God himself. With a sudden stroke, God wrenched Jacob's hip and brought him to an abrupt surrender. He then changed Jacob's name to Israel.

The location of this significant event was identified in the biblical account as Peniel, which means "face of God."

We followed a narrow dirt road up the Jabbok until we arrived at some Bedouin tents. The women were washing their clothes in the river while the men attended to the animals. We stopped and told them that we were looking for the ford of the Jabbok. They pointed further upstream and replied that there was only one ford on the Jabbok and that the Bedouin had used it for countless generations. They identified the place as Peniel.

I was astounded, feeling as though I had just stepped back four thousand years into the biblical story and physically walked in the footsteps of those who had gone before so long ago.

We drove a little further up the winding dirt road, manoeuvring around deep ruts, and pulled up beside a small wooden sign on which someone had painted the name *Peniel*. We ascended Tel Peniel and found thousands of pottery shards scattered everywhere, fragments that each told a story from ages past.

A Bedouin shepherd looked at us suspiciously as he led his flock around the base of the tell toward the stream. From the top, I saw a shallow place in the riverbed where the water danced and sparkled as it bubbled over stones. The ford.

We descended the steep slopes of Tel Peniel and returned to the Jabbok. I waded into the narrow river, the water splashing up against my knees, and crossed the ford as Jacob had done hundreds of years earlier. I then returned over the same ford and stood on a small, flat piece of land where I imagined Jacob might have wrestled with the Lord. I was certainly in the locality.

I felt an overwhelming sense of being in the presence of the Lord. It was surreal. These kinds of experiences revolutionized my teaching.

Fifty-Nine

OUR TRAVELS IN biblical lands came to play such a significant role in my teaching at the church that it warrants spending more time sharing the stories. When we returned from Jordan, I began putting together a tour itinerary. By this time, I knew which sites and places I wanted to bring people. I avoided the traditional religious sites, preferring to spend time experiencing the culture, walking the ancient paths, exploring the stones and ruins of biblical sites, dipping our feet in the water, mingling with local villagers, experiencing the hospitality of the Bedouin, interacting with shepherds, smelling the aromas of the Middle Eastern markets, tasting the food, and listening to the plethora of sounds.

I planned a tour that traversed the entire country from the western coastal plain to the Jordan valley in the east, from the Golan Heights in the north to the southern Negev. The excursion extended into Jordan, visiting Aqaba on the Red Sea and then up to Petra where we would encounter the Bedouins and familiarize ourselves with the way of life in biblical times.

I cannot overstate the concentrated work of organizing a tour intended to give every visitor a meaningful, even life-changing experience. I met with key people who helped me finalize the many logistical details. We designed and printed brochures, advertised the tour, arranged a nonstop flight to Tel Aviv, arranged for the Israeli guide, booked lodging, and planned a ten-day schedule. I spent many hours perusing and studying maps, thinking and rethinking the itinerary to maximize the adventure.

Diane partnered with me to assist with the administrative side of things, keeping an ongoing financial account as the tour progressed. She kept her ear attentive to the needs, concerns, and questions of every person on the tour. She watched and listened for things I may have missed. That role was incredibly important. It was a team effort.

My tours were not vacations. They were designed to be spiritual pilgrimages in the fullest sense. Time was devoted to reading one's Bible in the very location where a scripture passage originated. I assisted with this by preparing related scripture readings for each day. The setting and context granted an open window through which to view, contemplate, reflect, and meditate on how the experience of being in a particular spot impacted one's soul and heart.

A very meaningful moment came from just sitting silently in a boat on the Sea of Galilee, pondering and listening to the water lap against the sides of the vessel. Followed by lively singing and dancing on the deck of the small craft to the rhythm and melody of Middle Eastern music.

The tour was also intended to be more like a seminary course in biblical studies. I wanted it to be fun but full. At each site, I gathered my students around me, talked about the biblical significance of the location, opened my Bible, and shared insights. Most evenings, onsite teaching times were supplemented with notes, charts, maps, and discussion, reviewing the past day and preparing people's minds for the next.

One of my primary goals was to augment my teaching ministry back home at the Campus Church. Therefore I took numerous pictures from which to draw and incorporate into my teaching at the church. Many people would have loved to participate in the tours but were unable to join for various reasons, so I brought the experience back to them. I carried a Bible in one hand and a camera in the other.

My favourite locale was Galilee. Much of the region was relatively untouched over the centuries. The rolling fields and tranquil hills still largely reflected how it had looked in the time of Jesus. One could stand on the top of any high sloping hill and enjoy a panoramic view of the heart-shaped sea. At a glance, one could scan the northern shore where the bulk of Jesus's ministry occurred.

We strolled down the same hillsides that the Rabbi had walked with his disciples, and as we walked I told the parables of Jesus to give an idea of his peripatetic style of teaching. I pulled a thistle out of the soil on the side of the path and pointed to some stones on the ground as I recounted the parable of the sower and the seed. I drew attention to the birds chirping in the bushes as they picked seeds and the flowers growing in the field while talking about the Father's care and provision for them. I reminded my followers, as Jesus did his followers, that we need not worry, for our Father in heaven knows our needs and cares much more for us.

We lived it. There were often tears. There was always quiet reflection.

We arrived at one of the best kept secrets in Galilee: a small cave tucked into the side of the Eremos hill, facing out toward the lake. Although the Gospels don't say, I have no doubt that Jesus spent time in this cave praying or resting, sheltered from the sun's heat or from the cool night air. I thought of Jesus's words to his disciples:

"Let's go off by ourselves to a quiet place and rest awhile" (Mark 6:31). The Gospels record that Jesus got up before daybreak and went out to an isolated place to pray. How many times did Jesus come to this spot?

Above the cave was a high grassy slope that formed a natural amphitheatre. I could speak in a loud voice without shouting and be heard clearly by listeners far up on the hillside. Again, I wondered how many times Jesus had taught the multitudes in this very place. Some believe that this was the location for the feeding of the five thousand—although it was more likely about twenty thousand people.

I led the group further down a steep, treacherous little path to a clearing on the shoreline of the Sea of Galilee. This particular spot was visited by few tourists, which is why I liked to go there. It was the location of the original Capernaum fishing grounds where Jesus had called four fishermen to follow him. A spring gushed out from the side of the embankment, and one didn't need to use much imagination to visualize first-century fishermen washing their nets in its spray.

As I stood teaching on a rock out in the water, my tour group often removed their footwear and waded into the refreshing waters. They were experiencing in real time something they had read about countless times.

One day, while perusing a small shop in Galilee, I looked for a prayer shawl, or tallit. As I opened a shawl to see it, a woman approached me. She took the tallit from my hands and gently laid it over my head. She then rested her hand on my head and prayed the prayer of blessing in Hebrew over me. Her voice could be heard throughout the store as she articulated each word directly into my soul with intense emotion and authenticity.

> May the Lord bless you and protect you.
> May the Lord smile on you and be gracious to you.
> May the Lord show you his favour and give you his peace.

There are some things that stay with you and lodge in your heart. This was one of them. Her words still reverberate in me.

I had so many experiences filled with significant meaning that it's difficult to know which ones to mention. For example, Caesarea Philippi. The first thing that strikes any visitor to Caesarea Philippi is the streams of water and lush vegetation.

At the time of Jesus, Caesarea Philippi was a major centre in the north of Israel. Jesus retreated to this area with his disciples immediately following the murder of John the Baptizer. It was home to numerous pagan temples and a hub for idolatry. Today great stones are scattered among the ruins of stairways and foundations where ancient temples stood, against the arresting backdrop of an impressive sheer yellow cliff. Hewn niches that once housed pagan statues line its rocky face.

The city was situated at the base of Mount Hermon, the only snow-capped mountain in Israel, and benefitted from the streams of water that flowed from its melting snow. In ancient times, water gushed from the depths of the enormous gaping mouth of a limestone cave, still the dominant feature, to become the source of the Jordan River. The abundance of water here produced flourishing trees and plants. It was a tourist destination even in Jesus's day. Today the water no longer flows from the mouth of the cave, but a brimming supply of water still gives life to rich green foliage.

This is where Jesus brought his disciples and asked them a critical question: *"But who do you say I am?"* (Matthew 16:15) And Peter uttered the resounding confirmation that Jesus was the Messiah, the Son of the living God. Jesus replied that his Father had revealed this to Peter and that he would build his church upon this rock; even the gates of hades would not prevail against it.

When one visits Caesarea Philippi, the reason for Jesus's visit there becomes apparent. In the ancient world, the cavernous mouth of this cave was believed to be one of the gates of hades, an entry to the underworld where the souls of the dead were sucked down as by a giant vacuum. Jesus wanted to sear the singular truth into his disciples' minds that even death, as powerful as death is, would not overpower his church and kingdom. The kingdom would prevail over everything, and they would play a critical role in it.

Before ascending to Jerusalem, we travelled along the Jordan Valley to the traditional site of Jesus's baptism. The bus drove down a dusty road past ancient monasteries that had been built to memorialize the event. There were always people in the tour group who wanted to experience baptism in the Jordan River. The Jordan is very narrow in that location and one could swim over to the Kingdom of Jordan in fifteen seconds if it weren't for the Israeli soldiers watching.

Two things stand out in my mind: the glow on the faces of those being baptized as they came up out of the waters of the muddy Jordan.... and the fish nibbling my feet. I wondered if John the Baptizer felt the fish nibbling his feet as he stood in this same water and baptized thousands of people.

Jerusalem is arguably the greatest city in the world. Certainly it's the world's most contested city. Historically, more battles have been fought around its walls than any other city. It is a city sacred to three religions—Judaism, Christianity, and Islam. It still draws the attention of the world.

We drove into Jerusalem on every occasion with the same sense of awe the pilgrims in biblical times would have felt as they approached to celebrate the feast days and worship at the temple. Everyone on our bus looked out their window with wonderment and a certain solemnity as the bus driver cranked up the hymn: "Jerusalem, Jerusalem, lift up your gates of peace." We'd sing just like the ancient pilgrims sang the songs of ascent as they drew near to the city.

Jerusalem, the city associated with such names as Abraham, David, Solomon, Isaiah, Jeremiah, Ezekiel, Nehemiah, and of course Jesus—the city where Jesus was crucified, rose from the dead, and ascended back to heaven.

The place where the church was born.

The old city, surrounded by its high walls, is a maze of congested streets and an easy place to get lost. More than once I had to go looking for one of my lost sheep. It was also a fun place to shop in the booths that lined the narrow streets.

"Come to my shop," one shopkeeper called out. "I rip you off less!"

The streets bustled with throngs of people pushing and shoving past each other. We took in the sounds of shopkeepers calling, children playing, worshippers singing, donkeys braying, dogs barking, roosters crowing, and bells ringing. Then there were the smells of freshly baked bread just out of the oven, food cooking, incense burning, garbage smouldering, sewage seeping, and spices sending off their fragrances; these aromas, good and not so good, all blended into one.

An old woman wended her way along the street bent forward under a heavy bundle of sticks wider and higher than the doorways through which she had to manoeuvre. Soldiers carried heavy guns and prayer shawls over their shoulders. A man pulled a donkey laden with pots and pans through the streets. Hasidic men, with their long curly sidelocks, long black suits with black brimmed hats, and sometimes large fur shtreimels rushed off to worship. Young men pushed their way through the crowds with loads of freshly baked loaves piled high on their heads.

Street cuisine was readily available here. We could just stop any baker and hand him a few shekels for a tasty pretzel, or slip into a shop for a falafel or shawarma. We drank freshly squeezed pomegranate juice.

A person could spend weeks in Jerusalem and still only scratch the surface of what there is to see, explore, learn, and experience. Archaeology continually uncovers new things. Take, for example, the ancient city of David. King David's city was located just outside the present-day walls to the south of the Temple Mount. It's a long, sloping ridge overlooking the Kidron Valley to the east; it descends south to the ancient site of the pool of Siloam. Not long ago, the only evidence for the existence of David was the Bible. Sceptics debated and cast doubt that he ever actually lived. But new discoveries are being unearthed, accumulating increasing amounts of extrabiblical evidence of his existence. I find it intriguing how archaeology keeps digging up support for the trustworthiness of the account recorded in the Bible.

We walked through the labyrinth of tunnels deep beneath David's city, tunnels which date back to early biblical times. I always enjoyed wading through Hezekiah's tunnel, dug 530 metres through solid rock in the late eighth century B.C. At that time, Jerusalem was threatened by a siege by the Assyrians, so King Hezekiah had a tunnel dug to bring the waters from the Gihon spring inside the city walls. Two teams chiselled and chipped their way through the rock from opposite ends and met in the centre, only one metre off from each other. Even today, no one knows exactly how they accomplished it. But the tunnel exists, another remarkable piece of evidentiary support for the biblical text.

One of the unforgettable places we visited was the house of Caiaphas. The remains of this house are hidden beneath the Church of St. Peter in Gallicantu (Latin for "cock's crow"), situated on the eastern slope of Mount Zion. The church is easily identified by a golden rooster that stands atop the roof of the church, signifying the event of Peter's denial of Jesus and the crowing of the cock. Beside the church, ancient stone steps dating back to the first century wind their way up the steep slope from the Kidron Valley; they are, in all probability, the stairway up which Jesus was led in chains after his arrest in the Garden of Gethsemane. Caiaphas was the high priest who had Jesus arrested and condemned at an unlawful night trial. This is believed by many archaeologists to be the place where it all happened.

Beneath is a guard room where prisoners were interrogated and even tortured. Holes in the sides of the stone walls once held iron rings, bearing witness to the harsh conditions in which prisoners were chained. It may have been this very room where Jesus was interrogated and beaten. At one corner of the guard room is a small stone step where a guard would have stood and peered down through a window into a small holding cell below to keep an eye on his prisoner. That small chamber, more like a cistern or dungeon, may be where Jesus was detained until morning at which time he was taken to Pilate.

Spending a few moments in that room was among the most moving and sober times I have ever experienced. When it was time to go, it was often difficult to get people to leave. It was overwhelming to possibly be standing on the same stone floor where Jesus, bloodied and alone, was incarcerated for us. The truth and emotional impact of his substitutionary sacrifice struck with full force.

One of the places I enjoyed least, but which has tremendous significance, was the Church of the Holy Sepulchre. It is crowded with people from all over the world, noisy, and full of ornate drapes, flickering candles, and burning incense. It is not a place I would ordinarily visit except for the fact that it is traditional site of the crucifixion and resurrection of Jesus.

When you peel back the layers of history, one discovers a sequence of structures dating back from the present church to an old Crusader church, to a church that Constantine built in 325 AD, to two pagan temples built by the Roman Emperor Hadrian in 135 AD, to a first-century garden which contained a tomb and a small rocky hillock called Golgotha.

Hadrian built his temples to conceal all evidence of the crucifixion and resurrection of Christ. However, when Helena, Constantine's mother, came to Jerusalem two hundred years later, she purposed to find and put an X on the exact spot where Christ was crucified and resurrected to life.

The local inhabitants readily pointed to what lay buried beneath Hadrian's temples. Constantine removed everything covering the site and exposed the original location, perfectly preserved. He built a rotunda over the tomb as well as a basilica, leaving Golgotha in an open courtyard.

Today, two thousand years later, the Church of the Holy Sepulchre stands as an historical monument and evidentiary witness to the greatest, most consequential event in human history.

Just outside the present-day southern walls of the city is a wide stone stairway that ascends the steep rise. The Southern Stairs were used in Jesus's day as the main entrance to the Temple courts. Many of the stone slabs are original to the first century, intact and well preserved. Jesus himself would have climbed these same steps on many occasions. The thousands of pilgrims who came annually to the Temple for the festivals also ascended them.

I could envision Jesus sitting on these steps debating the Pharisees, or interacting with people as they entered and exited the Temple grounds. I had my groups sit on the steps as I opened my Bible and taught.

The Temple was the dwelling place of God. For centuries, he lived here. But on the Day of Pentecost, the Holy Spirit came and took up residence in a new temple—the lives of Jesus-followers. Paul the apostle later wrote that the body of a believer is the temple of the Holy Spirit of God.

I could image thousands of people listening to Peter preach on these steps. The Bible says that three thousand believed and were baptized. The baptism of so many new converts could have been accommodated in the many mikvehs, ritual immersion baths, situated immediately below the ancient stairs.

Let's go to the desert for a moment. The Negev in the south of Israel is a contrast between majestic beauty and complete desolation. The wilderness of Paran is where the Israelites spent part of their forty years after the Exodus. Travelling through the Paran in an air-conditioned bus didn't give anyone in my tour any idea of what it would have been like for two and a half million Israelites to trek on foot through such a scorching environment.

So I always had the bus stop. I'd ask my tour group to step out and follow me. They walked along behind me for about fifteen minutes across the hot gravel and stones to an acacia tree that stood alone.

By the time we arrived at the acacia tree, the response of people was what I had hoped. They were complaining about the severe heat, intense glare of the sun's rays reflecting off the sand, fatigue, and their need for more water. They were happy to finally rest under the shade of the tree.

I turned our short desert experience into a faith lesson, talking about what it must have been like for Moses to lead such a huge population through such an inhospitable region. In this desert, every Hebrew man, woman, and child could have—or should have—shrivelled up to a desiccated carcass within a few days. But they didn't.

Why not? God! The desert was a testimony to God's faithful presence, provision, and guidance. He kept them alive.

The desert is a unique classroom that teaches some of life's most important lessons. It analogizes those times of dryness, drought, and adversity when we recognize that I can't, but God can. That all will surely fail if God doesn't show up. In such times, we are brought to the end of ourselves. The harsh reality hits home: we can't make it on our own. We abandon ourselves to God. Our faith is stretched to rely totally on God's presence and provision. We drink water he provides from the rock, and eat manna he daily sends down from heaven. We find refuge and rest in the shade of his presence. As we stood under the shade of the acacia tree, we were reminded of the words of the Psalmist, "Those who live in the shelter of the Most High will find rest in the shadow of the Almighty. He alone is my refuge, my place of safety; he is my God, and I trust him" (Psalm 91:1-2).

The desert is a harsh place, but it is a good place because it's a testament to the truth that we need God in the midst of life's bitter, challenging, barren realities. In fact, we need him at all times.

When I had finished my lesson from the desert, we would return in silent reflection to our air-conditioned bus. Moses didn't have that luxury. He only had God. But that was enough!

Sixty

I HAD READ and studied my Bible often without fully appreciating the significance of the country of Turkey in the biblical narrative—that is, until we visited there. In New Testament times, this land was known as Asia Minor. It's the setting for most of the New Testament outside of the Gospels.

My brother and sister-in-law had moved to live and work there, and again they invited Diane and me to visit them and explore the country. We were excited to go.

We stayed at the charming Kybeli Hotel in the centre of the old historical district of Istanbul. It was a blue building, tall and narrow. The small rooms were brightly coloured in Turkish decor. The hotel had hundreds of lamps hanging from the ceilings. It was furnished with antiques and its floors were covered in Turkish carpets. One afternoon, we sat on the floor in a large room filled with carpets and listened to one of the owners explain all about Turkish carpets. It was fascinating to learn about the history of carpet making, the weaving and knotting, as well as the tribal and floral designs and colours. The older and more worn the carpet, the more valuable it was.

We enjoyed a Turkish breakfast every morning in the cafe. The table would be spread with figs and apricots, boiled eggs, meats and cheeses, Turkish yogurt, olives, tomatoes, sausage, flatbread dipped in olive oil, various freshly baked breads, honey, pastries, tea, and strong Turkish coffee. We quickly learned that breakfast was not to be missed.

The Kybeli was located on the peninsula jutting out into the Bosphorus Strait just south of a narrow stretch of water called the Golden Horn. A long bridge, lined tightly on both sides with people fishing, linked Europe to Asia. This part of Istanbul was once the old city of Constantinople, made famous by the first "Christian" emperor Constantine in the fourth century AD. The history and culture of the city are rich.

In the evening, we enjoyed sucking on sweet baklava with coffee or tea in the outdoor patios while watching the whirling dervish. The streets were always congested with shopkeepers darting back and forth, street vendors selling their goods, shoppers bargaining for a deal, worshippers heading to the mosque for prayers, beggars holding out tin cans, and tourists from all over the world roaming around. The call of the muezzin from the minaret summoned worshippers to prayer, adding to that Middle Eastern vibe.

The sites we wanted to see were all within walking distance.

The Hagia Sophia, built by the Byzantine emperor Justinian in 537 AD, is considered one of the world's greatest architectural marvels. One can still see the foundations of an earlier church building built by Constantine himself two centuries before that.

The high dome of the Hagia Sophia was supported by gigantic granite and marble columns imported from the spoils and ruins of older buildings and temples from other parts of the empire. I was intrigued by columns that originated from the great Temple of Artemis in Ephesus, the idolatrous city where the apostle Paul preached and founded a young church.

Hagia Sophia was turned into a mosque when the Muslims conquered the city in 1453 AD. When we visited, it was a museum. Today it is again a mosque.

We visited the Blue Mosque, opposite the Hagia Sophia.

That same day, we descended fifty-two steps into a large underground cistern built by Emperor Justinian in the sixth century AD. The ceiling here was also supported by great columns shipped in from around the empire.

The cistern was filled with mystery and intrigue, as well as fish that swam in the dark, shallow waters to keep the water clean.

Then there was the Grand Bazaar, one of the largest and oldest covered markets in the world, dating back to the 1400s. Throngs of people wandered in and out of its thousands of shops, bargaining for every item under the sun—colourful and fragrant spices, fish and meat, clothing, food, rugs, souvenirs, jewellery, bags, candy, Turkish tea, and Turkish coffee.

When we left Istanbul, we set off across the country through the heartland of Turkey to Cappadocia in Central Anatolia. Cappadocia is the region where Christians through the centuries found refuge from persecution. Isolated, its countless caves provided shelter. We lodged in a cave hotel ourselves and woke up on the first morning to the delightful sight of brightly coloured hot air balloons flying overhead. Breakfast was served on an outdoor patio shaded by an overhead lattice covered with grape vines. The large, ripe grapes hung in heavy clusters.

We were awestruck by the unique and surreal beauty that surrounded us. Unusual towering rock formations called fairy chimneys, sculpted from the soft volcanic rock over centuries of erosion, projected an air of mystery. Their spires rose forty metres and many looked like giant mushrooms.

The caves permeating the terrain gave it the appearance of Swiss cheese, and the remains of early dwellings, churches, and monasteries could be found within many of them. We were amazed to discover ancient graffiti of early Christian symbols scratched or painted on the walls.

At one point, I looked out over a valley from the mouth of a particular grotto that had provided refuge for a family, wondering what it had been like to be always watching out for approaching soldiers. Each space told a story lost to history, and yet the land felt strangely alive as we imagined the lives of these people who had occupied the caves.

One of the most intriguing places we visited was Kaymakli, a completely underground city that descended eight levels. Its origins are still a mystery, but 3,500 people could live inside its rooms and passages. People fled to this refuge to escape persecution and death. Entire armies could pass over the city without knowing what was beneath their feet. Even if the inhabitants below were to have been discovered, it would have been dangerous for enemy forces to enter; its defences were such that an entire army could be trapped inside and die.

We drove further inland to Hattusa, the capital city of the ancient Hittites. We passed the open air rock sanctuary of Yazilikaya, with its striking relief art depicting twelve Hittite gods and goddesses. Large containers from the Grand Temple's warehouses lay scattered about in the fields. Pillars of the Lions Gate, and other monumental gates, still stood as tributes to the magnificence and might of a glorious ancient civilization. Inside the expansive walls, stretching six kilometres, lay the evidence of a prosperous and wealthy city with temples, palaces, storehouses, and other great buildings.

Interestingly, the Hittites were forgotten for three thousand years. Hattusa and the existence of the Hittite Empire were believed to be a myth referenced only in the Bible. King Solomon was the middleman of a thriving trade of chariots and horses between Egypt to the south and the Hittites to the north. Today, thanks to archaeological discoveries, it is recognized as an historically great civilization and mighty military power.

We visited many of the places visited by the first Christian missionaries, cities where the apostle Paul and others evangelized and founded churches. For example, Lystra was where Timothy lived and Paul was stoned.

Antioch Pisidea was where Paul and Barnabas stayed for a week and taught in the synagogue, causing a great stir that resulted in their expulsion from the city. The foundation stones of the Jewish synagogue can still be seen today. As I looked down the road leading away from Antioch Pisidea, I imagined the two missionaries being chased out of town by a howling mob, pelted with stones and struck with sticks.

The ruins of Colosse lay silently at the top of a high tell, largely undisturbed to this day. The church founded there was the destination for two New Testament letters, Colossians and Philemon.

The book of Philemon is a tiny gem tucked away in the New Testament. Onesimus, a slave, had stolen goods and run away from his master, Philemon, a Christian in the church in Colosse. Onesimus had eventually arrived in the big city of Rome and met up with the apostle Paul in prison, where he heard the good news and came to faith in Christ. Paul sent him back to Philemon with a personal written plea to forgive his runaway slave and accept him back as a brother in Christ.

According to the thinking of the day, it was inconceivable to consider one's slave as a brother or sister. The first century was littered with social barriers. But this small book is a demonstration of the power of the gospel to cut through racial, ethnic, social, cultural, economic, gender, and religious barriers. The new Christian faith introduced people—whoever they were and whatever status they held, rich and poor, master and slave—to a family: the family of God. As Paul wrote to the Colossian church, *"Christ is all that matters, and he lives in all of us"* (Colossians 3:11).

After visiting the site, we spent a special time with a farmer and his family who had a small farm at the base of the tell, cuddling their young lambs and exploring some early tombs that surrounded the ruins of the city.

Ephesus is one of the best-preserved cities of the ancient world. The site is so well preserved that it leaves little to the imagination of what the city was like in the first century, including the agora, the street of Curetes, the terrace houses running up the slope above the street, the odeum, the temples, the baths, the gymnasiums, and of course the Great Theatre that stands out prominently; it looks much like it did when Paul lived there.

We walked down the marble-paved Arcadian Way, linking the theatre to the harbour. In the first century, the harbour was a very busy commercial port. Over the centuries, it has silted in and disappeared. It felt like we were walking along the streets with the apostles Paul and John, reviving life as it was in the New Testament period.

Something I found amusing was the public toilets. Each person did their business on one of the thirty-six holes lined along three stone benches with no dividers. It was a communal time. I envisioned the apostle Paul sitting on the loo and witnessing about Jesus to the person sitting beside or across from him. The New Testament says nothing about that!

There was no toilet paper at the time, but a trough of water flowed in front of one's feet. When the occupant was finished their business, a sponge on a stick was dampened in the trough and used to clean one's nether regions. The sponge was then rinsed off in the trough to be ready for the next person to use. Enough said!

We travelled eastward through the rugged Taurus Mountains past the city of Tarsus where Paul grew up. We crossed the great Euphrates River and stopped to take pictures.

As we were standing by the river's edge, a large group of men and women in black gowns stepped off a bus and walked down toward the river. When they saw us, they unexpectedly grew agitated, talking excitedly and pointing. Some even pushed and shoved their way back toward the bus. We felt uneasy but had no idea exactly what was happening.

Suddenly a man ran toward us, beckoning for us to follow him. We thought it best to obey as we were somewhat bewildered. He ushered us into his home and explained the situation. Those people were Iranians travelling the popular route through Turkey from Iran to Syria. When they'd seen us, they thought we were Americans and their first reaction was to feel alarmed and anxious. Our host had been watching the situation play out. Unsure of what might transpire, he had decided to harbour us in his home.

While under his roof, he cared for us and fed us. We experienced old biblical hospitality. I recalled the story in the Bible of the angels who came to Sodom and Gomorrah to rescue Lot from the coming judgment. They were assaulted by the Sodomites, but when Lot saw what was happening he quickly ushered them into his house to find safety under his roof.

That wasn't the only time we experienced biblical hospitality. Many times we were welcomed into homes and offered food, given water to drink, or invited to chat.

One day, a man welcomed us into his simple one-room stone and mortar dwelling. We were seated in two small circles, the men in the front circle and the ladies behind. He proudly served us hot unsweetened black tea in small tulip-shaped glasses, as was the custom. Men first, ladies second. The girls weren't impressed.

Another time, an elderly woman beckoned to us to come into her small cave home. Just inside the door, there was a bowl with water for washing our feet from the dust of the road. The inside of the cave was white-washed and simple, containing only a bed, a chair, and a tiny table with a candle on it. She asked us to sit on her bed and offered us the only food she had: corn on the cob. It was probably the toughest corn we had ever eaten. It would have been an insult to excuse ourselves from eating it, so we happily and gratefully ate our cobs clean. She had shared with us the best that she had.

As we travelled the countryside, many encounters evoked images from right out of the Bible. Women in their colourful dresses threshed wheat on a small mound where the breeze was blowing. They flailed the stalks of wheat with a stick on a blanketed dirt threshing floor until the grain separated from the stalks. Everything was then winnowed by taking the ends of the blanket and flinging the grain and broken stalks into the air. The straw and chaff were caught by the wind and carried away while the heavier grain dropped back into the blanket. They repeated the action until only the grain remained.

Our travels frequently kindled in us the image of the biblical shepherd. One morning, we got up close to the largest flock of sheep and goats I had ever seen. I estimated the size of the flock to be several thousand animals spread out in a procession about half a kilometre long. A single shepherd led them along a dusty path across a hot arid field.

I wanted to get up close to the shepherd, so we drove out into the field. I got out of the vehicle, pointed to my camera, and asked permission to take a picture. The shepherd nodded. The entire flock plodded along step by step, heads down, eerily silent. All I could hear was the muffled sound of thousands of hooves treading on the beaten surface. As I stood taking pictures, before I knew it I was surrounded by the massive flock; the animals paid little attention to me except to walk around me.

Throughout this encounter, several monstrous Kangal Shepherd dogs kept their eyes on me and I kept my eyes on them. Their job was to guard the sheep alongside the shepherd. They are also known for having the strongest bite of any dog in the world. A little unsettling!

Some of the sheep began to fan out around me, venturing a little too far. As the shepherd walked ahead, however, he led with only his voice and the graceful, mellow notes of his flute. In the words of Jesus, the sheep heard his voice and drew back in and followed him. This was an experience never to be forgotten.

About eighty kilometres east of the Euphrates, we arrived at the city of Sanliurfa, a devout Islamic centre. In the heart of the old city was a fish pool filled with "sacred" carp that tradition associates with the patriarch Abraham. In the same location was a large mosque enclosing a cave that housed a sacred spring. I spent a day sitting outside the mosque, captivated by the many people coming and going. Some approached me to chat, knowing that I was Western and wanting to practice their English. I actually had an opportunity to share my faith in Jesus with one interested person who wanted to know more about Canada and then inquired about Christianity.

Further south, we came to the ancient site of Haran, a major centre in Abraham's day. It's located on the Haran Plain, just north of the Syrian border. The region is watered by a major tributary of the Euphrates. The dwellings were an interesting feature, called kumbet houses, constructed of mud with beehive-shaped roofs. Kumbet houses date back thousands of years in northern Mesopotamia and are quite possibly the kind of house that Abraham occupied while living in Haran. The conical shape and clay material are suited for the climate, keeping the house cool in the hot summer and warm in the winter.

I had wanted to see Haran more than anything because it was associated so strongly with the lives of the patriarchs. Abraham lived here for a period of time before moving on to Canaan. Rebecca, Isaac's wife, lived in Haran as well.

It was at the well in Haran that Abraham's servant discovered Rebecca. The inhabitants of Haran told me that there was only one well in the whole area and it had been used to draw water for thousands of years. As I stood by the well that day, I was overwhelmed at the likelihood that I could be standing at the same well where Rebecca had come to draw water four thousand years earlier—and the women were still coming to the well to draw water.

Haran was also where Jacob spent a couple of decades in exile, married his wives Leah and Rachel, and raised a large family.

Our excursion into Turkey left me with an intense desire to return with tours of eager and interested people to investigate the many biblical sites, especially those related to the New Testament. It was ground zero for walking in the steps of the first-century missionaries, trekking the regions into which the earliest Christians had journeyed, exploring the remains of cities and towns where the early church grew and flourished, and understanding the suffering endured by Jesus-followers during the years of persecution that followed.

Sixty-One

I TRIED TO accomplish two things on my tours.

First, I wanted each member to grow in knowledge of the scriptures. I wanted them to understand the contextual setting for a scriptural passage so they could grasp what the original listeners heard. The originally intended message is often clarified when someone studies the historical, social, cultural, topographical, religious, political and archaeological setting and conditions at ground zero. Even one of these contextual components can shed light on the meaning of the text.

Second, I wanted them to place themselves into the story and feel it.

Let me be clear: one does not need to go to a biblical site to understand the scriptures or deepen one's faith. Many people never travel to any biblical land and yet have a sound knowledge of the Bible and strong, secure faith. But there is something immensely meaningful and memorable about standing where an event occurred, or where certain words were spoken, and simultaneously opening one's Bible to read about it. Something profound that I cannot explain happens at ground zero.

We walked to the spot just outside Hierapolis where the apostle Philip was martyred either by crucifixion or by being hanged upside-down. It gave new meaning to the words of Jesus to take up one's cross and follow him.

We sat on the foundation stones of the first-century synagogue in Antioch Pisidea, where Paul and Barnabas taught, and talked about the story in Acts 13:13–52.

At Miletus, I led my group down to the marble steps surrounding the first-century harbour where the apostle Paul made his emotional appeal to the elders from the church at Ephesus and said a tearful goodbye to them. We opened our Bibles to Acts 20 and the Holy Spirit opened the scriptures to us.

At Priene and the great Temple of Athena, we stood among the scattered stones and fallen columns as I spoke about how the temple had been constructed stone by stone. I opened my Bible to 1 Peter 2:5 where Peter used the same imagery for the spiritual temple that God is building out of living stones: *"And you are living stones that God is building into his spiritual temple."*

Didyma, just south of Miletus, was home to the largest temple in the ancient world, the Temple and Oracle of Apollo. People would travel from faraway places to this temple to ask Apollo for direction, counsel, or insight about their future. Requests were written down and handed to a priest. Petitioners then waited for an answer, sometimes for weeks. The answer would come from a priestess suspended directly above a sacred underground spring in a state of stupor, high on the gases that escaped from the spring below. The answer was written down and returned to the person in waiting.

I reminded my listeners that we can go directly to God, through Christ, to make our needs and requests known. Hebrews 4:16 says, *"So let us come boldly to the throne of our gracious God. There we will receive his mercy, and we will find grace to help us when we need it most"* (Hebrews 4:16).

This was the world of the New Testament. When people experienced these places in the light of the scriptures, their minds were enlightened and the impression was profound.

Our tour group ascended the imposing heights of the mesa upon which sat the acropolis of Pergamum, the most northerly city of the seven churches in Revelation. Everyone was stunned at the impressive sight. Pergamum was no longer just a name or word to them.

The city was home to a large library, second only to that in Alexandria, that housed more than two hundred thousand volumes. It was here that parchment was invented.

At the base of the city was a large complex and healing centre where the god of healing, Asclepius, who always carried a staff with a snake twisted around it, was worshipped. Pagan temples dominated the acropolis and it was also a key centre for the worship of Caesar.

Jesus identified Pergamum as the place where Satan lived and had his throne. Early Christians also lived and gathered there as a church, but it wasn't an easy place to be a Jesus-follower. It would have been easy to compromise one's faith.

We opened our Bibles to Revelation and read the passage where Jesus rebuked the church for tolerating those who were Balaamites and Nicolaitans (Revelation 2:14–15). These people followed a teaching of compromise with the world. There were others, however, who remained loyal to Jesus in the face of persecution and resisted the temptation to compromise with the cultural and social norms and pressures around them. Antipas was one of them and paid with his life.

We sat among the white marble ruins of the Temple of Trajan and on the huge steps of the square-shaped terrace that led up to the great altar of Zeus. We read Jesus's words:

> I know that you live in the city where Satan has his throne, yet you have remained loyal to me. You refused to deny me even when Antipas, my faithful witness, was martyred among you there in Satan's city. (Revelation 2:13)

We entered at the top of the steepest theatre in the Greek and Roman world, perched on the dizzying edge of the acropolis. When each person looked down over the benches that once sat ten thousand people, the sheer vertical slope gave each of us a queasy sensation in the stomach. We wondered whether this was where Antipas was dragged before the people and condemned as a Jesus-follower. Was he then thrown over the edge of the cliff or had something else happened?

All these sites enriched our understanding of how the early Christians lived, the challenges they faced, the persecution they endured, how they understood and applied the scriptures, and how they became a countercultural movement in their day. My prayer and desire was that the experience would challenge my hearers to follow Christ as those early believers did and impact our culture for him.

The Laodicean church was another of the seven churches addressed in the book of Revelation, and it's a good example of how understanding the contextual setting helps to clarify the original meaning of the text. Laodicea was a city of wealthy aristocrats, a centre for commerce and banking situated on the major trade route to Ephesus and other cities on the coast. There are ongoing extensive archaeological excavations occurring here.

Jesus said to this church, *"You say, 'I am rich. I have everything I want. I don't need a thing!' And you don't realize that you are wretched and miserable and poor and blind and naked"* (Revelation 3:17).

The letter from the apostle John to the Laodicean church was written during the reign of the Roman emperor Domitian. Domitian was the first emperor to call himself a god while still alive. Up to this time, emperors had been deified after their deaths. Not so with this madman. And Domitian enforced submission to the imperial cult of Caesar worship. If his citizens didn't cooperate, they could lose their wealth, status, trade associations, patronage benefits, or even lives. In this pressure-cooker environment, there were wealthy Christians in Laodicea who compromised their faith in order to retain possession of their earthly riches and securities. In doing so, however, they became spiritually wretched and poor.

Our group sat on the ancient benches along the top of the theatre, taking in the breathtaking view across the valley toward Hierapolis. We could clearly see the mineral hot springs of Hierapolis with their white calcium deposits glistening in the sun. I read the words of Jesus to his church:

> I know all the things you do, that you are neither hot nor cold. I wish that you were one or the other! But since you are like lukewarm water, neither hot nor cold, I will spit you out of my mouth! (Revelation 3:15–16)

The letters to the seven churches are rich with local allusions that the recipients would have recognized. Was the mention of lukewarm water one of them? Hierapolis had a good water supply. Laodicea did not.

Interestingly, archaeology has uncovered an ingenious aqueduct system. The Laodiceans had constructed an inverted siphon system that drew water uphill into the city from a hot spring about eight kilometres away. Some historians believe that hot water was also drawn from the hot springs of Hierapolis, ten kilometres away. By the time it reached Laodicea, however, it was tepid. Cold water came from springs to the south and even from as far away as Colosse, seventeen kilometres distant. It was also tepid by the time it arrived in Laodicea.

The Laodicean church knew all about lukewarm water and most probably quickly identified the allusion. Jesus rebuked this Christian community for their apathetic and dispassionate lukewarmness toward him, generated by an attitude of compromise and self-sufficiency that resulted from their wealth. Wealth will do that. They believed they were rich and needed nothing, not even God. They hadn't denied Christ, but their enthusiasm for him had become tepid, neither hot nor cold. In words that signify disgust, Jesus said, *"I will spit you out of my mouth!"*

My second goal for my followers on tour involved giving them more than an objective experience. I wanted it to be rich, subjective, and personal. Good storytellers do more than read words or entertain with an interesting plot; they draw listeners and readers into the story. They feel the story. They become engaged in the story.

Return to Israel with me for a moment and visit Beit She'an, one of the ten cities of the Decapolis. It is the best preserved Hellenistic city from the Roman era in Israel. When you walk down the columnated Palladius Street, you are quickly transferred back to an earlier time. The tracks of chariot wheels are worn into the stone pavement. Immediately in front of you is the high tell of the ancient city where the Philistines fastened King Saul's body after his death and defeat at Mount Gilboa.

But the place that caught my attention was the amphitheatre just outside the main site. There were none of the crowds there that visited the Beit She'an site. In fact, usually no one was there. In the Roman era, it seated more than ten thousand people who gathered to watch gladiatorial combats and wild animals fight. Most sobering, it was a place where early Christians were slaughtered for their loyalty to Jesus and their refusal to deny him.

The lower section of the stands where the spectators sat remains. Around the perimeter of the arena are rooms where the hungry wild animals were caged and released to tear their victims to pieces. The crowd roared in a frenzy when the beasts were set loose upon the Jesus-followers hovering together in the centre of the floor. The sight that followed was gruesome and bloody.

My concern was how to make this more than a place to learn a history lesson, take some pictures, and get back on the bus and head off to the next site. I wanted my audience to enter the story—to enter the lives of those early believers trapped in such a hostile societal and political environment. How had they felt while waiting to endure such a bloody end to this earthly existence? How would my followers feel in the same situation? What would they do?

So I had my group stand in the centre of the same arena floor, in the same spot where those early Jesus-followers had stood. I played the part of a Roman soldier and wrapped an imaginary rope around them. I instructed them to squeeze together and informed them about what was behind the doors in the rooms surrounding them. When the doors were opened, wild dogs, tigers, and lions would rush upon them and tear them limb from limb. The animals would drag them around the arena floor in their teeth, then eat them and their children alive. I appealed to the imaginary children, telling them that their parents were choosing a horrible death for them, and to beg their parents not to do so if they loved them. I played on their emotions, urging them to recant their faith and deny this Jesus, to save their lives and the lives of their children.

Before long, I could actually see dread in the eyes of my captives. They were visualizing themselves in the arena. They had stepped back into the lives of those early believers at ground zero. They had become participants. They were living the story, internalizing the experience. Some wept. Some showed strong determination to stand their ground and face death bravely. Others held tightly to the person next to them. Some looked heavenward and prayed. A few even stepped out of the group and walked head down across the arena floor to the exit, choosing life over death, their fear becoming stronger than faith.

The event was real.

When we finished, we sat in a shady spot on the arena floor and read from Hebrews:

> Think back on those early days when you first learned about Christ. Remember how you remained faithful even though it meant terrible suffering. Sometimes you were exposed to public ridicule and were beaten... You suffered along with those who were thrown into jail, and when all you owned was taken from you, you accepted it with joy. You knew there were better things waiting for you that will last forever... Patient endurance is what you need now... (Hebrews 10:32–34, 36)

We continued reading:

> But others were tortured, refusing to turn from God in order to be set free. They placed their hope in a better life after the resurrection. Some were jeered at, and their backs were cut open with whips. Others were chained in prisons. Some died by stoning, some were sawed in half, and others were killed with the sword. (Hebrews 11:35–37)

I could tell that my listeners grasped it!
Hebrews 11 goes on the say:

> Some went about wearing skins of sheep and goats, destitute and oppressed and mistreated. They were too good for this world, wandering over deserts and mountains, hiding in caves and holes in the ground. (Hebrews 11:37–38)

The reality of hiding in caves and holes in the ground is nowhere more actualized than at Kaymakli in Turkey. I touched on this compelling place in the previous chapter. It's one of many subterranean cities dug out of the soft rock, eight levels and eighty-five metres deep. A tangled network of passages connects numerous dwellings, food storage rooms, cattle stables, schools, churches, and kitchens. The city was totally self-contained with complex water and air ventilation systems. Early Christians fled to this city to hide from their persecutors. Thousands fled here for refuge from the Islamic Arabs during the Byzantine era in the seventh century AD. They endured months, even years, living in underground darkness.

Our group navigated the narrow, claustrophobic, musty tunnels, venturing up and down steep stairs, often on our hands and knees or stooped over in single file. The passage would suddenly open up into a large chamber or small room. The walls were black with soot from centuries of torch-lighting. Without exception, this excursion into the shadowy underground gave everyone a powerful sense of what many of our Christian brothers and sisters endured for faithfully following Jesus.

We surfaced from the depths to snake our way up a path that led to an ancient church carved out of the rock high up on a rockface. Upon entering the space, we immediately felt awe and reverence. The walls still revealed the colours of paintings relating stories from the life of Jesus.

Our group sat silently and contemplatively on the stone benches with our backs against the walls. Someone began to sing and others joined in. We prayed, read a few Bible passages, and reflected on them. We read quotes from early Christian martyrs. We imagined what it must have been like fifteen centuries earlier to be worshipping in this very spot.

But it was more than reflection; it was as though those voices from the past echoed from the walls and united with our voices as one in worship. We absorbed that surreal moment and cherished it.

Ephesus is a popular destination. Busloads of tourists arrive there from off the cruise ships at Kusadasi on the coast. But I truly wanted Ephesus to be more than a tourist attraction. It's an amazing place to visit, but most importantly for the Christian it's where the apostle Paul planted a church, one pastored by men like Timothy and the apostle John. It has an epistle bearing its name.

What was it like being a follower of the Way, as the early Christians were called? When you read the story in Acts 19, you become aware that persecution was a reality for the Jesus-followers in Ephesus.

That persecution became extreme under the rule of Domitian from 81–96 AD. The great Temple of Domitian stood on a high point of the city and could be seen from nearly everywhere in Ephesus. It was dedicated in 89–90 AD. The temple itself rested on a large second-floor platform supported by huge columns more than thirty-five feet high. On the same platform was a twenty-seven-foot statue of Domitian with his fist raised in defiance. Some of the massive supporting columns still stand today. Each column had the representation of a deity carved into it, symbolizing that Domitian was supported by all the other gods. He himself was lord of lords, god of gods, and king of kings.

The Temple of Domitian was a stark reminder of the reality of two opposing kingdoms. At the time, the one ruled and controlled the world with power and might; the other was a small fledgling group of people who taught and practised humility and compassion. One kingdom was ruled by Domitian, who carried the title of Caesar. The other was ruled by Jesus, who bore the title of Christ. Caesar was called the Saviour of the world and the one who brought peace. Jesus was also called the Saviour of the world, and the Prince of Peace. Caesar demanded submission to him as king. Jesus required the same submission.

But one cannot submit to two kings. This placed the early followers of Jesus in a dire predicament. They found themselves in the crosshairs of the emperor.

Ephesus became a leading centre for the imperial cult of emperor worship and Domitian persecuted the followers of the Way brutally. While the worship of Domitian flourished, the apostle John, the beloved disciple of Jesus, evangelized, preached, pastored, wrote his three epistles and his gospel, and opposed any acknowledgement of Caesar as Lord. He must have ministered with significant consequence, since Domitian ordered John exiled to the Island of Patmos.

I led my group to a square on the north side of the temple ruins where an altar once stood. All citizens assembled there annually and were ordered to sprinkle a pinch of incense upon the altar, thus declaring that Caesar was lord. I asked my audience how each one of them would have responded if they had been standing in the shadow of this great temple in the year 89 AD and ordered to declare Domitian to be lord and god. Would they submit to Caesar or remain loyal to Christ? Each person's face took on a sombre countenance as they contemplated the grim reality of the cost of following Jesus.

We then read the words of Jesus to the Ephesian church sent from John while exiled on Patmos: *"You have patiently suffered for me without quitting... You hate the evil deeds of the Nicolaitans..."* (Revelation 2:3, 6) The Nicolaitans were believers who compromised their faith and justified their behaviour. Most believers, however, didn't follow their example of compromise but remained loyal to Christ. It wasn't a perfect church, but it was a church that patiently persevered through suffering and refused to quit.

Some experiences came unexpectedly. Early one morning, we got on a boat to sail to the Greek island of Patmos where the apostle John was exiled and given the Revelation. About a hundred people sat on the boat clasping their coffees, some chatting with excitement while others were still waking up. The sun hadn't risen yet and the Aegean Sea was peaceful and calm.

That was about to change dramatically.

An hour into our journey, as dawn broke, a wind began to rise and increased in velocity by the minute. As the wind intensified, the Aegean became rougher and rougher. Soon the angry sea was heaving our craft up and down, thrusting us into the next surging wave. Each wave lashed against the boat and sent a frothy spray across the upper deck.

Angst filled everyone's minds as we sat holding tightly onto our seats. By this time most of the coffee was on the deck. I staggered across to the wheelhouse to obtain some degree of assurance from the pilot. My concern was only heightened when I saw he was anxiously struggling to navigate the vessel. That certainly didn't help!

Later, when we discussed the ordeal, more than a few shared the same thought: the unwelcome wind and waves had caused them to identify with what the apostle Paul endured on his voyage to Rome in these same waters. The Book of Acts says that the weather changed abruptly and a wind of great strength caught the ship. Paul's experience ended in shipwreck. Thankfully, ours didn't!

One of my personal highlights was to visit the ruins of Aphrodisias, about one hundred kilometres inland from the Aegean coast, particularly the ancient hippodrome. This hippodrome was built in the first century AD and is the best preserved of all ancient stadiums in the Mediterranean region. It is 262 metres long and seated thirty thousand people. It was designed for athletic contests such as chariot races, riding, boxing, the pentathlon (discus, javelin throw, jumping, wrestling, and running), and the brutal pankration. The stadium is virtually untouched and its visitors require little imagination to hear the roar of the spectators, the pounding of the horses' hoofs pulling the chariots, or the sound of the runners' bare feet beating the track.

As my group sat on the benches of the first-century hippodrome, I challenged them from Hebrews 12:1–3: *"And let us run with endurance the race God has set before us. We do this by keeping our eyes on Jesus... Think of all the hostility he endured... then you won't become weary and give up."*

And I challenged them with these words: "As you live your life and run your race for God, keep your eyes focused on Jesus. He ran his race for you; now you run your race for him. He didn't quit on you; don't you quit on him. He endured for you; now you endure for him. He gave his life for you; now you give your life for him."

I then presented the opportunity for anyone who wanted to run to the far end of the hippodrome and back in the footsteps of the ancient runners. Many did so, and as they ran I stood in the stands calling out to them, "Run! Run! Run!" I didn't want them to ever forget the lesson of running the race of life for Jesus.

Those days were rewarding and a sheer delight. I couldn't have imagined any of it when I was younger. I was always so humbled and grateful for the opportunity God provided for me to experience such places and things—and more so, to lead and teach and share with many others the same experiences, either personally or vicariously.

Sixty-Two

MISSIONS WAS A primary focus at the Campus Church. By missions, I mean living out and sharing the good news of Jesus's love and salvation wherever you are. In addition to local outreach efforts, we supported local missionaries who served the marginalized, missionaries who served in Canada's indigenous communities, and missionaries who served abroad in many other parts of the world. We kept their names and pictures in front of the church and prayed for them regularly. We gave people, especially our youth, many opportunities to experience missions firsthand and serve in cross-cultural ministry. Twice a year we had special missions-emphasis weekends. I continually taught and challenged our people to go into all the world with the good news. And many did.

I didn't want our people to think that missions was something somebody else did somewhere else. I wanted them to understand that missions was a personal responsibility. That's why the sign reading "You are now entering the mission field" always hung above the exit. Missions began just outside the door of the church building—in one's home with one's family, in the community with colleagues, friends, and acquaintances. We are to be light in the darkness, hope to the hopeless, a friend to the lonely, a good Samaritan to the hurt and wounded, and the hands, feet, voice, and heart of Jesus.

Our daughter Sarah once spent seven weeks in Zambia with an organization called Faith's Orphans Fund. Faith was a Zambian nurse who cared for approximately 4,500 orphans. She carried a heavy load of responsibility.

The organization was set up to allow orphaned children to remain within the familiarity of their own villages. Children were provided with clothing, blankets, and health supplies. School fees were also paid so they could receive an education.

Faith established a skills training centre in the city of Kitwe for older children to receive life skills training in areas such as agriculture, health, and nutrition. It was a mammoth endeavour. The purpose was to help break the cycle of poverty and give vulnerable children a fighting chance to obtain a meaningful future.

When I familiarized myself with the ministry, I was impressed with its focus on Jesus and the good news, not to mention the countless practical ways it displayed the love of God in a broken world.

When Sarah returned home from the mission, her heart was full—and her passion for this particular mission quickly spread to others in the Campus Church. Soon the church was supporting Faith financially and prayerfully. Faith visited us on several occasions and we sent missions teams to Zambia regularly to serve with her there. Some of our people took a very personal interest in what Faith was doing and often travelled to Zambia for longer periods of time. It was truly hands-on participation.

One day I received an invitation to go to Zambia as the guest speaker for the twenty-fifth anniversary of Faith's Orphans Fund. It was a wonderful privilege to be invited and I was eager to go.

After the long flight to Zambia, we drove into Kitwe, the location of FOF's main office and homebase. A lot of activities had been planned by my hosts and it was the beginning of a very busy but rewarding week.

As the week progressed I personally witnessed the many amazing ministries being done. I visited schools where many of the orphans were receiving an education. I saw the Kitwe Skills Training Centre, banana plantations, chicken barns, vegetable gardens, the dorms where the students lived, and the chapel where worship services were held daily and classes conducted for Bible teaching. I also quickly discovered that I needed to be ready to speak if called upon at any given moment.

Everyone broke out spontaneously into singing and dancing with every activity—in times of prayer and worship, on their way to chapel, on their way back from chapel, strolling to lunch, raking in the garden, or even walking to school. They sang to an up-tempo rhythm with a syncopated beat that was difficult to emulate. Often there was a call-and-response pattern where one person sang a line of music and the others responded in something akin to a musical conversation. It was unrehearsed but rich in harmony. And as they sang, they all swayed in unison.

On several days, thirty or more of us crammed into a bus with seating capacity for twenty. Boxes of medical supplies and clothing were also loaded into the bus. We bumped along the dusty roadways with no sense of traffic rules. Usually the surfaces were so bad, the ruts and potholes so deep, that we drove on the sides of the road or in ditches. Dust filled the bus as well as the heat.

Of course, everyone sang.

It became evident to me as we drove that large multinational corporations owned and controlled the copper-mining industry and that the Zambian people benefitted little from the raping of their land. They lived in dire poverty. Most rural villagers lived in mud huts. They dressed scantily with no shoes for their feet. They ate one meagre meal each day that was cooked slowly in a pot over a small outdoor woodfire. Most villages had no source of clean water.

And yet they always found a reason to sing.

I felt a growing admiration for FOF when I learned about the wells it had dug for many of these villages to provide clean water, as well as the trees it had provided for villagers to plant and replenish the vegetation around their homes.

We drove down narrow, dusty dirt trails into the jungle to visit some of the villages under the care of FOF. As we came into a small clearing with circles of mud huts, I encountered children already lined up awaiting our arrival. They welcomed us with big white sparkling eyes and wide smiles, singing and clapping. The harmony was beautiful.

When I stepped out of the bus, a cacophony of sound reverberated all around. Birds shrieked and squawked. Monkeys screeched and howled. The jungle was alive and asserting its presence.

After a ceremony of singing and dancing, performed for us by the children and women, we told them that we had gifts for them. They lined up in an orderly way, with no shoving or pushing. We handed out toothbrushes, shoes, and clothing, and each child took what was given with visible gratitude. Medical attention and medicine were administered to anyone who needed it. They were anxious to show us the gardens they had cultivated and proudly led us down a worn path into a space they had cleared out of the jungle. Rows of cabbage, spinach, carrots, and beans flourished. We were greeted with an amazing display of hospitality in every village we visited.

On the day of the twenty-fifth anniversary celebrations, dignitaries arrived early. A large tent had been set up. The mood was happy and festive and the music played loudly.

As if on cue, everyone began to form a line and dance their way into the large tent to assemble for the ceremony. There was an interesting balance of protocol and formality with informality. The dignitaries were seated and treated with great esteem while everyone was welcomed, including the children who ran everywhere. There was lots of music, rhythm, singing, clapping, and swaying.

The tent was packed. Flowers and deserving words of tribute and appreciation were showered upon Faith and others who helped carry the responsibility for the ministry. The impact of FOF was noted by various dignitaries who got up to speak. Faith attributed the success to God and thanked him for the difference he had made in so many young lives.

When I was introduced to speak, I got up with a great sense of humility. I felt very unworthy to be in this privileged position. I'd had such a small part. I told the people exactly that. Speaking through an interpreter, I shared from the scriptures what can be accomplished when the faithfulness of God is aligned with the faithfulness of his servants. I commended Faith and all who worked alongside her for their vision and persevering service over twenty-five years—for making such a difference in so many young lives. I paid tribute to their faithfulness, courage, and passion to reach into their fragmented world with the love, compassion, and selflessness of Jesus who came to bring good news to the poor, to comfort the broken-hearted, and to free those oppressed and imprisoned in the brokenness and injustice of this world's system. I shared what God had given me to say.

Everyone listened intently, periodically breaking out with "Amens" and clapping. At one point, a man got up and began dancing and praising his way around the room. No one seemed to give him any attention; it was just a normal Zambian response to what was being said from the platform. So I kept going as though I noticed nothing.

After the service, we gathered for a feast. And what a feast it was! All sorts of traditional food was piled high. There was nshima and maize, fish, chicken, sweet potatoes, corn, scones, fruit, and much more that I could not recognize. I had no idea what I was eating, but I felt an overwhelming sense of blessing that the Campus Church had had even a small part in such a vital ministry for changing lives and impacting the world for God and good. I was extremely grateful to have been there to participate—and I returned home with a full heart.

Sixty-Three

AS OUR AIRCRAFT flew over Sudan on our way to Ethiopia, I looked over at my friend Daniel, who had clasped his hands and was shaking. His lips moved as though praying. I asked him whether he was okay and he replied that when flying over Sudan he always shook with the dark memory of what he had endured there. So he took that time to pray for his nation and the many suffering Sudanese Christians.

Daniel was born and raised in Sudan. His Sudanese name was Alla Eldin Omer Agbma. He had been a devout Muslim and, in fact, had fought as a devoted jihadi soldier against the enemies of Islam. He had believed strongly in that cause—that is, until one night he had a dream. In his dream, he saw an image of Jesus and an inscription appear before him: "John 3:16." He had no idea what it meant, but for some reason he was greatly disturbed by it.

He began a search for the meaning, a search that led him to discover a verse in the New Testament Bible: *"For this is how God loved the world: He gave his one and only Son, so that everyone who believes in him will not perish but have eternal life."* The words struck a chord that resonated nonstop in his heart. In fact, the words were so impressed upon his heart and mind that he couldn't escape them.

This was the beginning of Daniel coming to a deep and profound faith in Christ. After his conversion, he gave himself the Christian name Daniel.

This was also the beginning of a long and difficult journey of persecution. He was disowned and disinherited by his father, shunned and ostracized by his family and community. He was imprisoned and subjected to beatings and torture. The cost of becoming a Jesus-follower was high and came with a lot of personal loss.

He finally fled his home country and reached Amman, Jordan, where he was again incarcerated for several months. We figured out the timing of his imprisonment and I was struck to realize that I had walked past his prison while visiting downtown Amman several years earlier—while he was being held there.

When Daniel was finally released, he made his way to Canada. He was welcomed into a Christian home, the home of Diane's aunt and uncle, and adopted as a son. This is how I was introduced to Daniel and became aware of his story.

Over the next couple of years, he attended a Bible seminary in Toronto and soon married and began a family of his own. But he couldn't shake the burden for his home country of Sudan. God used this burden to stir him to begin a ministry of support, teaching, and encouragement to the Sudanese church and its leaders.

Our two stories tangibly intersected when the Campus Church began to support Daniel and the work he was doing. I got to know him well and one day offered to help him in whatever way he could best use it. He invited me to accompany him on his next trip abroad.

Hence I found myself flying with Daniel that day over Sudan on our way to Addis Ababa, Ethiopia. The plan was to spend five full days with eight Sudanese pastors. The trip and its purpose had to remain closely guarded because of the vulnerable nature of the situation and the risk that these pastors faced upon their return to Sudan. Adding to the many challenges already existing there, a brutal conflict had been raging in Sudan for many years. Persecution was rampant against Christians and Christian pastors in the Darfur region particularly, many falling victim to displacement, violence, and humanitarian atrocities.

We arrived ten hours before the arrival of our guests and found our way to the place where we planned to spend the week. It was in such dismal shape, however, that we decided not to subject our friends to it. We decided to change the venue. Daniel made some phone calls and found another location at a hotel about fifteen minutes away.

We jumped into a cab and off we went. Garbage blew about everywhere. Poverty was widespread. The roads were broken asphalt and most buildings were in a state of disrepair.

Our short ride to the hotel was an event to be remembered. Our cab driver seemed knowledgeable of the perils of the road as he manoeuvred his way around the minefield of potholes. The absence of any suspension in the small car gave us no cushion. We felt the jolt of every bump.

Even the poor vehicle bore scars from years of abuse. The taillights hung by their wires and something was dragging and sparking underneath. Our cabby had to peer through a maze of cracks in the front windshield. The floor was filled with rusted holes allowing me to look down at the road passing beneath my feet. The smell of exhaust was strong. I sat in the front passenger seat, my door held together by duct tape. In fact, the entire vehicle was held together by duct tape. Everything rattled.

But it got us to our new abode.

We pulled up to a small hotel, the name of which I cannot repeat because of the clandestine nature of our purpose. I had a room on the top floor. The window on one side of the room looked out over a congested street with small shops and boutiques; the other looked upon a mammoth slum of shacks with tin roofs held down by stones to keep them from flying off in the wind.

My heart felt heavy for the many people living in these cramped conditions. Jesus loved each one of them. Was there someone telling them that good news and showing them his love? Even in this woeful squalor, from my perch in the sky I heard the children laughing and watched them running and playing in the alleys, kicking soccer balls and skipping. Women swept in front of their doorways. Young girls carried pails of water.

While in flight a few hours earlier, we had been sitting among a group of Somalian basketball players. They were from the Greater Toronto Area (GTA), but all were originally from Somalia, and were returning to their homeland to play in a tournament.

I wanted to learn more about them and Somalia. I knew that Somalia wasn't a safe country to visit due to civil unrest, terrorism, and kidnapping. It was hostile to the gospel and closed to the Christian faith.

We somehow got onto the subject of long-distance running. I told them that I had written a book called *Run! The Amazing Race*, about the most amazing race of all, the race of life. I even had an opportunity to share a little of my Christian faith with these young Muslim men.

At the end of the flight, we said goodbye and parted ways.

But when Daniel and I arrived at the hotel, I was shocked to walk into the lounge and meet, you guessed it, our new Somalian friends. Some might call it coincidence, but it's amazing how many coincidences occur when God is in something. What were the chances of meeting this same group of young men at the same hotel in a city with many hotels, and furthermore, a hotel where we hadn't originally planned to stay? And it turned out they were only resting at this hotel for a few hours before catching another flight.

These are the kinds of encounters I believe God sovereignly puts together for his purposes.

The coach gave me his address, and when I returned home I sent him enough copies of *Run!* for the entire basketball team.

Later that evening, our eight Sudanese pastors arrived. As we greeted them, I was impressed by their humble spirits.

That week I experienced one of the most profoundly moving weeks in my life. Every day for five days we gathered together in a room on the third floor. There, I had the opportunity and privilege to open up the scriptures and teach and share with these men of great persevering faith. They listened to every word with earnest attentiveness. They shared their stories of terrible mistreatment, harassment, and oppression. We prayed together. We encouraged one another. Their stories touched my heart at a deep level and opened my eyes to the kind of followers Jesus calls us to be.

These men were the epitome of those whom Jesus spoke about in the beatitudes, as part of his sermon on the mountain (Matthew 5–7): the poor in spirit, those who mourn, the humble, those who hunger and thirst for justice, the merciful, those whose hearts are pure, those who work for peace, and those who are persecuted for doing right. They were the salt of the earth, lights in the darkness. They were a contradiction to the world. They gave when others took from them, loved when others hated, and helped when others abused. These men were blessed by God because they were willing to give up everything for the sake of Christ. The kingdom of heaven is theirs. They blessed and humbled me. I received so much more from them than I gave.

We departed with tears, warm hugs, and a bond of brotherhood rarely felt. I gave each of them a copy of my book, *Hitting the Wall*, and a small bottle of Canadian maple syrup. I then returned to the safety and security of Canada and they returned to the uncertainty and peril of being a Jesus-follower in Sudan.

Only one year later, two of my Sudanese brothers, two of the kindest, humblest men I have ever known, were imprisoned. They spent one full year in prison under harsh, overcrowded conditions with a lack of food, water, healthcare, and sanitary facilities. They endured abuse and torture. Why? Because they wouldn't compromise their faith or love for Jesus.

> God blesses you when people mock you and persecute you and lie about you and say all sorts of evil things against you because you are my followers. Be happy about it! Be very glad! For a great reward awaits you in heaven. (Matthew 5:11–12)

Sixty-Four

SOON AFTER OUR return home from Ethiopia, Daniel and I began planning another leadership development conference, this time in Egypt. It was important to vary the location for these events for the sake of security. Egypt was an accessible destination for most people in North Africa and the Middle East.

The focus was on leadership development for Sudanese pastors and church leaders, but we wanted to expand and include church leaders from other parts of the Middle East and North Africa. We sent out private invitations and about fifty men and women responded. We were thrilled!

My responsibility was again to offer encouragement and provide daily Bible teaching. It was planned as a five-day conference or retreat, there and back, in and out.

We arrived in Cairo two days early, only because of travel logistics. I was happy because this gave us the opportunity to explore the city and its environs. My brother Roger had accompanied me, so the two of us maximized our time travelling to many places of interest.

I enjoyed walking along the edge of the Nile, since the famous river figured prominently in so many stories of the Bible. It felt like seeing the Euphrates for the first time. We visited the large souk in the heart of the bustling city. And of course we saw the Cairo Museum, which was within walking distance of where we were lodging.

It was overwhelming to see thousands of years of history on display. Hundreds of sarcophagi and statues and thousands of artifacts filled room after room. The burial chamber and gold mask of Tutankhamun stood out in their brilliance. There were rooms of mummies thousands of years old, many of them still with their teeth and hair.

We don't know the precise dates for the life of Moses in the Bible, but we can make an approximation.

It felt surreal to stand and stare into the face of the powerful Thutmose III (1479–1425 BC), possibly the Pharaoh Moses had stared down. Thutmose was predeceased by his oldest son, which fits the record of the tenth plague in the book of Exodus. What stood out to me were his long fingers.

Or did Moses rather face the great Ramases II (1279–1213 BC)? If so, his mummy showed a good amount of hair, strong chin, and aquiline nose. It gave an exceptional idea of the facial appearance of the living pharaoh.

Visiting the pyramids of Giza and enigmatic Sphinx was an amazing experience. I slid down a long slanting passageway into the burial chamber of a smaller tomb, all the while feeling like Indiana Jones.

Next to the three Giza pyramids was something that caught my attention. One of the oldest-known planked boats from antiquity, constructed around 2500 BC when the Great Pyramid was built. I found it particularly interesting because it dated back to before the time of Joseph in the Bible (Genesis 39–50).

We then travelled south of Cairo to Saqqara to visit Egypt's oldest pyramid, the Step Pyramid of Djoser, built in 2660 BC. No doubt, Joseph stood and looked at this very same tomb. So old! So mystifying! So intriguing!

After a long day, we returned to Cairo to have an early night. I needed to refocus on my reason for coming, and further prepare for my part in helping to host the conference.

Early the next morning, our small group departed in several vehicles, picking up people along the way, to a region called Wadi El Natrun about one hundred kilometres northwest of Cairo. Wadi El Natrun is a desolate desert depression below sea level. It was historically one of early Christianity's most sacred places. Being an isolated desert, it attracted many early desert fathers who established monastic communities. Between the fourth and seventh centuries AD, thousands of people came to this region and joined these monasteries. They believed the solitude and harshness of the desert would teach them to place less value on worldly things and to practice God's call to a simple, holy, virtuous life.

My brother and I wanted to visit one of the monasteries, so one afternoon we took a break from the conference and made a brief excursion to the oldest Coptic Orthodox monastery in the area, the Monastery of Saint Bishoy.

When we arrived, we were met by a fascinating monk who led us on a tour and shared a wealth of information—and he wouldn't take a penny for it. The monastery had been founded by Bishop Bishoy in the early fourth century AD, during the time of Constantine. His body was still interred there and is believed to be preserved and uncorrupted since his death hundreds of years ago.

Also located on the grounds is the Well of the Martyrs. Back in 444 AD, the Berbers, ethnic groups indigenous to North Africa, attacked and killed forty-nine elders at this well. It is said that they washed the blood from their swords in the water from the well before throwing the dead bodies into it. It is twelve meters deep and has continued to produce freshwater since the time of Bishop Bishoy.

After this wonderful digression, I was anxious to get back to the conference. The Spirit of God was moving in wonderful ways, and I was engrossed in mingling with people who followed Jesus in some of the most difficult places on earth to be a Christian. I sought out their stories, asked about their families, and listened to their testimonies of personal struggle and church life under times of persecution and war. Each day was tiring but energizing.

I greatly looked forward to my times of teaching. My audience sat and listened with intense interest, seemingly feeding off every word. They were hungry. They had an unquenchable thirst for knowing God's Word and made me want to keep going. They would have allowed me to keep going for as long as I wanted, for time seemed irrelevant.

Each day, time was given to pray for one another. During these times, they shared their stories of suffering, loss of employment, seizure of possessions and houses, intimidation, imprisonment, torture, and even death. But the message that came through was their commitment to endure to the end. They were determined to live for Jesus whatever the cost. I felt acutely challenged.

Near the end of our week, we had to contend with a disturbing turn of events. It shouldn't have happened. We had invited two reporters who worked for Christian publications to accompany us to Egypt. Their purpose was to report on the suffering and challenges of the church in North Africa and the Middle East from firsthand accounts, and to tell the story of what God was doing in the midst of it all. They had been clearly informed of the risk of sending online reports back to their publishers in North America and were prohibited from doing so. They'd been told to hold all information until the conference was over and they had returned home. They had agreed to this as a prerequisite for attending.

On the morning of the last full day of our conference, Daniel got up to speak. His voice trembled. He sounded both troubled and angry. When I understood the problem, I also understood the degree of responsibility he felt for the lives of all his guests.

During the previous night, a particular radical Islamic newspaper had apparently picked up the story of what we were doing and our location. They reported it. We were exposed. This put our Sudanese attendees at grave risk when they returned home. In fact, it put all of us at risk. There were known radical groups residing in the very region we were in. Our safety could no longer be guaranteed.

An acute feeling of agitation pervaded the room and we began to pray. We prayed for safety. We prayed for each other, especially our Sudanese brothers and sisters. We prayed that God would surround us with his protective shield and that his peace would fill every heart and mind. We prayed for a safe return to our homes and families. In that moment, I experienced in a small way the reality many of these believers lived with every day in their homeland.

A decision was then made by all to continue with our plans for our last day and push forward as intended.

The culpable party, one of the reporters, came to Daniel and confessed his negligence and irresponsibility. He had in fact sent a report back to Toronto the past evening, wanting to get the story out on the day we left. This was a clear breach of protocol and Daniel reprimanded him. He was genuinely remorseful and understood the uncertainty and endangerment he had created for everyone. He stood before the whole group and admitted his fault. He expressed deep regret for the risk he'd placed everyone under and asked forgiveness.

I was stunned at everyone's response. One by one, each person walked forward and embraced him. They stood around him and prayed for him and for the whole situation.

Someone then lifted their hand and spoke aloud, "We do not fear!" His words reflected the words of Romans 8 like soothing oil.

"If God is for us, who can ever be against us?" the man said. "For Jesus's sake, we live under the threat of death every day. We are being slaughtered like sheep. But despite all these things, overwhelming victory is ours through Christ, who loves us. Nothing can ever separate us from God's love." He then added the reassurance of Psalm 118:6: "The Lord is for us, so we will have no fear. What can mere people do to us?"

The rest responded in agreement as one voice: "Amen! Amen!"

We then left the desert valley of Wadi El Natrun to return to our families. I arrived home to a country that is sheltered, secure, and free, and for which I am truly grateful. I don't know how it went for the others. I never heard. But for that brief time, I felt a profound oneness and identification with them in their suffering—and a deep appreciation for the lives they lived.

Sixty-Five

THESE EXPERIENCES ABROAD are among the ministry highlights I will never forget and always miss. I was passionate about these opportunities and was so grateful for them. But they were over and above my regular pastoral duties, leadership responsibilities, and teaching role at the Campus Church. My priority remained steadfast to build an effective witness for Jesus in Aurora and the surrounding region. To achieve this, the Campus Church needed to be healthy.

And it was. Both sites were flourishing and embracing the blessings, activities, pursuits, demands, and challenges that accompany a thriving church.

At the Bathurst site, we were running out of space again. It seemed a good time to begin planning for a third campus. For some time, the Holy Spirit had been focusing our minds on a particular location about twenty minutes north of Aurora near the town of Bradford on the perimeter of a large wetland called the Holland Marsh. The GTA was stretching northward and the rate of population growth was exponential. Developers were drawing up plans for large residential housing projects and were breaking ground for thousands of new homes.

There were a few other churches established in the area, but we believed significant need existed for more. We investigated various venues for a place to meet every Sunday morning. Before long, a remarkable door opened. A Christian school in the area invited us to use their facility. It seemed perfect. At each step, we shared our ideas with the church. Everyone was enthusiastic. We prayed that God would continue to open doors to confirm his will.

With the prospect of operating three sites, we wanted to investigate the best system of government under which our church should operate. No organizational structure is perfect for operating a multisite church; any structure has its advantages and drawbacks. We researched and weighed the advantages and disadvantages of a centralized administrative framework versus each site having its own management autonomy, and we came to believe that the benefits of autonomy outweighed the benefits of centralization. Each site had its own unique personality, challenges, strengths, and opportunities. The community in which the site was situated was distinctive. Each individual site needed the ability to set its own goals and strategies.

With this organizational structure, it was critical for the leadership to reinforce a unified vision. As the lead pastor for the whole church, I met with the staff of all three sites every six weeks to coordinate, plan, pray, and ensure that we stayed on the same page. I met monthly with the site pastors. We drilled into our congregations the slogan, "One church in multiple locations." All the campuses embraced one mission—to love and serve God and people. They adhered to one doctrinal statement of beliefs. They came together for common projects, events, and activities.

Each campus site had control over its own finances, but we shared resources whenever necessary. When a new site was starting up, it was supported by the mothership, the Bathurst campus, financially and with essential staff until it was large and healthy enough to sustain itself.

I compared our model to the concept of a family. When children are young, they are dependent on their parents to care for them, provide for them, feed them, and clothe them. But as children grow and mature, they become less dependent and more independent. They begin making small choices for themselves. Then larger choices. In time, they acquire the resources to provide for themselves. They determine their own direction, setting their own goals and ambitions.

Children gradually move away from the security and familiarity of their parents to a state of autonomy. But despite this autonomy they still belong to the same family. They still share the same sense of identity, the same history, the same core values.

The Campus Church was like a family. It spread out like a family tree. The branches grew in different directions, each one autonomous, each one bearing its own fruit, but all the branches came from the same trunk and roots.

And with maturity, we would discover that our strength as a family was not in independence but in our unity and interdependence.

Our people caught the vision. They were enthusiastic about a third site. There were many logistics to be worked out, but we began to prepare and lay the groundwork. Our goal was to raise $100,000 for startup costs. Over the next several months, we raised $80,000 through two special freewill offerings. The momentum and generous giving was a positive confirmation that the church supported the new endeavour. People will give financially to something they support.

I prayed much about who would fill the critical position of site pastor, and the Holy Spirit kept impressing one name upon my mind: Keith.

Keith was our worship pastor. I knew he had the maturity and gifts to step into this significant position and move the church forward. He was a gifted musician and a strong, passionate, visionary leader. He was deeply dedicated to any task he took on and always followed through on what he agreed to do.

One day I called him into my office and presented the idea to him. He was very reluctant at first, but he promised that he and his wife Beth would pray earnestly about it.

Through their time of fervent prayer, they came to believe that God was calling them.

Keith began almost immediately to take on the leadership for what we were calling the Campus Church North. He and Beth prepared themselves and their family to embark on this notable shift in ministry. They even sold their home in Aurora and purchased a new home in the area where the new campus was to be established so they would be part of the community there. That was the type of person Keith was—an all-in kind of guy.

The staff at the Bathurst campus generously planned to take on the additional work of providing leadership, support, and training until the new site was able to sustain itself. We prayed for willing individuals and families to volunteer to venture out of the familiar box and commit themselves to the new undertaking. Soon about eighty dedicated and motivated people had signed up to become an integral part of Campus North.

I planned to do the same as I had done for the Bayview campus when it began, which was to shoulder the weekly Sunday preaching and teaching responsibilities for the first year to help get the church on its feet. We arranged the service times to accommodate this plan. It meant that Sunday mornings would be taxing and tiring for me, having to drive back and forth between sites and preaching three times. But I believed the effort was needed to make the venture sustainable in the short-term and successful over the long-term.

Everything was rolling forward when storm clouds suddenly threatened on the horizon.

Sixty-Six

THE APOSTLE PAUL penned some sobering words near the end of his ministry: *"Alexander the coppersmith did me much harm..."* (2 Timothy 4:14) The same happened to me. My plans were to see the Campus North site get on its feet and then pass the torch and retire from forty-five years of full-time pastoral ministry, thirty-three of those years at the Campus Church. I didn't want my time in pastoral ministry to end on a low note.

But it did.

The problem surfaced with one of my pastoral staff. He had been gathering a loyal following around him for some time and it was beginning to stir up unhealthy attachment issues and agitation in the church. I certainly felt uneasy with some of the things I was hearing. But I wanted to avoid problems for the present while putting my energy into planning and focusing on the new campus.

And I didn't have much gas in my emotional tank. The Holy Spirit was telling me that it was nearing my time to let go. God had done so many wonderful things in this story and his faithfulness was evident every day. It was truly his story.

But he uses frail vessels, and there comes a time when God, who knows our load line and limits, leads us to the point of understanding that enough is enough. I was almost there.

This particular group of followers began to question the justifiability of the new campus site. They became increasingly factious and influential. I knew most of them well and was aware that they had been manipulated into an abnormal loyalty that centred around the needs of one particular individual. They argued that the location of the proposed site was wrong. They were adamant that the region would grow in a different area and that our plans were misguided and ill-advised. They accused us of stepping carelessly into a new endeavour without sufficient investigation or thought.

They were wrong. We had investigated and made a decision based on research we had shared with the church.

Some questioned the cost. Others repeated the same arguments we had heard when we'd begun the Bayview campus, parroting the same criticism that one doesn't grow a church by dividing it. This escalated into the typical maligning of my character, the questioning of my motives, and a persistent attempt to undermine my leadership.

The attacks became more aggressive with each passing week. The church leadership tried to meet with each person in an attempt to appease, answer objections, and correct misinformation and disinformation. I met with some of them myself. I believed that the opposition to the new campus was only a surface issue, that there were underlying heart issues at play.

One day I met with the staff person in question to try to get to the bottom of what was going on. He informed me that he believed he should have been the one considered to be the new site pastor. He argued that he was very familiar with the Bradford area and that he would be the best fit for ministry there. He didn't understand why he had been overlooked. I told him that he had only been in the church for a short time and that we needed him in the role for which he had been hired.

He disagreed and then informed me that some of the pastors in the Bradford region were close friends of his. They also felt disregarded and ignored in the decision to establish a campus in the area. I assured him that we needed to correct this and asked him to organize a breakfast meeting with all the pastors of the area so we could build relationships and answer their questions.

He reluctantly agreed.

I thought this would be a way to include him in the process, and I asked him to give me the date and time as soon as the meeting was scheduled.

On the morning when the breakfast meeting was to take place, I showed up along with Pastor Keith. Only four other pastors attended. I was taken aback when the pastor who had planned the meeting didn't even show. We introduced ourselves and began by telling them what the Campus Church was all about. We reassured them that our desire was to work alongside them in building God's kingdom in a growing community. We encouraged their questions and sought to offer clarification on anything they asked.

It was a peculiar and uncomfortable breakfast. The pastor of the Baptist church sat across from us and didn't look up except to put his fork into his pancakes. His face was buried in his phone and he seemed to be taking notes the entire time.

A couple of the other men asked a few questions.

Finally the same pastor whose chin had been buried in his chest and who had been to this point preoccupied with his phone, looked up and murmured something to the effect that churches in the area, including his own, were struggling, and that it seemed to him that the Campus Church was charging thoughtlessly into their space without consulting them. I gently reminded him that the purpose of this meeting was to begin that conversation and find common ground upon which to work together. His neck stiffened and he charged that even one of our own pastors was resistant to the new site.

I realized then that the roots of this disaffection went deeper.

This man added that he believed the end result would be that people would leave their existing local churches, including his own, and gravitate toward ours. There seemed to me little sense of cohesion or oneness of kingdom purpose around the breakfast table that morning, only a myopic and parochial mindset. I didn't know quite how to respond except to again reassure those present that our purpose was not to compete with or infringe upon what they were doing, but only to partner with them to build God's kingdom in a rapidly expanding town.

When I returned to my office, I spoke to the staff member who had scheduled the meeting. I had assumed he'd be present and wondered why he hadn't shown up. He was evasive and gave no clear answer. I shared that it was also disturbing during the breakfast meeting to have heard about his personal disapproval for the new site from another pastor. Apparently that particular individual was his friend and someone in whom he confided.

The attempt that morning to make a meaningful connection with these other pastors seemed to have been a dismal failure. What was worse was that the problem clearly wound its way back to our own inner core.

When I opened my computer later that same morning, there was an email waiting for me from the Baptist pastor whom I had met at breakfast. He stated that he spoke for the association of pastors in the Bradford region and did not support our plans. He added some very negative comments about me and judged, or misjudged, the motives of the Campus Church. Clearly, he didn't welcome us.

There is a sidebar to this story, an ironic development that I can't help but briefly mention. Several years following this episode, something quite unexpected and surprising occurred. The same Baptist church closed its doors and gifted its entire facility and property to the Campus Church North site. It was a significant and extraordinary gift! We gratefully received this wonderful provision and today use it as our base of operations in that area. The pages of life are layered with ironic twists and turns and absurd outcomes. The supernatural and ironical often blend.

Returning to my story, I was invited one day to lunch by a successful businessman who attended our church. Upsettingly, he shared with me about a disturbing conversation he had been drawn into firsthand by the staff member in question. He was adamant that the man's actions needed to be confronted immediately.

This issue seemed to be mushrooming and coming at me from all directions.

I asked his advice and he agreed to meet with the leadership team himself.

The result was that the board took action, arranging a special meeting to confront this disaffected pastor. During that meeting, he listened but could not understand the wrongness of what he had done.

After much discussion, the leadership team couldn't resolve the matter and was forced to make the difficult decision to ask for his resignation.

The reaction was immediate. His loyalists turned their intense hostility on me and the chairman of our board. They began a campaign of blame, slander, and abusive behaviour.

Over the next few months, the church sustained some severe blows. We received letters from a lawyer representing the pastor who had been terminated, demanding higher severance pay and ludicrous amounts of money for damages. All I could think about was the damage we had suffered on our end. The church was forced to hire a lawyer to represent us and mediate a resolution. Our leadership debated greatly about how to respond to such unreasonable demands, but in the end they made the decision to pay out a significant sum of money to put it all behind us.

The church lost the $80,000 that had been put aside for the new campus. Furthermore, some of the people who had volunteered to participate in the Campus North now felt nervous about the new endeavour and backed away from their commitment to it. We understood.

We still had fifty people, however, locked and loaded and ready to go. They were committed and enthusiastic to get started.

The consequences of all this upheaval extended beyond the church. One day the superintendent of our denomination knocked on the door of my office and asked to sit down with me for a few minutes. He had been informed about recent occurrences and seemed sympathetic toward me and the church leadership. He talked for a few minutes about the stresses of pastoral ministry and how I was in his prayers.

And then he dropped his reason for coming.

To put it in context, up to this point I had always enjoyed a fruitful one-week summer teaching ministry at the denominational conference grounds and retreat centre. I had been invited to return for another full week of ministry that coming summer.

The superintendent looked at me sheepishly and asked me to voluntarily forgo my week of teaching ministry this year. He would substitute for me himself. What was the reason for this? The family of the pastor who had been dismissed from our church was influential at the conference grounds and was stirring up agitation over my invitation to teach. For the sake of peace and harmony, a decision had been made to ask me not to return.

I looked at him in disbelief. I remained outwardly calm, but inwardly I felt shocked and deeply disappointed. The decision was not mine to make, though. The course of action had been made for me and without me by a board of directors. I hadn't been asked to defend or explain the actions of the church and its leadership. Nor should I have been required to do so. Denominational politics reigned. My ministry that summer was forfeited in order to placate and oblige those who had caused so much conflict and distress in our church.

That still wasn't the end of it. When our next regular church business meeting arrived, the whole opposition party showed up with arguments to counter the dismissal of their friend as well as to persuade and pressure the church to abort its plans for the new campus. Accusations were made against the church leadership, staff, and myself. There was a lot of theatrics and at times it got very heated and personal. One man even arrived intoxicated and every so often emitted a volley of profanity.

They were a minority, but a very argumentative and forceful one.

The board chairman gently but firmly upheld the recent decisions of the church leadership. The group exited the meeting that evening unhappy and angry. They moved en masse to another church on the other side of town, which welcomed them with open arms.

Our church was left numb. But we recovered. Being able to pick up and move forward manifested the health of our congregation.

Campus Church North was born. Its commencement delivered a sense of relief to a people who had endured intense labour pains. Birthing a new baby brings renewed joy and fresh perspective. Pastor Keith and his congregation worked eagerly and tirelessly. When people arrived at the door on Sunday mornings, they were met with a warm welcome and invited to enjoy coffee and doughnuts or homemade cookies. They sat in the gymnasium and participated in a moving time of worship. And I would arrive just in time to preach.

The new campus grew and thrived. All three sites flourished. God's blessing was upon the Campus Church in noticeable ways.

It's difficult to describe my feelings when I recall the early days when Diane and I met in a classroom with only a small number of people in attendance. Now we witnessed hundreds of people gathered on Sunday mornings over three campuses, as well as weeklong kingdom ministry. There are probably no better words to express my sentiments than *gratification* and *humility*. I am profoundly humbled that God would call and use us in the way he did. His hand was constantly on us and his grace was always sufficient.

Our ambition was never to build a large church. Our mission was simply to grow a church that was a light in the darkness of Aurora and the surrounding region. Our passion was to lead people to Jesus and make disciples who would grow in their knowledge of God and his word and live their lives as committed Jesus-followers. We planted and watered the seed and God caused it to grow and increase. God brought these dreams and aspirations to fruition in ways that abundantly exceeded everything we asked or thought. It was truly a story of something God did for his glory.

Sixty-Seven

WE HAVE BEEN retired from full-time pastoral work for several years now. I don't regret the years I served as a shepherd to feed and care for God's flock. Yes, there was upheaval, formidable challenges, and behaviour that could only be labelled as abusive, but there was also reward and rich fulfillment. The motives of my heart were steadily refined to please God alone. Over and over, our eyes turned toward Jesus, knowing that we were partners with him.

We learned through the trauma of some very thorny and perverse circumstances not to place our confidence in man, but solely in God. He instilled courage in us to do what he entrusted to us. We followed God's call and he empowered and equipped us for everything. It was gratifying and humbling to witness firsthand the power of faith and prayer and be given insight into the ways of God. We watched God tear down walls, destroy weapons fashioned against us, and silence accusatory voices.

I have found, in the midst of some very dark places, the treasure of resting in the safety of his arms, and the peace of depending on him to provide and care for my family. Resting, trusting, and depending are not things I have always done well. It has been a process and still is. But I have made progress. And he has never failed.

I admit that I have a bit of a complicated relationship with the church. There are memories that trigger me in a negative way. The church has not felt like a safe place for me. I know what can lie behind the curtain. Even today when I walk into a church space, it provokes a feeling of discomfort. I am most relaxed sitting in the back row and observing. I still have a way to go on my journey of restoration and healing.

As long as human nature exists, the church will experience the negative impact of pride, hypocrisy, divisiveness, judgmentalism, self-interest, manipulation, control, gaslighting, and apathy. There will always be wolves in sheep's clothing. People who claim to love Jesus don't always love each other. The church is not tidy; it's messy. It's broken… sometimes very broken.

Every Sunday, buildings fill with churchgoers, some of them deeply committed Jesus-followers, and others just warming seats. Some attendees are engaged, devoted worshippers while others are devoted to the status quo of religious life and going through the motions. Some are filled with the Spirit of God, while others are filled with the spirit of self-centredness and self-righteousness. Some are true searchers for truth, and others are merely "house-trained' in a particular religious group or culture.

While I don't want to sound too critical, the church in North America in this early twenty-first century is not the Christ-centred counter-culture movement that Jesus intended it to be and that the early church was. It does not resemble the Anabaptist movement of the sixteenth-century that I studied in seminary and university and which ignited my passion and spurred my enthusiasm.

The church should be different than every other institution and organization known to man. It should be a contrast to every other community that exists. A community of faith. A community of faithful obedience to God. A community that loves and serves God and people. A place that welcomes the downtrodden. A refuge where burdens are lifted. A people who display the beauty, power, and righteousness of Jesus and the unity of the Spirit. A community that lives and breathes to worship and glorify the one true God.

It is time, however, for the church community at large to pay serious attention to the message of Jesus to the seven churches in Revelation, lest he remove its lampstand from its place (Revelation 2:5).

Jesus said to the church in Laodicea,

> I know all the things you do, that you are neither hot nor cold… I will spit you out of my mouth! You say, "I am rich. I have everything I want. I don't need a thing!" And you don't realize that you are wretched and miserable and poor and blind and naked…
>
> I stand at the door and knock. If you hear my voice and open the door, I will come in, and we will share a meal together as friends. (Revelation 3:15–17, 20)

The image of Jesus knocking on the door and asking to enter is often thought of as Jesus knocking on the heart's door of the unbeliever. But it's not. It's spoken to a church—and Jesus is on the outside looking in.

Be certain, however, that God has not abandoned his church. She is still the bride of Christ. Jesus is still Saviour and King. His kingdom is expanding, encompassing men, women, and children of every race, colour, social, and cultural background. He is building his church and all the gates of hades will not overpower it. The true church is still a force to be reckoned with and will endure to the end. The church still gives reason for the powers of darkness to tremble.

Many faithful Christians around the world are deeply committed to following Christ whatever the cost, and often at great personal sacrifice. The church is Jesus's heart, hands, and feet, reaching into a hurting and broken world with love and compassion. It plays the pivotal role of God redeeming the world to himself.

The church is still God's means of carrying the good news of salvation to everyone everywhere. The good news is still the power of God to save and transform lives and it is still impacting every corner and crevice of this planet. The truth and power of Christ's resurrection are still greater than all other powers and authorities in the heavens and on earth.

God's word is alive and powerful. His promises never fail. Faith still moves mountains. The Holy Spirit still fills and works in and through the church with divine love, power, and influence. God is still sovereign with ultimate authority, wisdom, and loving control.

Sixty-Eight

ALLOW ME TO close with one more story that I think capsulizes what I've written. The story really begins back in 1978.

I mentioned earlier that Diane and I began our first full-time pastoral ministry in a small church in a small city called Peterborough about one and a half hours northeast of Toronto. The location is important to remember.

One day I picked up a peculiar stone that caught my eye. It was smooth and greenish in colour with a distinct shape that resembled the head of a hatchet. It was about five inches long. At one end, it was shaped inward on both sides to form a narrow edge that looked like a blade. It certainly looked like it could be an old stone tomahawk head, but I had no idea.

I decided to keep it and store it in a box. And that's where it remained… for forty-five years.

I'll return to the stone later.

In 2022, after forty-five years of pastoral ministry, Diane and I made a significant change in our lives. We packed up our possessions and moved from Ontario, where we had always lived, to Charlottetown, Prince Edward Island. The move was unforeseen and quite unexpected. It certainly caught me off-guard. We live in a small but comfortable condominium right on the harbour, affording us a wonderful view of Port Charlottetown. We overlook the wharf where cruise ships dock during their North Atlantic trips. There is always lots happening around us, with tourists coming and going all the time.

I make it part of my morning to go for a walk along the water's edge, meeting people from all over Canada and many other countries around the world. I retired from pastoral ministry, but one does not retire from life or serving Jesus. If you are still aboveground, then God isn't finished with you here on earth. There is always more that he wants to do in you and through you.

Diane and I asked the Lord to show us what he wanted of us at this stage in our lives. The thought that persisted was to look for people around us who needed light, hope, a friend, or someone to be like Jesus to them. That became our ministry. It wasn't a ministry inside the established church, but it was very much a part of Jesus's kingdom work.

Another story was unfolding during this period of my life, concerning a man named Levi. While strolling on one of my morning walks, I quite unexpectedly ran into him. Levi wasn't a tourist. He worked for the city. He was under a tent out behind our condo, carving a large red wooden lobster to be placed on the waterfront. Levi was Indigenous and had lived on PEI most of his life.

After introducing ourselves to each other, I asked him a few questions about himself—just to make small talk. He answered with brief yes-or-no answers. He didn't ask me anything about myself. He wasn't friendly. In fact, he seemed cautious of me. But we chatted.

I visited Levi each morning and began to regularly take him coffee, or sometimes a bottle of water. I soon learned that his favourite food was egg salad sandwiches and a quart of milk.

He took note of everything happening at the harbour, including on the yachts moored at the docks. He knew who was doing what and would inform me about what the police were up to in the neighbourhood, or what the harbour authority was doing. He knew all the municipal political drama, the plight of the homeless, the town gossip, and he had strong opinions on Indigenous affairs. Then the next minute he would draw my attention to a bald eagle circling a group of seagulls, readying itself to fall from the sky and scoop up its squawking breakfast in razor-sharp talons.

The easiest topic of conversation with him was his carving. What he carved. How he carved. Why he carved. That last question opened up some better conversation. He hadn't known that he could carve until he was in his thirties. He told me the story. He had been asked by an elderly gentleman to carve a bear head on the end of a walking stick. He hadn't carved anything before, but he did it and the gentleman was very pleased with the result.

A few weeks later, out of the blue, he received a phone call from the curator of the art museum in Charlottetown, who told Levi that he had seen the carving of the bear head and thought it to be very good. Would Levi carve a few more things? If they were good enough, he would get Levi into exhibitions all across Canada, familiarizing him with the industry and introducing him to the general public as an Indigenous carver.

Well, Levi carved a few more things—and he was good enough. The curator made good on his promise and helped Levi over the next few years to become a recognized Indigenous carver. Levi sold his work to museums in Ottawa and London,

England, and even to various celebrities. Now he worked for the city of Charlottetown carving seals, sea turtles, lobsters, or whatever else the city asked for to welcome the thousands of tourists who visited every year.

There was something else Levi didn't know about himself, at least until he was in his twenties—and that's the fact that he was Indigenous.

I remember the day that this part of his story began to unfold, because at first he was hesitant to tell me about it. But once he got started, the story began to spill out. He had been born on an Algonquin reserve called Golden Lake near Bancroft, Ontario, close to Algonquin Provincial Park.

Most of the Indigenous people living on Prince Edward Island are Mi'kmaq, and Levi made it clear that he was not Mi'kmaq. He was Algonquin. His Indigenous name was actually Billy White Bear. When he had been only three years old, he and his three siblings were picked up by the police and taken from their home as part of what became known as the Sixties Scoop. During this time, Indigenous children were taken from their homes and placed in residential schools or foster homes.

Levi remembered, on that fateful day, a nice lady coming into their home and taking him by the hand to put him in a police car. One of the policemen asked him whether he would like to ride in the front seat. Little Billy thought that would be fun, so he willingly and happily jumped in. As did his older brother and sister. His little brother, still in diapers, was held by the lady in the back seat of the vehicle.

Billy White Bear didn't realize it at the time, but he would never see his family as it was again. He and his younger brother were adopted by a white family and resettled in a place he knew nothing about: Prince Edward Island. A small, beautiful, tranquil island little disturbed by civilization.

But little Billy's life was disturbed. It had been turned upside-down.

Given the name Levi, he was too young to know what was really going on, only that he wasn't with his family. But as time went by, and because of his young age, Levi began to adjust to his new name, unfamiliar family, contrasting community, foreign surroundings, different lifestyle, and divergent values. He grew up white.

He also grew up abused. He and his younger brother had been abused both physically and sexually by their adopted father through their growing up years. The family seemed to know, but nobody had said or done anything.

Levi struggled in school. In fact, he never finished secondary school. He just knew that there was a lot wrong in his life. He felt unloved, alone, and purposeless.

When he grew older, he bought a Harley and that motorcycle became his friend and escape from his reality.

Things were about to get worse for him. While in his twenties, he learned that he wasn't white. He was Indigenous. In some ways, the circumstances of his life now began to make some sense—why he had always felt like a misfit, a nonconformist, an outsider, different.

He didn't know how to describe *it*. Whatever *it* was, he just hadn't ever seemed to fit in with everyone else. But his primary emotion was anger. Anger that important information had been withheld from him. Anger at what had happened to him as a young boy. Anger at what had originally happened to his family and being separated so brutally from them. Anger that he didn't know who he was. Anger at the abuse he had endured. Anger at white society for what it represented to him.

For a few years, Levi vented his anger in a rebellious way, burning through life without care or concern for anything or anyone.

At some point, Levi decided that he would turn his anger into something more positive. He immersed himself in learning the Indigenous history of Canada, absorbing everything he could on his people's customs, traditions, and ways. He gained understanding of his heritage, values, and spiritual beliefs.

Levi decided that he needed to complete his secondary education. He enrolled in Holland College in Charlottetown to finish those studies. It wasn't easy being a full-grown adult sitting at a desk in a room full of younger people, learning what he should have learned years earlier. But he had some dedicated teachers who wouldn't let him quit when he felt like giving up. They constantly encouraged him to keep going. And he did! He persevered—and he graduated.

One day Levi told me that he had begun writing a book about his life. I had previously shared with him that I had written a few books, so he wondered if I would be willing to review his first chapter. He had only written one chapter and didn't know whether or not to proceed. Would I advise him?

This was the first evidence of trust I received from Levi. I guarded that handwritten ten-page manuscript with my life. I read it over and found the details of his early life to be disturbing. When I returned it to Levi, I told him that I believed it to be a story that needed to be told. It contained the makings of an important book—both personally and therapeutically for him, and also a story to awaken awareness for future readers.

He thanked me for the feedback.

Over time, Levi became chattier, offering more information about himself and his life. I made it a point not to say anything about myself, who I was, my work as a pastor, or even my faith. Because of his history and pain, I felt that some of those things would be a cause for him to push me away and keep me at a distance. Too many walls had been built up in his life. I was going to let him lead the way and only respond to his questions when and if they arose. I needed to build trust with him first.

The next evidence of trust came one day when he was carving a life-sized figure of a fisherman, pipe poking through his full beard, wearing a vintage yellow sou'wester rain hat, long oilskin coat, and large black welly boots.

Levi asked if I would give his new creation a name. In Indigenous culture, to be asked to name someone is a great honour and sign of trust.

I thought it through carefully and decided to give him the name Herbert, after my grandfather, who was a sailor and had boasted of sailing the seven seas.

Levi was pleased with the name. "Captain Herbert Payne it is!" Today Captain Herbert stands on the wharf and his photo is taken by hundreds of tourists coming off the cruise ships.

I had been praying all along that God would help me break through the wall Levi had built around himself. That prayer began to be answered one morning when, out of the blue, Levi informed me that he would like to make an Algonquin tomahawk for me as a gift—a replica of one that would have been used back in the seventeenth or eighteenth centuries.

I was surprised. This was the first time Levi had ever offered to do something for me. He instructed me to find a stone to use for the tomahawk head. He would do the rest.

So I went out onto the beaches and found two stones that I thought looked the right shape and gave them to him.

At that point, something unexpectedly came to my mind. Do you remember the old stone I'd found in Peterborough, the one I'd stored in a box forty-five years earlier? I suddenly remembered it. Or was it the Holy Spirit who stirred my memory?

"I just remembered," I told Levi. "I have a stone that I found years ago and always wondered if it was an authentic tomahawk head. If it is genuine, that would be great to use for the tomahawk you're making me. Would you like to see it?"

"I would love to see it," he replied.

I searched for it, and sure enough, it was still at the bottom of the storage bin where I had placed it so many years before.

I excitedly brought the stone to Levi for inspection. He handled it carefully and gave it a close examination.

He finally looked up at me with a smile on his face. "It's real. Can I show it to my son? He's an expert on these kinds of relics."

Levi also wanted to show it to some Indigenous elders and get their thoughts on it, to which I agreed.

He returned the next morning.

"You need to be sitting down," he said with gratifying eagerness.

I sat down. "What's the verdict?"

He began to inform me that the piece of stone was indeed an authentic relic. It had been ground and smoothed by another piece of harder rock—as opposed to knapping, where the craftsman strikes the stone with a harder tool or rock to chip away and shape the stone piece. It was Ojibway or Algonquin, most likely Algonquin because of where it was found. It probably dated back to the seventeenth century. Its size determined that it had most likely been a tomahawk used for hunting and throwing at small game.

It was also the opinion of the elders, because of its sacred nature, that it should be kept in a museum or placed in the possession of someone Indigenous. To their people, such relics have spiritual implications and carry a sacred component. For instance, a sacred object might be believed to carry the spirits of the ancestors and must be handled with great care and respect.

I listened with keen interest. My first response was to incorporate the stone tomahawk head into the replica Levi was going to craft for me. I thought it would be an amazing conversation piece. But then I told him that I would think about what he had said.

That afternoon, the Holy Spirit kept impressing one thought upon me: "Give it to Levi. Give it to him."

But it was mine. And I had kept it all these years.

"Give it to Levi," the voice persisted.

My mind began to change. Maybe God had kept it in my possession for such a time as this. As mentioned, I had been praying that God would help me to find a way to soften Levi's heart. Maybe this was the reason I had found the relic all those years ago. Maybe this was God's way of breaking down the wall Levi had built. Maybe this was the way to seal his trust in my friendship.

It was decided. I would give the tomahawk head to Levi.

I got up from my chair and returned to his tent, where he was carving.

"Levi, I want you to have the tomahawk head," I said. "I want to give it to you."

For the first time, I saw a tear in the corner of his eye. I was chipping at the wall.

"I don't think that I could take it," he said. "I'd have to really think about that."

"Well, I have thought about it and I want to give it to you. Now I would like you to think about it and give me your answer tomorrow."

He said that he would.

The next morning, I went out to see Levi with a sense of anticipation. I asked him what he had decided and he told me that he'd thought long and hard about it.

He had a question: "Why do you want to give it to me?"

I thought about my answer for a minute and then replied that I could think of four reasons.

First, I believed that it belonged to him. He was from the Algonquin tribe and we had already determined that the relic was of Algonquin origin. Possibly one of his ancestors had sculpted the head. Certainly someone from his tribal ancestry had done so. It really belonged to him, not me.

Second, I believed that there was a bigger hand behind all this. I didn't use the word *divine*, but Levi knew what I meant. More than sixty years ago, he had been cruelly and rudely uprooted from his reservation, home, and family near Bancroft and brought to Prince Edward Island. More than forty-five years ago, I had found an ancient relic of Algonquin origin in the Peterborough area, only an hour from his home of origin. Many years later, Diane and I had moved from Ontario to Charlottetown to live in a condominium on the harbour right next to a tent under which Levi was working and carving for the summer. We had met. By accident? By chance? I don't think so. There was something bigger at play.

Levi listened intently.

Third, I believed that he was a good man.

And fourth, I liked him.

For the second time, I saw a tear in the corner of Levi's eye. But he caught himself and wiped it quickly away.

"Okay," he replied. "I receive it as a gift. Thank you."

The softness in his voice echoed a deep and genuine appreciation. The relic gave him a tangible connection to his ancestors and heritage. It gave him a newfound sense of strengthened identity and helped him gain back something that had been taken from him. It was personal. It was sacred to him.

He told me that he would craft a unique and special tomahawk handle and incorporate the head into it. He would handle it with sacred care and one day bequeath it to his son. It gave us a bond.

After that, it seemed that Levi couldn't do enough for me. That same week, he welcomed me to join him at an Indigenous council event. I attended and enjoyed the dancing and drumming. He crafted for me another beautiful tomahawk, a replica from the seventeenth century. I mounted it in a shadow box and hung it on the wall of my home for all to appreciate.

He wanted to do something for Diane as well. He told me what it was, but he wanted it to be kept a secret from her.

A few weeks later, he handed her a replica of an ornate papoose from the seventeenth century, beautifully and skillfully crafted. Levi beamed with delight when he gave it to Diane, and so did she.

A month later, he gave me a painting that he himself had painted, called "The Blueberry Field." It depicted Indigenous dancers around a fire in a blueberry field.

And he crafted for Diane what he called a "talking stick." He said that this was the most sacred object he could give anyone. It was seventeen inches long with an eagle head carved on the top, signifying wisdom, and a small stone embedded in the base to symbolize staying grounded. It was decorated with small eagle feathers. It was something that should be cradled in the left arm—and when in one's possession, it gave that person the authority to speak. He was proud of his work.

He was extremely appreciative of the gift I had given him, and he discovered himself enjoying an unexpected friendship and relationship of trust with this white man.

Today the tomahawk hangs proudly on a wall in Levi's home above a plaque that reads "When the tomahawk hangs on the wall, there is peace; when it is taken down from the wall, there is no peace."

I haven't talked to Levi about Jesus to this point. I'm sensitive to Levi's readiness and letting God look after the timing of such things.

There are signs, however, that he is getting closer to me approaching the subject. The chapter isn't over. Mostly I have tried to be like Jesus to him. To show him Jesus. To be a friend. To find ways of blessing him, affirming him, and instilling a sense of worth in him. To build trust.

It took two whole years, but Levi finally asked me what I did for a job throughout my life. I told him that I was a pastor. He just stared incredulously at me. I wasn't sure what would come out of his mouth next, but he was good with my revelation. And I think he was a little surprised that he had actually come to trust and make friends with a Christian pastor.

God is in control of all things in our lives from beginning to end. This story reflects that truth. Something that happened seemingly randomly many years ago was part of a divine unfolding that is still evolving today. When I found that tomahawk head many years ago, God had Levi in mind. That's not something I could have foreseen. But God saw it all and coordinated the narrative.

This is an important lesson for us all. Diane and I have found this to be true in the unfolding and chronicling of our shared life and ministry.

Know that behind, in, and through all the details of your life, God's divine hand is intentionally, mysteriously, and lovingly working all things out, fulfilling his purposes in accordance with his perfect timing, for his glory and for your good.

Pamukkale (biblical Hierapolis) in southwest Turkey. The white calcium carbonate cliffs are deposits from the thermal hot springs.

Teaching in the ancient theatre at Hierapolis across the valley from Laodicea, home of one of the seven churches of Revelation.

A shepherd in Anatolia, Turkey.
David learned much from studying the ways of Middle Eastern shepherds.

Mount Carmel overlooking the Jezreel Valley in northern Israel.
Site of Elijah calling down fire from heaven.

Teaching on the shore of the Sea of Galilee, where Jesus called five of his disciples to follow him.

Teaching at Banias in northern Israel (site of biblical Caesarea Philippi) where Peter made his great confession that Jesus was the Christ.

Zambia, ministering with Faith's Orphans Fund.

Our family (Jeremy, David, Diane, Sarah, and Rebecca) at our Campus Church retirement event in June 2017.

About the Author:

DAVID PAYNE IS a family man and pastor of forty-five years. For thirty-three of those years, he was the founding and lead pastor of the Campus Church, a multisite congregation in Aurora, Ontario. He draws from his own personal journey, experience as a pastor and Bible teacher, and extensive travel in biblical lands studying its sites, people, and cultures. David has written two previous books, *Hitting the Wall: Finding Perspective When Life Stops Working* and *Run! The Amazing Race*. Reach out to him at davidspayne00@gmail.com.

Also by David S. Payne

ISBN: 978-1-77069-739-3

HITTING THE WALL is inevitable in life and a necessary ingredient in the journey of faith. Each wall is unique and embraces such words as brokenness and pain. But each wall also carries the potential for positive change in your life.

When life stops working and you lie broken and confused at the wall, this book will open your heart to a profound hope in a loving, all-knowing God. *Hitting the Wall* will open up a new perspective, empowering you to begin to move forward again. There is usually no quick fix at the wall. Rather, you must begin a slow, steady growth over it. This book will nourish that growth.

ISBN: 978-1-77069-738-6

THERE IS A path that God has set for you to run that will raise your life to the highest plane of quality, fulfillment and significance. It is not an easy or painless run. It can be demanding and tough. The Bible says, "Run with endurance the race that God has set before you." God's race has an astounding eternal destination. This book focuses on the amazing journey of getting there. We often think the greatest races are reserved for the gods we read about in books or watch in the movies, not for mere mortals like us. Not true. The most amazing race is reserved for everyday folk like you and me.

It is a sad reality that many people run the race of life far below their potential. Too many begin well but fail to finish well. They tire over the distance. They settle for the mediocre. The ordinary. They feel the pain of the run, but not the exhilaration. They become discouraged. Slowly dismayed. Easily distracted. Gradually sidetracked. They live aimlessly and soon find themselves running on empty. But God did not put you here to simply exist. He put you here to thrive.

This book will encourage, challenge, and inspire you to participate, endure, enjoy, flourish and go the distance in life's most amazing race.

www.ingramcontent.com/pod-product-compliance
Lightning Source LLC
Chambersburg PA
CBHW030103170426
43198CB00009B/470